UNLEARNING LIBERTY

UNLEARNING LIBERTY

Campus Censorship and the End of American Debate

Greg Lukianoff

ENCOUNTER BOOKS
New York • London

First American edition published in 2012 by Encounter Books,
an activity of Encounter for Culture and Education, Inc.,
a nonprofit, tax exempt corporation.
Encounter Books website address: www.encounterbooks.com

Manufactured in the United States and printed on
acid-free paper. The paper used in this publication meets
the minimum requirements of ANSI/NISO Z39.48–1992
(R 1997) (*Permanence of Paper*).

FIRST AMERICAN EDITION

LIBRARY OF CONGRESS CATALOGING-IN-PUBLICATION DATA

Lukianoff, Greg.
Unlearning liberty : campus censorship
and the end of American debate / by Greg Lukianoff.
pages cm
Includes bibliographical references and index.
ISBN 978-1-59403-635-4 (hardcover : alk. paper) — ISBN 978-1-59403-649-1 (ebook) (print)
1. Academic freedom—United States. 2. Teaching, Freedom of—United States.
3. Freedom of speech—United States. 4. College students—Civil rights—United States.
5. Universities and colleges—Law and legislation—United States.
6. Education, Higher—Moral and ethical aspects—United States. I. Title.
KF4242.L85 2012
378.1'2130973--dc23

2012017076

For Michelle

Contents

Chapter 7
Don't Question Authority
137

Chapter 8
Student Activities Fair
159

Chapter 9
Finally, the Classroom!
185

The Dangerous Collage

IN THE SPRING OF 2007, Valdosta State University took vigorous action against an undergraduate student it believed was a "clear and present danger" to campus. What had Hayden Barnes, a decorated paramedic in his early twenties, done to terrify the VSU community? He had publicly protested the decision by the university's president, Ronald Zaccari, to build two parking garages on campus. Believing that the $30 million price tag was an exorbitant expenditure ($15,000 per parking space) and that more environmentally friendly parking options were available, he had written a letter to the editor of the student newspaper and contacted members of the board of regents to voice his objections, politely, by all accounts.[1]

One of his protests—and a very broad definition of *protest* is necessary— was a collage depicting the dangers he believed the parking garages posed: smog, a bulldozer, an asthma inhaler, and the words to the classic liberal fight song "No Blood for Oil." On April 13, Barnes posted this collage on Facebook under the headline "S.A.V.E. – Zaccari Memorial Parking Garage."[2] S.A.V.E. referred to Students Against Violating the Environment, the VSU environmental group that Hayden believed should be opposing the garage. "Memorial" referenced Zaccari's claim that the garage was to be part of his legacy.

On May 7, Hayden found an official notice slipped under his door, telling him that he had been "administratively withdrawn," effective immediately.[3] Stapled to the note was the only evidence offered for this decision: the collage, which President Zaccari claimed was an "indirect" threat against his life because it used the word "memorial." Within a few days, Hayden was locked out of his dorm room and ordered to leave campus. The notice's promise of an appeal if he received a "certificate of mental health" from a psychiatrist proved a false hope. Not only did Hayden provide the certificate and letters verifying his mental health from both a psychiatrist and a psychologist, but he also wrote a detailed and impassioned appeal, arguing that his sudden expulsion because of political speech without so much as a hearing, formal charges, or a chance to respond was a violation of his constitutional rights to due process and free speech, not to mention the university's own policies. Despite the fact that the law was overwhelmingly on his side and that he had done everything the university asked him to do, his appeal was denied.[4] The euphemistic term "administrative withdrawal" was revealed for what it was: permanent expulsion.

The punishment of Hayden Barnes for a collage on Facebook may seem like an extreme case, but it isn't all that exceptional. A popular misconception is that battles for free speech on campus were fought and won in the 1960s, and that free speech emerged victorious again after a challenge by politically correct speech codes in the 1990s. I am sorry to report that this is not the case. The VSU president's attitude towards dissent is replicated by administrators both high and low at too many colleges across the country, where differences of opinion are not viewed as opportunities to learn or to think through ideas. Instead, dissent is regarded as a nuisance at best, and sometimes as an outright threat—even when it's only about a parking garage.

That's why there is plenty of work to do at my organization, the Foundation for Individual Rights in Education (FIRE), which defends free speech rights and other student rights on campuses around the country. FIRE learned about the troubles of Hayden Barnes in fall 2007 through an article in a Georgia newspaper. When I first met Hayden in the winter of 2008, I felt like I was being reacquainted with an old friend from college. He was mellow, with a scruffy hippie beard, and lived with his irresistibly lovable girlfriend in a small apartment in southern Georgia. We liked the same music, we were both Democrats and environmentalists, and we even studied the same kind of Buddhism. His understated and calm manner made it all the more impressive to me that he was an EMT—and all the more strange that Valdosta State University had called him a "clear and present danger" to the campus. For First Amendment lawyers, students of history, and fans of Tom Clancy, "clear and present danger" is a legal doctrine arising from World War I that refers to grave threats to the nation itself, such as encouraging sabotage, espionage, outright revolt, or other forms of terrorism and treason.

FIRE researched the case thoroughly and wrote a letter to the university demanding an explanation.[5] After VSU failed to adequately respond to our letters, we started issuing press releases, our standard weapon in fighting abuses on campus. FIRE's unofficial motto is that colleges cannot defend in public the rights violations they commit in private, and as president of FIRE, I have seen hundreds of colleges and universities back down in the face of public embarrassment. But VSU would not budge.[6] Finally, we enlisted the help of Robert Corn-Revere, an eminent First Amendment attorney, and after he filed suit in January 2008, the VSU Board of Regents finally reversed the university's decision against Hayden and offered him readmission.[7] Hayden—who was by then completing his education at another college—understandably declined.

The court's opinion revealed a number of previously hidden facts that made the case even worse than we at FIRE had known. Internal documents and testimony showed it was Hayden's opposition to the parking garage, not fear of mortal danger, that led the VSU president to expel him.[8] Zaccari even called Hayden into an hour-long meeting to harangue him about the parking garage, asking him, "Who do you think you are?" and stating that he "could not forgive" him. This attempt to browbeat and guilt-trip a student out of a strongly held position is fairly typical in my experience, and if it fails, campus administrators have a toolkit of policies and rationales they can use to punish students who do not back down.

Over the course of just a few weeks in the spring of 2007, Zaccari held meeting after meeting with his administration on what to do about Hayden, despite being told repeatedly by his staff that Hayden was not a threat, that Hayden deserved due process if Zaccari planned to punish him, and that the president couldn't just kick a student out of school over a disagreement. According to the court's opinion, Zaccari even ordered staff to look "into Barnes's academic records, his medical history, his religion, and his registration with the VSU Access Office."[9]

The VSU Access Office is the university's department for students with disabilities. Zaccari learned that Hayden had sought counseling for depression and anxiety, which he tried to use as justification for ruling him a threat. He talked to a campus counselor and to Hayden's psychologist, both of whom told him in no uncertain terms that Hayden was not a danger to himself or anyone else. Indeed, for all the prying Zaccari did, it would have been difficult for him to miss that Hayden was a decorated EMT and a believer in nonviolence.

Finally, Zaccari seemed to give up trying to convince anyone that Hayden was a threat and instead announced that he would exercise his presidential authority to expel him unilaterally, without a hearing or even prior notice, both of which are required by Valdosta State policy and by the Bill of Rights.

In light of this evidence, the court ruled that President Zaccari had violated Hayden's due process rights so clearly and brazenly that he should be held personally and financially liable for damages. This is a severe penalty, as government employees are usually protected by "qualified immunity." The ruling showed that the judge believed Zaccari knew, or at least should have known, he was violating Hayden's constitutional rights by kicking him out of college. Zaccari appealed the ruling, but in February 2012 the Eleventh Circuit Court of Appeals upheld the finding against Zaccari.[10] At this writing, Hayden is poised to graduate from law school (inspired to attend because of his experiences in this case) and that lovable girlfriend is now his wife.

But while things are working out for Hayden, it took an aggressive campaign by FIRE and a federal lawsuit to vindicate his rights—rights that were firmly established by the Supreme Court even at the time he was punished in 2007.

Campus Censorship: Alive and Thriving

On college campuses today, students are punished for everything from mild satire, to writing politically incorrect short stories, to having the "wrong" opinion on virtually every hot button issue, and, increasingly, simply for criticizing the college administration just as Hayden Barnes was. In the coming pages, you will see a student punished for publicly reading a book; a professor labeled a deadly threat to campus for posting a pop-culture quote on his door; students required to lobby the government for political causes they disagreed with in order to graduate; a student government that passed a "Sedition Act" empowering them to bring legal action against students who criticized them; and students across the country being forced to limit their "free speech activities" to tiny, isolated corners of campus creepily dubbed "free speech zones." You will see Christian students being banned from watching *The Passion of the*

Christ, while another college financially sponsored an angry mob's censorship of a play making fun of *The Passion of the Christ*. Meanwhile, schools as venerated as Yale and Harvard have gotten into the censorship act for things as seemingly inoffensive as quoting F. Scott Fitzgerald. And all of this is happening at the very institutions that rely most on free speech, open exchange, and candor to fulfill their mission. At the same time, we are paying more and more for higher education, which, perversely, expands the very campus bureaucracy that fosters this anti-free-speech environment.

Most campuses still cling to speech codes and other restrictions on expression that violate First Amendment principles, seemingly without understanding that these policies not only chill speech but also teach students that an open exchange of ideas might not really be such a good thing. Administrators have been able to convince well-meaning students to accept outright censorship by creating the impression that freedom of speech is somehow the enemy of social progress. When students began leaving college with that lesson under their belts, it was only a matter of time before the cultivation of bad intellectual habits on campus started harming the dialogue of our entire country. The tactics and attitudes that shut down speech on campus are bleeding into the larger society and wreaking havoc on the way we talk among ourselves. As I will expand on throughout this book, the punishment of dissenting opinions or even raucous parodies and satire has surprising downstream effects, encouraging the human tendency to live within our own echo chambers. It turns out the one institution that could be helping elevate the national discussion may actually be making it worse. To put it bluntly, I believe that three decades of campus censorship has made us all just a little bit dumber.

This book grew out of my experience reviewing thousands of instances of campus censorship and defending faculty and students at hundreds of colleges across the country over the last eleven years. The overwhelming majority of accounts here are based on primary documents ranging from police reports, to letters from campus administrators and judicial boards, to university policies, contracts, and student handbooks that FIRE has collected and posted online.

Over the past two decades, the topic of censorship on campus has often been treated as a "conservative issue," because the fact is that socially conservative opinions are the ones most likely to be stifled at colleges and universities today. While many attempts at censorship are apolitical, you are far more likely to get in trouble on campus for opposing, for example, affirmative action, gay marriage, and abortion rights than you are for supporting them.

Political correctness has become part of the nervous system of the modern university and it accounts for a large number of the rights violations I have seen over the years. For decades, our universities have been teaching students that speech with a chance of offending someone should be immediately silenced; but the slope for offensiveness has proven remarkably slippery, and the concept of hurtful speech is often invoked by campus administrators in the most self-serving ways. The press has gotten so used to such cases that they are often shrugged off as the same old "political correctness" on campus. But the problem is much more serious than that dismissive definition. When students risk punishment for speaking their minds, something has gone very wrong in the college environment.

One thing that makes this book a little different than one might expect is that I am not your stereotypical social-conservative critic of "political correctness run amok." I am a lifelong Democrat and have something of a liberal pedigree. I have never voted for a Republican, nor do I plan to. I am one of only a few dozen people honored by the Playboy Foundation for a commitment to free speech; others include Bill Maher, Molly Ivins, and Michael Moore. In March 2010, I received the Ford Hall Forum Louis P. and Evelyn Smith First Amendment Award on behalf of FIRE, which has also been bestowed on Ted Turner, Maya Angelou, and Anita Hill. I have worked at the ACLU and for EnvironMentors, which is an environmental justice mentoring program for inner-city high school kids in Washington, D.C. I have worked on behalf of refugees in Eastern Europe and volunteered for a program educating incarcerated teens in California about the law. I believe passionately in gay marriage, abortion rights, legalizing marijuana, and universal health care. Playing even more into the liberal stereotype, I am a board member of an edgy Philadelphia theater company, I belong to the notoriously politically correct Park Slope Food Co-op in Brooklyn, and I have been a regular blogger for the *Huffington Post* since 2007.[11]

Why is it odd that a liberal should fight for free speech rights? Isn't freedom of speech a quintessentially liberal issue? Some members of the baby boomer generation may be horrified to learn that campus administrators and the media alike often dismiss those of us who defend free speech for all on campus as members of the conservative fringe. While I was once hissed at during a libertarian student conference for being a Democrat, it is far more common that I am vilified as an evil conservative for defending free speech on campus. I remember telling a New York University film student that I worked for free speech on campus and being shocked by his response: "Oh, so you're like the people who want the KKK on campus." In his mind, protecting free speech was apparently synonymous with advocating hatred. He somehow missed the glaring fact that the content of his student film could have been banned from public display if not for the progress of the free speech movement.

The transformation of free speech on campus to a conservative niche issue is a method of dismissing its importance. Sadly, we live in a society where simply labeling something an evil conservative idea (or, for that matter, an evil liberal one) is accepted by far too many people as a legitimate reason to dismiss it. This is just one of the many cheap tactics for shutting down debate that have been perfected on our campuses and are now a common part of everyday life.

How Campus Censorship Harms Us All

What happens on campus doesn't stay on campus. After all, colleges and universities are grooming schools for future leaders and training grounds for the great national debate; and higher education, more than ever, shapes our general culture. Never before in our history have so many Americans held or pursued a college degree.[12] Our national discussion is dominated by people with a college education. So, if we assume that colleges and universities are supposed to make us deeper, more creative and nuanced thinkers, we should be enjoying a golden age of American discourse. But I doubt that anyone believes this is the case. Indeed, critics as various as the *New York Times* columnists David Brooks and Paul Krugman, the comedian Jon Stewart, the *Washington Post* columnist Kathleen Parker, the media icon Tom Brokaw, and even former and current presidents of the United States have lamented the sorry state of American dialogue.[13]

A corollary of this failure of dialogue is that our country's polarization across political lines has gone from controversial conjecture to a fact documented by research. Bill Bishop's *The Big Sort* (2008) laid out extensive data to demonstrate America's growing political polarization and showed that the problem extended beyond our relatively new ability to live in cyber environments where likeminded people confirm our pre-existing opinions (something dubbed by MIT's Nicholas Negroponte as "the daily me").[14] Since the 1970s, there has even been a trend of physical separation, as people move to communities that are more and more ideologically homogeneous. Charles Murray cited a dizzying number of statistics in his 2012 book *Coming Apart* to show that affluent and highly educated people in particular are sequestering themselves into likeminded communities and social circles, and thus becoming both physically and culturally isolated from their fellow citizens.[15]

Like most Americans, I have seen the results of this hyperpolarization and groupthink in my own life. Take, for example, the shooting of Congresswoman Gabrielle Giffords and eighteen others by a psychopath on January 8, 2011. I was on Twitter as the events unfolded, and I was stunned at how many friends—people I follow for their opinions on art, science, and politics—started ranting, before any meaningful information was known about the case, that the shooting was the result of right-wing rhetoric. One Tweeter whom I had never before seen resort to all-caps asserted, "There is NO DOUBT WHATSOEVER that Palin/Tea Party created this political climate." Some of us on Twitter tried to remind everyone to take a minute to just be sad and recognize the human tragedy rather than twist it into a weapon to bash the "ignorant masses." But our comments had little impact. Conservatives soon joined the fray, using bits and pieces of information that they had uncovered about the shooter, Jared Loughner, to argue that he was a "left-wing nut job." It was as if the primary significance of the shooting for countless people was the justification of their hatred for everyone who disagreed with them.

As the days passed after the Tucson massacre, the evidence began to show that Jared Loughner was mentally ill and had political beliefs that didn't neatly fit anyone's preconceptions. Some of those who had been so quick to blame the shooting on Glenn Beck and Sarah Palin started to back off. The truth, however, did nothing to stop the chancellor of UC Berkeley, Robert J. Birgeneau, from blaming the tragedy on "xenophobia" and the climate of "hateful speech" in our nation. As key evidence of this climate, he cited the failure of the "DREAM Act," a bill that would have opened up citizenship for illegal aliens who were enrolled in college or had served in the military and lived in the United States since the age of sixteen.[16] While I also support the DREAM Act, there is no indication of even the slightest connection between the shooting and the failure of that legislation. Chancellor Birgeneau used his position as a respected educator to transform a tragedy perpetrated by a madman into an excuse to vilify those who disagreed with him, rather than using it as an opportunity to have meaningful discussions about a relevant topic, like our failure to effectively identify and care for the mentally ill. What was even more worrisome was how many students and politicians agreed with the chancellor.

The response to the Tucson tragedy was just another in a long line of knee-jerk reactions I have seen over the past decade. And this typical rush to judgment is an indication that, in truth, we live in *certain* times. I know the saying is that we live in *uncertain* times, but that is not the case today. America's metaphorical culture war increasingly feels like a religious war, with too many crusaders and high priests and too few heretics on each side. And I believe that an unsung culprit in this expansion of unwarranted certainty and group polarization is thirty years of college censorship.

How, you might ask, would censorship on campus contribute to political polarization and the failure of the Golden Age of American Dialogue to blossom? It may seem like a paradox, but an environment that squelches debate and punishes the expression of opinions, in the very institution that is supposed to make us better thinkers, can lead quickly to the formation of polarized groups in which people harbor a comfortable, uncritical certainty that they are right.

The potential for this damage to open and free-flowing dialogue does not require that every citizen experience censorship personally. Even a single conspicuous case of punishing speech can have dramatic consequences. This is what we lawyers call "the chilling effect." If people believe there is *any* risk of punishment for stating an opinion, most will not bother opening their mouths; and in time, the rules that create this silence become molded into the culture. While few outside the university setting know the reality and scale of campus censorship, students are quite aware of the risks. A study of 24,000 students conducted by the Association of American Colleges and Universities in 2010 revealed that only around 30 percent of college seniors strongly agreed with the statement that "It is safe to have unpopular views on campus."[17] (The numbers are even worse for faculty, the people who know campus the best: only 16.7 percent of them strongly agreed with the statement.) Meanwhile, the fact that this generation of students is more reticent about sharing their opinions than previous ones has been a subject of scholarly research for over a decade now.[18]

So what happens when students get the message that saying the wrong thing can get you in trouble? They do what one would expect: they talk to people they already agree with, keep their mouths shut about important topics in mixed company, and often don't bother even arguing with the angriest or loudest person in the room (which is a problem even for the loud people, as they may not recognize that the reason why others are deferring to their opinions is not because they are obviously right). The result is a group polarization that follows graduates into the real world. As the sociologist Diana C. Mutz discovered in her book *Hearing the Other Side* (2006), those with the highest levels of education have the *lowest* exposure to people with conflicting points of view, while those who have not graduated from high school can claim the most diverse discussion mates.[19] In other words, those most likely to live in the tightest echo chambers are those with the highest level of education. It should be the opposite, shouldn't it? A good education ought to teach citizens to actively seek out the opinions of intelligent people with whom they disagree, in order to prevent the problem of "confirmation bias."

As students avoid being confronted with new ideas in the one place where it's the most crucial that they do so, they develop an even greater unreflective certainty that they must be right. The work of Cass Sunstein explores this problem, highlighting decades of research indicating that isolation from diverse points of view can lead to a runaway process of group polarization, extremism, and groupthink.[20] This process further robs people of the intellectual growth that comes from subjecting one's own ideas to challenges. As the Zen maxim goes, "Great doubt, great awakening. Little doubt, little awakening. No doubt, no awakening."

And this is decidedly not a problem that affects only liberal elites. Damage to the level, scope, and sophistication of debate and discussion harms us all, whether we are liberal, conservative, libertarian, or independent. As Professor Mark Bauerlein observed in his book *The Dumbest Generation* (2008), campus polarization promotes a low level of intellectual rigor on the part of campus Republicans just as it does for everyone else.[21] When higher education is failing to raise the standards for discussion, the state of dialogue in the nation as a whole is bound to suffer.

The stifling of expression on campus and the resulting consolidation of self-affirming cliques are harmful to higher education and to our country for three primary reasons:

First, when you surround yourself with people you agree with and avoid debates, thought experimentation, or even provocative jokes around people you disagree with, you miss the opportunity to engage in the kind of exciting back-and-forth that sharpens your critical thinking skills. The failure of universities to cultivate critical-thinking skills was starkly brought home to the public by Professor Richard Arum of New York University and Professor Josipa Roksa from the University of Virginia in their 2011 book *Academically Adrift*. It features a multiyear analysis of the "critical thinking, analytical reasoning, problem solving and writing" skills of over two thousand students at fourteen colleges of all different sizes, regions, and rankings. The study found that most students showed very little improvement in critical-thinking skills, with 45 percent of them showing virtually *no* improvement in *a single one* of the basic competencies.[22] Underscoring my concern, Arum and Roksa noted that the majority of students could not demonstrate simple debate skills, and were unable to effectively take arguments from multiple points of view or break them down. Other extensive studies, including one out of Wabash College, have shown similar results.[23] I believe a college education that did a better job of encouraging people to seek out debate and discussion, both inside and outside class, would never produce such miserable results.

Second, the deadening of debate and the fostering of self-affirming cliques also promotes a shallow and incomplete understanding of important issues and other ways of thinking. As John Stuart Mill pointed out a century and a half ago, without free and open debate and discussion, people hold on to their opinions like they hold on to prejudices: believing themselves to be right, but not really understanding *why* or ever seriously considering the possibility that they might be wrong. The mind rebels at the thought it might be wrong, and overcoming this natural defensive resistance requires constant, rigorous practice in challenging our opinions by leaving our comfort zones. Higher education is supposed to serve this function, but omnipresent speech codes and punishment of controversial viewpoints do the opposite. They create a feedback loop that rewards unreflective ideological conformity and simple avoidance of difficult disagreements. A mind at rest tends to stay at rest. By blotting out challenging ideas or arguments, colleges are holding back their students' intellectual development.

Collegiate censorship is, of course, not the *only* reason why American national discourse is suffering. There are numerous reasons why we seem to have devolved into a culture of smug certainty, partisanship, sound bites, and polarizing überpundits. There is plenty of blame to be foisted upon the right wing, left wing, and every point in between, not to mention far-reaching social and technological changes. What I am arguing is that higher education is our best hope to *remedy* oversimplification, mindless partisanship, and uncritical thinking, but it cannot do so if students and professors alike are threatened with punishment for doing little more than speaking their minds. Indeed, what should be the cure for calcified political discourse is likely making the problem even worse.

Third, and perhaps most importantly, campus censorship poses both an immediate and a long-term threat to all of our freedoms not just because free speech is crucial to every other freedom, but also because it teaches students the wrong lessons about living in a free society. Free speech is a far more fragile right than most people know. When bad examples and flat-out misinformation characterize the lessons that students get about free speech, due process, and the other essential elements of liberty, it can be expected that rights will erode in our larger society just as they have been eroding on campus. The values, habits, and practices that allow you to live and function in a free society are things that you must be taught. Despite our country's veneration of the term "free speech," the importance of free expression is neither obvious nor intuitive. It has been the exception in human history, not the rule.

In order for free speech to thrive, students need to experience on a regular basis how open discussion and debate and even random bits of comedy can increase tolerance and understanding more effectively than any speech code, residence hall initiative, or ideological "training" ever could. Modern universities are producing college graduates who lack that experience of uninhibited debate and casual provocation. As a result, our society is effectively *unlearning* liberty. This could have grave long-term consequences for all of our rights and the very cohesion of our nation. If too few citizens understand or believe in free speech, it is only a matter of time before politicians, activists, lawyers, and judges begin to curtail and restrict it, while other citizens quietly go along. Perhaps no one has summarized what is at stake more clearly than FIRE's cofounder Alan Charles Kors: "*A nation that does not educate in liberty will not long preserve it and will not even know when it is lost.*"

Beginning Our Journey
through the Modern College Experience

In the process of offering a theory on how the world of higher education today is harming American discourse and increasing polarization, this book will reveal the many ways that today's universities violate basic rights and betray the principles that undergird fundamental liberties. I will expose violations of due process, intrusions into the realm of private conscience, and programs that require investigating and "reforming" people's deepest moral beliefs and convictions. What all of these violations have in common is that they arise from and reinforce an unscholarly kind of certainty. After all, if you already know that a student must be guilty, why do you need due process? Or if you're certain you know the moral and factual truths about the issues at hand, why bother with debate and discussion? Students and campus administrators are losing sight of the important role that the skeptical, questioning mind, aware of its own failings, has played in every aspect of human progress. Those who are responsible for higher education need to be reminded that we want bright, ambitious, iconoclastic thinkers, not more foot soldiers for a seemingly endless culture war.

Throughout this book, I'll be linking what has been happening on campus to larger controversies involving a diverse cast of characters—Herman Cain, Bill Maher, Juan Williams, Dave Barry, Glenn Beck, Margaret Cho, Rush Limbaugh, Richard Dawkins, even Robert De Niro—and issues as varied as the "Ground Zero mosque" and the Penn State rape scandal. There is even a case in which Jon Stewart's *Daily Show* saved the day for one student. You will also see how the problem with free speech on American campuses has international implications from the Middle East to India, as it did in the wake of Harvard's decision to fire a famous Indian politician because of his public response to terrorist attacks on Mumbai.

The time frame of the cases in this book spans my career over the last eleven years. For the definitive text on campus censorship in the 1980s and '90s, I recommend *The Shadow University: The Betrayal of Liberty on America's Campuses,* with its numerous additional examples of violations of free speech, due process, and other rights on campus.[24] The book was authored by FIRE's cofounders, Alan Charles Kors and Harvey Silverglate.

Because FIRE plays such an important role in this book, you should know a little about it. Founded by a conservative-leaning libertarian professor at the University of Pennsylvania (Kors) and a liberal-leaning civil rights attorney in Boston (Silverglate), FIRE is a unique organization in which liberals, conservatives, libertarians, atheists, Christians, Jews, Muslims have successfully worked together for the common cause of defending rights on campus. I am a Democrat and an atheist, our senior vice president is a Republican and Christian, while our legal director, a Democrat and former

Green Party activist, works harmoniously alongside our other top lawyers including a Jewish libertarian and a Muslim-raised liberal. I have worked at nonprofits almost all my life and have never even heard of, let alone worked at, a cause-based organization successfully run by people with such different personal politics. But we all agree on free speech and basic rights without hesitation, and we live the benefits of having different perspectives in the office every day. True, it can get a little heated in the office around election season, but we wouldn't have it any other way.

At FIRE, we see every day the tribulations of college students who get in trouble for assuming that higher education involves speaking candidly about serious topics, or that telling jokes is always permitted on campus. This book invites you to experience the confusing challenges that students face today. Each chapter opens by putting you in the shoes of a fictional modern student as you progress through high school to the last day of your first semester in college. All of the opening fact patterns are based on real-life stories and will help illustrate the bad lessons that students are learning about what it means to live in a free society—even before they set foot in a classroom.

So let's start our journey through the modern collegiate experience. Imagine you are a sophomore in high school . . .

CHAPTER I

Learning All the Wrong Lessons in High School

You are a fifteen-year-old sophomore in high school and it's the night before you take your PSAT exam. While you know it will be the most important test you have taken in your life, your mind is on something very different. You work for the student newspaper, and earlier this week the editor-in-chief was told by the principal that the paper could not run an investigative article about the student body president. The article was carefully researched and did its best to be fair, but found that the president had failed to deliver on any of his campaign promises. The principal told your editor that the article was "hurtful" and didn't provide any further justification for rejecting it. The newspaper staff couldn't help but believe this rejection had something to do with the fact that the student body president was the son of the vice principal. In an attempt to circumvent the clamp-down, your editor tried to hand out an underground edition of the article, but he had been caught doing so and was now suspended. None of this seems right to you, so now you are sitting in front of your computer, an instant away from publishing the entire article on a blog that you and a few students run.

You've spent the last few hours online and on the phone with classmates trying to figure out what you should do. Your closest friend warned you that you could get kicked out of school for posting the piece. She has heard about students being punished for what they posted on Facebook, what they printed in the student magazine, or even the T-shirts they wore to school. Soon you get an angry phone call from the vice president of the student government, who learned via Facebook that you're planning on posting the article. He gives you a serious dressing-down, saying that publishing such an article would be "cyber bullying" and that you could be suspended for it. This sounds like self-serving nonsense to you, but then he says, "Do you seriously think you'll get into a good college if you have a suspension for bullying on your record?"

You have been dreaming about going to college almost as long as you knew what the word meant. You are a serious student, which can sometimes make you feel like an outcast in high school, and college holds the possibility of being your "island of misfit toys," a place where you will fit in. But you know that the competition for a good college is brutal, and could you really afford to suffer the wrath of the school administration?

You think about your grandparents, who went to college in the 1960s during the "free speech movement," and about how different college must be—freeing and exciting. It will be such a relief to be able to speak your mind without having to worry about getting in trouble . . . if you can make it in. Maybe this isn't your fight. You switch off your computer and crawl into bed.

High Schools and Unlearning Liberty

You can't fully understand what lessons colleges are teaching students about living in a free society without knowing what students have learned before they even step foot on campus. The news isn't good. By the time they graduate from high school, American students already harbor negative attitudes about free speech. A survey of 100,000 high school students by the John S. and James L. Knight Foundation in 2004 found that 73 percent either felt ambivalent about the First Amendment or took it for granted.[1] This should not come as a surprise, given how little high school students learn about free speech rights and how many negative examples they get from administrators.

Lessons taught by example are most powerful, and high school administrators have offered students some of the worst examples of censorship. In the past few years, high school student newspapers have been punished, censored, or shut down on a fairly regular basis not only for being critical of their administrations but also for publishing articles on everything from abstinence education, to the popularity of tattoos among students, to abortion and gay marriage.[2] Of course, some lessons are more direct than others. Take, for example, this quote from a high school principal explaining his decision to confiscate an edition of the student newspaper because of an editorial supporting marijuana legalization: "I feel like censorship is very important." He elaborated, "Court cases support school censorship of articles. And we feel like that's necessary for us to censor editorials in the best interest of our program and the best interest of our school and community."[3] I believe this statement reflects the opinion of many other high school administrators: not only may a high school censor opinions, but it *should* do so for reasons ranging from harmony, to patriotism, to convenience.

And here is one of the great truths about censorship: whatever reason is offered to justify a speech code, such as the prevention of bullying or harassment, time and time again the school administration ends up using the code to insulate itself from mockery or criticism. People in power bamboozle the public (in this case, parents and students) into supporting rules that will ultimately be used to protect the sensibilities (or sensitivities) of those in power.

With high school administrative censors claiming the moral high ground, it should be no surprise that the Knight study also found that high school students were far more likely than adults to think that citizens should not be allowed to express unpopular opinions and that the government should have a role in approving newspaper stories.[4] After all, if protecting everyone from the hurt and difficulty of free speech is a laudable goal, shouldn't the government be empowered to do that?

Meanwhile, there is precious little education in the philosophical principles that undergird our basic liberties, which might otherwise counteract these bad examples. Civics has not been stressed at high schools in recent years, and ignorance of the basics of American governance is widespread. In 2009, the First Amendment Center's survey of knowledge about basic rights found that 39 percent of Americans could not name even *one* right protected by the First Amendment.[5] An online survey by the Bill of Rights Institute in 2010 found that 42 percent of adult Americans identified Karl Marx's "from each according to his ability, to each according to his needs" maxim as a line from America's founding documents.[6] A more recent large-scale study rated less than a quarter of twelfth graders as having a decent understanding of our system of government.[7]

A shameful level of civics knowledge, in combination with the miserable state of student rights in K–12, leaves students uninformed about the importance of free speech and distressingly comfortable with censorship. The result is that students show up at college with little idea of what their rights are and even a little unsure if this freedom is a good thing. So before we embark on our college odyssey, there are some fundamentals that every student, and every citizen, needs to know about free speech.

"Seriously, Why Is Free Speech Important Again?"

Many of us are good at paying lip service to freedom of speech, but without having a fully developed idea why we should. Others, especially among academics, view it as a right whose importance is exaggerated and that might even stand in the way of progress. So let's start with some fundamental questions that seldom get asked these days: Why is free speech such a big deal anyway? And why is it so important in college? Given that the age difference between a senior in high school and a college freshman is sometimes negligible, why should there be any difference in their rights? Isn't protecting students from offensive or hurtful speech an important goal as well? To most high school students, the answers to these questions are not obvious. They can be found in areas of law, philosophy, and history that are seldom explored by today's students, or even by high school or college administrators.

The Legal Landscape

In law, there is a stark distinction between the free speech rights of college versus high school students. The law accepts K–12 as a sort of training ground for adulthood and citizenship, but higher education is the big time, with students from eighteen to eighty years old and beyond taking part. The function of high school is preparation, while the function of higher education is nothing less than to serve as the engine of intellectual, artistic, and scientific innovation. Any limit on the expression of college students is understood to endanger the entire academic endeavor. The Supreme Court has recognized this in unusually powerful language, declaring in 1957:

> The essentiality of freedom in the community of American universities is almost self-evident. No one should underestimate the vital role in a democracy that is played by those who guide and train our youth.

To impose any strait jacket upon the intellectual leaders in our colleges and universities would imperil the future of our Nation. . . . Scholarship cannot flourish in an atmosphere of suspicion and distrust. *Teachers and students must always remain free to inquire, to study and to evaluate, to gain new maturity and understanding; otherwise, our civilization will stagnate and die.* [Emphasis added.][8]

Of course, some kinds of speech are unprotected even under our First Amendment, including child pornography, obscenity (meaning hard-core pornography, not simple swear words), and libel. However, the Supreme Court takes special pains to limit these restrictions to a handful of narrow categories in order to protect as much speech as possible and is hesitant to create new exceptions. Also, state officials, including administrators at public colleges, have the power to place reasonable "time, place, and manner" guidelines on some speech as long as it is done in a "content neutral" way. So a college is within its rights to stop a protest that is substantially disrupting the university. For example, nothing prevents colleges from stopping student takeovers of administrative buildings, from kicking a disruptive student out of class, or from punishing students for trying to disrupt a speech. (Throughout this book, you will see administrators exploit even that humble power beyond recognition.)

The First Amendment guarantees an exceptionally broad range of speech on campus. A unifying theme within First Amendment law is that those in power cannot shut down speech simply because they dislike the views being expressed. This is called "viewpoint discrimination" and it forms the very essence of what we normally mean when we say "censorship." Despite the First Amendment's clear prohibitions against singling out certain viewpoints for punishment, however, public campuses do precisely that on a regular basis.

Some of you may be wondering why I keep referring to public colleges and not private ones. The First Amendment does not directly bind private colleges. California is the only state (through a law known as the "Leonard Law") to apply First Amendment standards to private universities.[9] Yet, even though private colleges face different legal obligations than public ones, their actions are governed by their own promises and policies. The overwhelming majority of colleges promote themselves as intellectual centers that place academic rigor, free speech, and intellectual freedom at the very pinnacle of their priorities.[10] Top colleges promise free speech in glowing language.

Harvard, for example, advertises: "Free interchange of ideas is vital for our primary function of discovering and disseminating ideas through research, teaching, and learning. Curtailment of free speech undercuts the intellectual freedom that defines our purpose."[11] Schools make such promises in part because of the long tradition of freedom of speech on campus, but also because they know that most students will not be interested in attending, most faculty will not be interested in teaching at, and many alumni will stop giving to universities that choose sides on popular debates and silence dissent. Only a comparative handful of colleges, usually deeply religious ones, can get away with advertising themselves as schools that place other values above free speech.

Just like any other business, colleges have to be truthful about how they present themselves. They have to live up to their contractual obligations, and they cannot fraudulently induce people to attend their institutions. When a private college promises free speech, many courts have rightly found this to be binding.

Beyond the Law:
The Grand Philosophy behind Free Speech

Learning the state of the law is all well and good, but it only scratches the surface of why free speech is so important. Today, many fall back on circular defenses of freedom of speech that sound something like, "free speech is important because it is protected by the First Amendment." Far too few of us learn—let alone appreciate—that free speech is a crucial intellectual innovation that allows for peace, prosperity, liberation, creativity, and invention on an unprecedented scale.

While the philosophical case for freedom of speech has been compellingly made by authors as revered as John Milton, John Locke, James Madison, Thomas Jefferson, and Oliver Wendell Holmes, I always recommend the one presented in Jonathan Rauch's 1993 book, *Kindly Inquisitors*.[12] Rauch saw the West's mixed and often unenthusiastic condemnation of Ayatollah Khomeini's fatwa against Salman Rushdie on account of *The Satanic Verses* as symptomatic of a larger crisis.[13] Jimmy Carter, for example, had lamented that the book had "violated" the beliefs of Muslims and caused them "suffering."[14] The chief rabbi of the United Kingdom opined that it "should not have been published."[15]

While it was no surprise that a fundamentalist theocrat like Khomeini would so adamantly oppose free speech, it was a relatively new phenomenon that he would find sympathetic voices in the industrialized democracies among people who call themselves political liberals. Something had changed in the 1980s. As scholars advocated the suppression of pornography and "hate speech," they launched a new, overarching commitment to fighting speech deemed "offensive" to historically disadvantaged groups. Thus, Muslim fundamentalists strangely found common ground with some liberal Western professors: the conviction that "insensitive" speech should be stopped.

So, what's the big deal? What's really at stake? Everything.

If you take a step back and view history broadly, you see that free speech is an essential component of how we order our society and how we come to decide what is true or false. As Rauch explains, the intellectual system that gave birth to the Enlightenment—which in turn gave birth to the American economic and political system—has been around so long and has been so successful that we don't even have a name for it. Rauch calls this system "liberal science." (For conservatives reading this, don't get too worried—he means "liberal" in its nineteenth-century sense, which was all about greater freedom and less control by government.) Often equated with the scientific method, this intellectual system is actually much broader, and possibly the most radical and brilliant system ever devised for resolving disputes and inching closer to the truth. Other systems too easily result in stagnation, ignorance, and oppression, or in division, tribalism, and warfare.

A society has to choose methods of settling disputes or deciding what is true, and the options are not infinite. Historically, the most common system for resolving these disputes was what Rauch labels "fundamentalist," which is based on the supremacy of authority. Some people may associate "fundamentalism" with religion, but Rauch explains it as a broader refusal by those in power to recognize (at least publicly) the possibility that they might be wrong. Governments and social structures that relied on different kinds of "fundamentalist" systems dominate the world's bloody history. Islamic theocrats, the pharaohs of Egypt, the emperors of China, the divine-right kings of Europe, the head priests of the Mayans, Stalin, and Hitler have all ruled with the conviction that they were uniquely attuned to the truth. Most importantly, a fundamentalist system places knowledge and the search for truth in the hands of the few—an order with horrible drawbacks. The history of fundamentalist systems at their worst is characterized by arresting and punishing or even wiping out people who disagree, often in defense of calcified ideas and often in pursuit of power for its own sake.

An alternative system is one in which all opinions are more or less equal. This is an asinine system because people believe contradictory things and everyone cannot be right at once. Two plus two equals four; people who say otherwise are wrong. Believing that all opinions must be *protected* allows for a flowering of rich debate, discussion, and artistic expression, but believing all opinions are *true* leads to nonsense. Unfortunately, a lot of students these days fall into this kind of uncritical relativism—in part because they are afraid of punishment, whether official or merely social, if they debate or disagree.

Among the scores of examples of mindless relativism on campus that I have seen, the one that haunts me the most comes from personal experience. During my time at Stanford Law School, when I took International Human Rights Law with Professor Thomas Ehrlich, there was a constant tension in the class between the value of human rights and a potent cultural relativism that insisted we had no right to judge the norms of other cultures. One day in class, this relativism was challenged by discussion of the practice of "female circumcision," the euphemistic term for female genital mutilation (FGM), which in its various forms involves tearing or cutting out all or part of a girl's clitoris or labia. The World Health Organization has rightfully described FGM as a horrific human rights violation, affecting between 100 and 140 million girls and women worldwide, according to the research.[16] Nevertheless, one of my classmates disagreed that we should condemn it. The student was not a Muslim from a country that practiced FGM, but rather a white, probably upper-middle-class woman. She argued that there was no way we as Westerners could understand the "beauty" of this practice and its cultural meaning and therefore we should not oppose it. I was stunned by how few people in the class were willing to challenge her. She had evoked the "beauty" of another culture, and by some strange social compact we were not allowed to challenge that argument. Of course, perfect relativism makes it impossible to decide anything. But the class wasn't canceled due to our newly discovered nihilism; instead, double standards became a virtual necessity. The very same student would thunder against far less horrific abuses as long as they were committed by people in America. A commitment to the idea that all opinions are largely equal is distressingly popular on campus, at least when someone wants you to drop your argument so they can make theirs. "Selective relativism" is a convenient tactic that educated people use over and over again to shut down debate and discussion, from the classroom to the cocktail party.

Another organizing principle that Rauch considers is the "radical egalitarian principle," which says that all opinions have equal claim to respect, but the opinions of "historically oppressed classes or groups get special consideration." There is also the "humanitarian principle," which can be combined with the relativist or fundamentalist systems, with the caveat that the first priority is to "cause no hurt." The radical egalitarian and the humanitarian principle are both especially seductive on campuses, where they are commonly used to silence the very discussions a society most urgently needs. After all, most serious discussions may involve facts or ideas that someone could claim are "hurtful." Yes, some words are genuinely hurtful. But colleges too often call upon some form of the humanitarian principle to justify speech codes that are then used to punish mild speech that simply annoys the administration. In this way, they manipulate students into supporting their own censorship.

The "liberal science" system, developed slowly over centuries, avoids the pitfalls of these other systems by adhering to this crucial principle: "checking of each by each through public criticism is the only legitimate way to decide who is right." In other words, the path of progress is a system of free speech, public disclosure, and active debate. It follows two important rules: First, no one gets the final say; we all must accept that no argument is ever really over, as it can always be challenged if not disproved down the line. Second, no one gets special, unchallengeable claims of "personal authority." No one individual is immune to the criticism of others and none can claim to be above intellectual reproach. No one is omniscient or infallible, so we are all forced to defend our arguments with logic, evidence, and persuasion. No one gets the final say, even if he claims to be the head priest of Zeus.

The radically open-minded "liberal science" approach to deciding what is right stands as one of the most important innovations in human history. In the broad view, societies that rely on this approach have flourished artistically, scientifically, and politically, while authoritarian orders have eventually languished.

The grand blossoming of philosophy and science in the modern academy began with the "liberal science" approach. Colleges and universities were built on the recognition that you have to leave knowledge open to continuous debate, experimentation, critical examination, and discussion. Ideas that don't hold up to this scrutiny should be discarded. It is a ruthless and tough system in which ideas that once gave us great comfort can be quickly relegated to the dustbin of history. It isn't concerned with your feelings or your ego, as it has a much more important job: discerning what is true and wise.

Interestingly, to succeed, liberal science relies on people being unafraid of being wrong on a regular basis.[17] You are never going to get to the right answer if people aren't constantly positing new hypotheses on top of new hypotheses. Even coming up with a "stupid" hypothesis is all part of the process of teasing out the truth—and sometimes those "stupid" hypotheses turn out to be right. Thought experiments are key to the system's wild success. If you limit the process to ideas that are comfortable to everyone, you suffocate innovation and, yes, progress.

Beyond Rauch's big-picture philosophy, there are many more reasons for believing in free speech, including:

THE SPIRITUAL: Free expression is especially important in the discussion of religious issues, since the desire to silence opposing spiritual views is very powerful. Amazingly, some people express sympathy on campus for "blasphemy" laws that prevent speech considered insulting to Islam, without understanding that almost everyone's beliefs are blasphemy to someone.

THE POLITICAL: A system that allows for censorship must necessarily put actual, flawed people in charge of deciding what does not get to be said. This is probably *the* most important reason to take that power out of the hands of authority. Even if we think authorities should be empowered to regulate opinion, they are likely to be too self-interested and self-deceived to do it fairly or, even, competently. Time and time again, those with the power to censor see criticism of themselves as what needs to be banned.

THE ARTISTIC: Art without the ability to push boundaries and buttons can hardly be called art at all.

THE COMEDIC: Free speech is the comedian's best friend. After all, how much of comedy is about saying what we all know we shouldn't say? Censorship is the natural enemy of comedy.

THE PSYCHOLOGICAL: Free expression allows a crucial "safety valve" for society where people can vent frustrations. In less free societies, disagreements often fester to explode in violence or revolt.

Polarization, and the Special Importance of Free Speech in the Internet Age

If you told me a few years ago that I would find fresh reasons for why free speech makes the world (and knowledge itself) better from the author of a book called *Democracy and the Problem of Free Speech,* I might have looked at you funny. But when I read several of the works of Cass Sunstein, a law professor at Harvard, I was surprised to find a treasure trove of new research on the importance of protecting dissent and a diversity of viewpoints.[18] Most importantly, take Sunstein's book *Infotopia.*[19] It was written in the early days of what we call Web 2.0, way back (in Internet time, that is) in 2006, and Sunstein's enthusiasm for advancing information technology is palpable throughout. In *Infotopia,* he explores the remarkable potential opened up by the communications revolution of the last several decades, whether it be in the form of open-source software, Wikis, prediction markets, or simply the access to thousands and thousands of opinions aggregated and presented to you on websites as basic as *Zagat* and *Rotten Tomatoes.*[20]

Infotopia, however, also emphasizes something that might seem to be bad news for free speech advocates: much research shows that group deliberation (that is, discussion of topics among groups) often does not do a very good job of making opinions better or more accurate. Group deliberation sometimes amplifies a particularly vocal member's incorrect opinions, it sometimes makes us more vulnerable to various logical fallacies, and it often results in group polarization.[21] Several famous studies have shown that when you bring together like-minded people and have them discuss a topic, they tend to become even more extreme in their positions.[22] It has been demonstrated that when a group of mixed viewpoints is broken into liberal and conservative groups that are then left to talk among themselves, the liberals emerge decidedly more liberal, and the same happens to conservatives, even when the individuals in the larger group had initially been much closer to agreement on the issues discussed. *Infotopia* illustrates how group deliberation may be no better at getting to the truth or to a wise course of action than other methods, including a simple vote among all the members of the group, and often it is worse.[23]

The importance to free speech of Cass Sunstein's voluminous research is what it reveals about *why* group decisions go wrong. Repeated throughout *Infotopia* is the idea that groups often fall short because they fail to get the full benefit of the wisdom and information of their individual members.

When groups start to grow cohesive, they often discourage and even silence dissenting voices or ones with contrary, but potentially important, information. The result is what another social scientist, Irving Janis, famously dubbed "groupthink," which is lethal to good decision making since it blinds us to holes in our logic, or to potential bad consequences of our decisions.[24] Sunstein and others have diagnosed this problem in historical mistakes from the Bay of Pigs disaster, to the tragedy of the Space Shuttle *Columbia*, to the wild underestimate of the difficulties that would come with the war in Iraq.[25]

Groupthink can result from forces as subtle as social pressure, an emphasis on group cohesion, the perception of someone's status, or even who speaks first. The techniques that Sunstein recommends to reduce or eliminate these effects are precisely the remedies to uncritical certainty. They include appointing a devil's advocate with the explicit role of taking the other side of any position, breaking up a group into opposing teams, and stressing critical thinking as a goal of greater importance than group cohesion.[26]

Given the subtle forces that can stifle candor and impede the exchange of ideas, adding an outright threat to punish speech—which happens all too often on campus—is poison to the process of getting to better, more interesting, and more thoughtful ideas. After all, how on earth can you have someone play devil's advocate on thorny public policy issues if everyone knows that the "wrong" point of view can actually get you in trouble? If we want our universities to produce the best ideas, we must do more than just *protect* diversity of opinion; we must train and habituate students to *seek out* disagreement, *seek out* facts that might prove them wrong, and be a touch skeptical whenever they find a little too much agreement on an issue. Campuses, however, are often doing the precise opposite: rewarding groupthink, punishing devil's advocates, and shutting down discussions on some of the hottest and most important topics of the day.

Universities take our best and brightest and put them through what is supposed to be an intellectual decathlon that helps our entire society develop better ideas. We are squandering this opportunity if we discourage dissent and if we do not train students to be brave in the face of ideas that upset them, to welcome challenging ideas, and to engage in endless thought experimentation.

I cannot emphasize enough the importance of comedy, satire, and parody to the whole process of experimenting with ideas. Today, students can get in trouble for making jokes (admittedly, sometimes the jokes aren't funny), but even a bad joke can have a remarkable ability to get people talking about issues they would otherwise never have discussed and to draw conclusions they would otherwise never have reached. I suspect that many readers can think of genuine insights they have gained from the work of Woody Allen, Gary Shteyngart, Lenny Bruce, George Carlin, or, for that matter, *South Park, Seinfeld,* or *Curb Your Enthusiasm.* These sources might even provide more real-life wisdom than anything we ever studied about Hegel, George Berkeley, Heidegger, or Foucault.

To be smarter, to be wiser, we need to accept the roaring rapids of information we now live in and learn to navigate them better. Colleges could be teaching us how to fully utilize today's unprecedented flow of data, opinion, emotion, and art to make for a better, smarter world. Hiding from it, pushing it away, looking for some safe harbor free from challenge or pain will only result in more illiberal ideas and fewer students prepared to live in a breathtaking, chaotic, tumultuous world.

J. S. Mill and a Warning to Colleges

In his transformative work *On Liberty* (1859), John Stuart Mill brilliantly makes the case for maximizing human freedom for the benefit of all humankind.[27] His arguments regarding free speech are timeless and yet especially vital today. Mill pointed out that dissenting voices must be protected because of one simple fact: any of us might be wrong. But he also went several steps further, pointing out that open debate is useful even when we are right from the start. The process of open debate and discussion can refine your understanding of the issues and help you recognize in detail why you believe what you do. An opposing argument may hold some kernel of truth, and even if it doesn't, it may deepen your understanding of your own beliefs.

Without free speech and discussion, people cling to their beliefs the same way people maintain prejudices, holding them to be true but not critically examining why, and never learning to defend them. The resulting inability to articulate why we may be right makes us even more emotional and hostile when anything questions our certainty. In *Academically Adrift,* Richard Arum and Josipa Roksa found that precious few college students knew how to argue or think critically and that they lacked the ability to argue more than one side of an issue. Students had a depressingly poor ability to "make an argument" and then "break an argument."[28]

So what would Mill predict for a system that has fallen away from a culturally enshrined process of debate and discussion? He would expect a society in which people of different beliefs do not talk to each other, because doing so might harm their certainty about what they believe. He might guess that opposing camps would surround themselves only by media sources that reflect and reinforce their views, which was possible even in Mill's day but is a thousand times easier today. He might argue that we would be unable to reach common ground, and we might even doubt that a common ground could be possible. He would predict that those in one camp might regard the name of the other camp as a dirty word, yet often be unable to describe the views of the other side (or, often, even their own side) very accurately. Does this sound familiar to anybody? It sounds like the America I live in. And it will continue to be this way if the institution that should be our best hope of remedying uncritical certainty—higher education—is only making the problem worse.

How the Road to Censorship Is Always Paved with Good Intentions

History may be the best weapon to overcome some of the most seductive and common arguments made these days to defend censorship. Probably the simplest but most successful argument for restrictions on speech I hear today is that censorship can protect people from hurtful or bigoted speech. The implicit question I run into all the time on campuses is, "Can't censorship be acceptable if one's intentions are pure, compassionate, and generally good?"

History tells us that the answer is flatly "no." I cannot think of a single anti-free-speech movement in American history that did *not* sprout from someone believing that they were fighting for truth, justice, decency, and goodness itself. This is so common a friend of mine has an acronym for it: the "GIRA Effect," standing for "Good Intentions Run Amok." John Adams thought he was saving the country from ruin by instituting the Alien and Sedition Acts. Northerners who believed that abolitionists needed to be silenced thought they were preventing a bloody civil war. The Victorians who censored everything from the use of curse words to the merest mention of contraception assumed they were saving the nation's soul. The communist-hunters of the two Red Scares thought they were guarding the nation from totalitarianism and, eventually, nuclear destruction.[29]

Having pure intentions, steadfast goals, and an unwillingness to consider that you might be wrong is the formula for some of the worst evils mankind has ever wrought upon one another, from inquisitions to the twentieth century's disastrous experiments with totalitarian utopias. As pushy as those of us who defend civil liberties may seem, the right to freedom of speech and freedom of conscience rests on a deep-seated humility: I know I am not omniscient, and I suspect you aren't either. Therefore, I have no right to tell you what you can't say, certainly no right to tell you what you *must* say, and I wouldn't even imagine telling you what you must think, believe, or hold in your heart.

Intentions matter little if you are still doing the wrong thing, and there is no need to genuflect to good ones. Prohibitions on hateful speech do nothing to stop hate, but they let resentments simmer, and they also prevent you from knowing who the hateful people even are. "I want to know which people in the room I should not turn my back to," says FIRE cofounder Harvey Silverglate, who was raised Jewish, speaking about the principle of allowing anti-Semites or other bigots to express themselves. It may be very tempting for high school students entering college to have sympathy for the advocates of speech codes, but that is only because they misunderstand the purpose of the First Amendment and lack knowledge of the legal, philosophical, and historical principles that support it. The First Amendment exists to protect minority points of view in a democracy, and anything that undermines it necessarily gives more power to the authorities. It is ultimately the best protection of the weak, the unpopular, the oddballs, the misfits, and the underdogs. If the only price that we have to pay for this freedom is that we sometimes hear words that we find offensive, it is well worth it.

Another historical fact that students need to know is that just because we have a First Amendment doesn't mean that the country has always enjoyed or will always enjoy robust protections of expression. People are often surprised to discover that prior to 1925, the First Amendment was considered to bind only the federal government, and even then it was interpreted so weakly as to have little practical effect. But in a line of cases extending from the 1925 decision in *Gitlow* v. *New York* to the present, the Supreme Court has interpreted the First Amendment as strongly protecting political dissent, satire, and parody—the very types of speech that are most often attacked on campuses.[30] Free speech, therefore, has not always been the rule, and we should not assume it will always remain the rule.

The Acceptance of Censorship by College Students

That most students don't care a great deal about freedom of speech and some-times are even hostile to it has been evident in case after case at FIRE. Here are just a few cases where you might think students would have risen up in outrage, but they didn't.

A student at Auburn University was told by the administration in late 2011 that he could not put a Ron Paul banner in his window.[31] When the student pointed out that other students had been allowed to put up banners, the university claimed (like they typically do) that this policy had always been in place—even though it was only being enforced, coincidentally, against this particular student. While the student continued to produce evidence that Auburn was not enforcing this policy against other students, the attempt to prevent him from engaging in the election process was met by an eerie silence on campus, except for objections from a libertarian group.[32] Imagine telling students in the 1960s or '70s that they could not be openly political; those students probably would've literally rioted.

The restriction on political speech defied parody in 2008 when the executive vice president of the University of Oklahoma announced that no university resources, including email and presumably Internet access, could be used for "the forwarding of political humor/commentary."[33] For those of us who have a hard time imagining what we would forward if we weren't allowed to forward anything political or anything from *The Daily Show* and *The Onion*, this was a startlingly broad restriction. Nonetheless, it took an article I wrote in the *Huffington Post* and a letter from FIRE to get the university to reverse course.[34] If there were protests over this policy, we can't find them. Likewise, we can find no evidence that any student objected to Case Western Reserve University's policy stating that "University facilities and services may not be used . . . to advocate a partisan position," despite FIRE naming the code our December 2010 Speech Code of the Month and publicizing that fact widely.[35] (More about our Speech Code of the Month project in the next chapter.)

On the even sillier side, the silence was deafening in 2006 when a university in Wisconsin tore down a quote from the humorist Dave Barry that a Ph.D. student had posted on his door. Marquette University claimed that the quote was "patently offensive"—a term reserved in law to refer to XXX pornography. The quote? "As Americans we must always remember that we all have a common enemy, an enemy that is dangerous, powerful, and relentless. I refer, of course, to the federal government." Marquette has yet to back down from its decision, even citing sensitivity to the victims of 9/11 as justification.[36] The censorship was absurd, and it garnered national attention and calls from reporters, yet the students and faculty did not register a peep.

But worse than ambivalence and apathy are the cases where students see free speech as an obstacle to progress, and censorship as the kind of thing that good, enlightened people do.

At San Francisco State University in 2006–2007, members of the College Republicans who stomped on hand-drawn Hamas and Hezbollah flags during an antiterrorism protest were brought up on charges of "incivility" by the campus judiciary.[37] When Debra Saunders, a columnist for the *San Francisco Chronicle*, called SFSU to ask how it could be possible to punish the students when the Supreme Court has held that even burning an American flag is protected expression under the First Amendment, university spokesperson Ellen Griffin responded, "I don't believe the complaint is about the desecration of the flag. I believe that the complaint is the desecration of Allah."[38] This is the first time I know of in American history that a public official tried to justify a violation of the free speech clause of the First Amendment by violating the First Amendment's clause banning the "establishment of religion" by mandating an Islamic norm. Apparently, the word for God appears in Arabic script on one of the flags, but when the College Republicans discovered this, they let a Muslim student mark out the word. Because there really could be no question that the students had the First Amendment right to show their contempt for two designated terrorist groups in this way, the College Republicans ultimately prevailed in the campus judiciary and in a First Amendment lawsuit against the university.[39]

But what interested me most were student reactions to the protest. The non-Muslim student who filed the complaint asked this question of the disciplinary board: "How can we let the College Republicans have such a rally that was politically motivated and one-sided?" (I believe a non-politically-motivated rally is called a party.) The outrage machine at SFSU is powerful, and it was clear from the moment that the College Republicans engaged in their intentionally provocative protest that the students and administration were going to find something to charge them with.

The overwhelming majority of the cases in this book involve student bodies that didn't care enough to react when they saw their fellow students' rights being violated. More disturbingly, the victims themselves often didn't know they have the right to be free from viewpoint-based censorship, from being pressured to say things they don't mean, and from speech codes. The K–12 system has little interest in producing students who know they have rights, and college and university administrators take full advantage of that fact. In the short term, they gain tremendous power to avoid campus controversies, stifle disagreeable opinions, and dodge criticism. In the long term, however, they are neglecting to cultivate the difficult intellectual habits of robust inquiry and critical reasoning. By keeping students in the dark about their rights and about why they have those rights in the first place, schools are failing to prepare them for the rigors of being educated citizens in a diverse, dynamic, and powerful democracy.

A Personal Aside:
How Multiculturalism Demands Free Speech

One thing that has always struck me as bizarre is that respect for multiculturalism and diversity is one of the most common rationales that people use when defending the policing of campus speech. I find this strange because my experiences growing up as a first-generation American in a multicultural environment are what led to my lifelong interest in freedom of speech. My second earliest memory relates to this very topic.

I was four years old and it was Christmas, and my auntie Rhona had given me a plastic drum as a present. It was the first gift I ever remember truly disliking. But as I looked at my mother and father, I didn't know what to do. My father is a Russian refugee who grew up in Yugoslavia and who believes it is more important to be honest than polite, while my mother is ethnically Irish but was raised in England and always emphasized the absolute importance of politeness. I was stuck. I hated that drum, but when my mother asked me, "Do you like your present?" I didn't know what to say. Under the cultural values of my father I had to say "no," but under the cultural values of my mother I had to say "yes." This dilemma bounced back and forth in my head, getting harder and harder every second that my mother waited for my response. So I did what any sensible four-year-old would do: I started crying. I remember my older sister saying, "Poor baby, doesn't like his present, starts crying." I didn't have the vocabulary at the time, but if I had, I would've said, "No, it's not that—it's my first experience with a cultural paradox!"

The other kids my age in my neighborhood all came from different backgrounds. The coolest kid in my neighborhood was Peruvian, while some of the other children were Vietnamese, Korean, Italian American, Puerto Rican, or African American, and several of the other white kids were from the American South (which, to a first-generation Russo-British American, is certainly another culture). One thing that became crystal clear in this environment is that no two cultures and no two people entirely agree on what speech should and should not be allowed. Indeed, ideas about politeness and propriety differ from economic class to economic class, between genders, among cultures, between different regions of the country, and certainly from one era in history to another.

If we were to put someone in charge of policing politeness or civility, whose ideals would we choose? My British mother's, which emphasizes politeness at all costs? My Russian father's, which values honesty over politeness? Danny Nguyen's? Nelson Beledo's? If we tried to ban everything that offended someone's cultural traditions, class conceptions, or personal idiosyncrasies, nobody could safely say a thing. It has been obvious to me ever since I was little that free speech must be the rule for any truly pluralistic or multicultural community. Far from requiring censorship, a true understanding of multiculturalism demands free speech.

What High School Students (and Parents) Need to Know before They Go to College

A high school environment that often portrays free speech as a problem, that does not teach the philosophy or law or utility of free speech, and that presents punishment of students for bad opinions as morally righteous is an environment that naturally produces students who are cautious about what they say and who may even favor pressure towards conformity or silence.

Here are a few things a student should know before heading off to college:

1. When it comes to rights, K–12 schools and colleges are as different as night and day. At a public college, you have far more constitutional

rights to freedom of speech and due process than you did in high school. At private universities, you are generally recognized to have far greater rights and autonomy, and are often contractually promised these rights in the student handbook or other materials.

2. Crucially, these rights do not arise simply because someone put ink on paper ages ago. They are not mere legalisms, and they developed from a profound understanding of the processes by which we get to better and more reliable ideas, as well as more creativity and innovation. Pointing out to college administrators or classmates how they rely on freedom of speech every second of the day is helpful when you need to explain to them that they can't just throw away the system every time it produces a thought or expression someone dislikes.

3. Colleges are supposed to provide at least as much, if not more, freedom of speech and thought as society at large, not the other way around. Campus administrators have been successful in convincing students that the primary goal of the university is to make students feel comfortable. Unfortunately, comfortable minds are often not thinking ones. Students should, however, be able to feel comfortable with engaging in devil's advocacy and thought experimentation, and, perhaps most importantly, with the possibility of being wrong. Making it safe for people to be wrong is one of the first steps in creating an atmosphere that is intellectually vibrant enough to produce good ideas and meaningful discussion.

4. Wisdom comes from surprising places, and certainly no person in power is going to be able to guess which comments or demonstrations or satires will lead to an interesting discussion that you would not otherwise have had. University administrators will argue that some speech is simply "worthless," forgetting that words and ideas exist only in interaction with other words and ideas. Even the stupidest joke you have ever heard can sometimes lead to an interesting discussion and call forth information or opinions that you would never have known about otherwise.

5. Be sure to read the university's promotional materials and student handbook before attending. If you see that a public college has policies that limit pamphleteering or demonstrations to a tiny corner of the campus or has codes that prevent "annoying" language (more on these in the next chapter), ask how such policies can be squared with the

college's obligations under the First Amendment. If you are applying to a private college that promises freedom of speech in glowing language in its promotional materials but then find questionable policies that seem to impose arbitrary, vague, and broad limitations on speech buried deeper in the student handbook, write to administrators before applying and ask what this means. If you apply to a college with promotional materials that make it pretty clear that the college values, say, its Mormon identity or evangelical Christian identity, and in language that is stronger than any mention of freedom of speech, you should know that you'll probably enjoy very few rights there, particularly if it publishes restrictions based on its distinct identity. By enrolling at such an institution, you have given your informed consent to forgo certain rights while you attend.

6. Be sure to check out FIRE's *Guides to Student Rights on Campus*, including our *Guide to Free Speech on Campus*, which is available for free online, and research any school you're considering applying to on our campus database to see its record on freedom of speech and whether it maintains a speech code. You can find these both at www.thefire.org. Again, the cases I discuss in this book are a small fraction of those listed on the FIRE website.

7. Remind administrators that the goal is to facilitate candid interaction between people who disagree and come from different experiences, and that making students fearful of disagreement, or holding out the threat of punishment for an unpopular opinion or even a joke, is undermining their intellectual experience.

Now, moving on in our march towards college, do you remember what it was like the first time you received one of those glossy college brochures in the mail?

Chapter 2

Opening the College Brochure

Y<small>OU ARE A SOPHOMORE IN HIGH SCHOOL</small>, and your attention has long since shifted away from the incident with the student newspaper. Turns out, you did quite well on your PSAT exam and you've been coming home from school every day to a mailbox full of glossy promotional materials from colleges around the country. The brochures show happy students making friends, playing Frisbee on the quad, or studying in a grand library. At night, when your other friends are watching episodes of *Tosh.O* on Hulu, you have been scanning info about your dream schools. You doubt that you have the scores to get into Yale, but you pore over its website, watching its promotional video over and over. It is a musical produced by students, very much like the TV show *Glee*. While combing through another section of the website, you stumble upon Yale's policy on "Free Expression, Peaceful Dissent, and Demonstrations." It bravely declares the essentiality of free speech:

> The history of intellectual growth and discovery clearly demonstrates the need for unfettered freedom, the right to think the unthinkable, discuss the unmentionable, and challenge the unchallengeable. . . . We value freedom of expression precisely because it provides a forum for the new, the provocative, the disturbing, and the unorthodox. Free speech is a barrier to the tyranny of authoritarian or even majority opinion as to the rightness or wrongness of particular doctrines or thoughts.[1]

Your heart jumps a little. Think the unthinkable, challenge the unchallengeable! Actual debate and discourse, actual self-expression! You think to yourself, college will be so different from high school. At college, you will finally be free to debate, argue, and discuss anything without fear of punishment.

Then you Google a little more and come across a term you hadn't seen before: "campus speech codes." That doesn't sound right. At college? You look a little further and realize it is no cause for concern. "Speech codes," whatever they were, were apparently abandoned, like, a gabillion years ago.

PC Went to War with Free Speech in the 1990s, and Free Speech Lost

The most pervasive myth about campus censorship and speech codes is that this war was fought long ago and free speech won. In the late 1980s and early '90s, America was distracted, disturbed, and sometimes delighted by a new craze: political correctness. Comedians and authors joked about the sudden commitment to a novel PC vocabulary designed to be less offensive: the gender-neutral "flight attendant" replaced "stewardess," the non-skin-tone-related "African American" became the stand-in for "black," and the non-heterosexist term "partner" attempted to replace "boyfriend" and "girlfriend." These terminology shifts were benign, but it wasn't long before America realized that political correctness had a more sinister side.

Colleges and universities across the country were at the vanguard of the PC movement. Many schools began proudly and publicly passing "speech codes" as a way of demonstrating their commitment to diversity and tolerance. This was in stark contrast to the reputation that higher education had enjoyed since the explosion of the campus free speech movement in the 1960s. The most common legal theory behind speech codes was one that characterized some kinds of protected speech as punishable harassment. Speech regulations came in a variety of forms, but their purpose was the same: to prohibit speech that might be offensive on the basis of race, gender, sexual orientation, or an ever-increasing list of other characteristics. The University of Texas at El Paso, for example, has expanded the list of protected classes to absurd lengths by including "race, color, *religion*, national origin, gender, age, disability, citizenship, veteran status, sexual orientation, *ideology, political views,* or *political affiliation.*" (Emphasis mine, to show the conscious targeting of core topics of debate.)[2]

While bizarre cases of "PC run amok" were frequently reported in the early '90s, it was not until 1993 that these abuses got their mascot. That year, the University of Pennsylvania threw its resources at punishing a student for shouting, "Shut up, you water buffalo!" out of his window.

Unfortunately, the student had directed his comments at members of a black sorority who were "serenading" his dormitory late at night. For sororities or fraternities, "serenading" means loud singing, stomping, and general clamoring in celebration of some group milestone. The sorority in this case had kept it up for more than twenty minutes while the student was trying to study, and while many others had yelled at them to keep it down. Even though no one could figure out how "water buffalo" was a racial epithet, the student was charged with racial harassment and threatened with expulsion. An Israeli scholar who heard about the case explained that "*Behema* is Hebrew slang for a thoughtless or rowdy person, and, literally, can best be translated as 'water buffalo.' It has absolutely no racial connotation." As it turned out, the student had in fact attended a yeshiva, where, he said, "we called each other *behema* all the time, and the teachers and rabbi would call us that if we misbehaved."[3]

Penn's efforts to punish the student over his English version of a Hebrew colloquialism brought international media attention, including coverage by *Time, Newsweek,* the *Village Voice, Rolling Stone,* the *New York Times,* the *Financial Times,* the *International Herald Tribune,* the *New Republic, The Times* of London, NPR, and NBC Nightly News.[4] Even *Doonesbury* and Rush Limbaugh came to a rare meeting of minds, agreeing that Penn's handling of the incident warranted mockery.[5] In the face of criticism from around the world and across the political spectrum, the school ultimately backed down.[6]

The defense of the student was successfully led by Alan Charles Kors, a Penn professor. Kors teamed up with Harvey Silverglate to author *The Shadow University: The Betrayal of Liberty on America's Campuses,* which shed more light on "the Water Buffalo Case" and described dozens of additional examples of violations of free speech, due process, and other rights on campus. After publishing *The Shadow University* in 1998, Kors and Silverglate received so many additional reports of students being punished for exercising free speech on campus that they founded the Foundation for Individual Rights in Education in 1999. I joined FIRE as its first director of legal and public advocacy in 2001.

To most of the public and the media, however, campus political correctness appeared to be in retreat after the "water buffalo incident." Beginning in 1989, every court-challenged campus speech code was struck down as unconstitutional.[7] In 1991, President George H. W. Bush warned that "free speech [is] under assault" on college campuses. Congress, the California legislature, and the U.S. Supreme Court all struck blows of their own against curbing free expression on campus.[8] This decisive turn against campus speech codes and political correctness led many people, including Robert O'Neil, a leading expert on campus free speech issues, to conclude that "most of the codes were either given a decent burial by formal action or were allowed to expire quietly and unnoticed."[9]

Unfortunately, O'Neil and others who celebrated the end of PC censorship were dead wrong. Speech codes did not retreat; in fact, they quietly increased in number to become the rule rather than exception at colleges around the country. As for cases of PC censorship run amok, they only got worse and more common.

Hidden Speech Codes, Everywhere

Despite the glowing promises of free speech touted by most of the nation's universities, if you dig deeper into university websites and student handbooks, you are likely to find policies seriously restricting speech. That is, if you know where to look.

FIRE defines speech codes as *any campus regulation that punishes, forbids, heavily regulates, or restricts a substantial amount of protected speech, or what would be protected speech in society at large.* Such a straightforward definition is necessary as, understandably, campuses do not place these restrictions under the heading SPEECH CODES in their student handbooks. In the most extensive study yet conducted of campus speech codes, FIRE's constitutional lawyers announced in a 2012 report that 65 percent of the 392 top colleges surveyed have policies of this kind that severely restrict speech protected by the First Amendment.[10]

Some of these speech codes promise a pain-free world, like Rhode Island College's policy stating that the college "will not tolerate actions *or attitudes* that threaten the welfare of any of its members" (emphasis added).[11] Banning actions that "threaten the welfare of others" is vague enough to be used against almost any speech, while banning "attitudes" is far beyond the legitimate powers of a state college. Meanwhile, Texas Southern University bans any attempts to cause "emotional," "mental," or "verbal harm," which includes "embarrassing, degrading or damaging information, *assumptions, implications,* [and] remarks" (emphasis added).[12] How exactly one enforces a rule about "embarrassing assumptions," I have no idea. Likewise, the University of Northern Colorado bans telling "inappropriate jokes" or "intentionally, recklessly *or negligently* causing physical, emotional, or *mental harm* to any person" (emphasis added).[13] The code at Texas A&M prohibits violating others' "rights" to "respect for personal feelings" and, in an oddly Victorian phrase, "freedom from indignity of any type."[14]

Many universities also have wildly overbroad computer use policies, like those at the College at Brockport (State University of New York), which bans "[a]ll uses of Internet/email that harass, annoy or otherwise inconvenience others," including "offensive language or graphics (whether or not the receiver objects, since others may come in contact with it)."[15] Similarly, the Lone Star College System in Texas maintains a policy that prohibits any use of "vulgar expression," including in electronic communications.[16] Fordham University forbids using any email message to "insult" or "embarrass" someone—a rule that most students likely violate nearly daily—while Northeastern University tells students they may not send any message that "in the sole judgment of the University" is "annoying" or "offensive."[17]

Vague and broad prohibitions against racial or sexual harassment remain the most common features of campus speech codes. Murray State University, for example, bans "displaying sexual and/or derogatory comments about men/women on coffee mugs, hats, clothing, etc."[18] (I am *dying* to see the coffee mug that inspired that rule.) The University of Idaho bans "communication" that is "insensitive."[19] New York University prohibits "insulting, teasing, mocking, degrading, or ridiculing another person or group," as well as "inappropriate . . . comments, questions, [and] jokes."[20] Davidson College's sexual harassment policy prohibits the use of "patronizing remarks," including referring to an adult as "girl," "boy," "hunk," "doll," "honey," or "sweetie" (so I guess performing *Guys and Dolls* is out). It also bars "comments or inquiries about dating."[21] How exactly one dates without commenting or inquiring about dating is a question I have been asking the Davidson administration for years, but this policy remains unchanged. Perhaps Davidson prefers an antisocial student body.

San Francisco State University states that "[s]exual [h]arassment is one person's distortion of a university relationship by unwelcome conduct which emphasizes another person's sexuality."[22] This rule gives students no idea what could get them charged with harassment. Asking someone out for a date? Turning someone down? For obtuseness and childlike drafting, however, the University of Iowa takes the cake: sexual harassment "occurs when somebody says or does something sexually related that you don't want them to say or do, regardless of who it is."[23] The University of Tulsa's harassment policy prohibits any "statement which, when viewed from the perspective of a reasonable person similarly situated, is offensive."[24] Again, the law is clear that offensive speech is precisely the kind of speech in need of protection. We don't really need a constitutional amendment to protect speech that is pleasant, popular, and agreeable to all.

Going above and beyond, Western Michigan University's harassment policy actually banned "sexism," which it defined as "the perception and treatment of any person, not as an individual, but as a member of a category based on sex."[25] I am unfamiliar with any other attempt by a public institution to ban any perception, let alone perceiving that a person is a man or a woman. The plain language of this policy would outlaw anything but unisex bathrooms. While colleges should protect students from actual harassment, absurdly broadening the meaning of harassment trivializes real harassment by recasting the concept as a catchall for any expression that offends someone.

FIRE has been naming a Speech Code of the Month every month for over seven years, and there is no risk that we will run out of outrageous codes. Here is a list of some of the colleges that were awarded the dubious distinction of "Speech Code of the Month" by FIRE.[26] Note the hasty throwing together of crimes, like assault, or unprotected speech, like threats, with clearly protected speech, like jokes:

Month	School	Policy States / Bans
Oct-05	Northern Arizona University (Flagstaff, AZ)	"[p]rohibited harassment includes, but is not limited to, stereotyping, negative comments or jokes, explicit threats, segregation, and verbal or physical assault when any of these are based upon a person's race, sex, color, national origin, religion, age, disability, veteran status, or sexual orientation."
Feb-06	Jacksonville State University (Jacksonville, AL)	"No student shall threaten, offend, or degrade anyone on University owned or operated property."
May-06	University of Miami (Miami, FL)	"Any words or acts, whether intentional or a product of the disregard for the safety, rights, or welfare of others, which cause or result in physical or emotional harm to others, or which intimidate, degrade, demean, threaten, haze or otherwise interfere with another person's rightful actions or comfort is prohibited."
Jul-06	Macalester College (St. Paul, MN)	"speech acts which are intended to insult or stigmatize an individual or group of individuals on the basis of their race or color, or speech that makes use of inappropriate words or non-verbals."
Aug-06	Colorado State University (Fort Collins, CO)	"expressions of hostility against a person or property because of a person's race, color, ancestry, national origin, religion, ability, age, gender, socio-economic status, ethnicity, or sexual orientation."
Sep-06	Drexel University (Philadelphia, PA)	Harassment includes "inconsiderate jokes" and "inappropriately directed laughter."
Apr-07	Florida Gulf Coast University (Fort Myers, FL)	"expressions deemed inappropriate."
Sep-07	Ohio State University (Columbus, OH)	"Do not joke about differences related to race, ethnicity, sexual orientation, gender, ability, socioeconomic background, etc."

MONTH	SCHOOL	POLICY STATES / BANS
Oct-07	Lewis-Clark State College (Lewiston, ID)	"Any practice by a group or an individual that . . . embarrasses . . . a member of the College community . . . and which occurs on College-owned or controlled property or while the violator is attending or participating in a College-sponsored event or activity is prohibited."
Nov-07	Saginaw Valley State University (University Center, MI)	"degrading comments or jokes referring to an individual's race, religion, sex, sexual orientation, national origin, age, marital or familial status, color, height, weight, handicap or disability."
Apr-09	San Jose State University (San Jose, CA)	"publicly telling offensive jokes."
Nov-09	Keene State College (Keene, NH)	The College "will not tolerate language that is sexist and promotes negative stereotypes and demeans members of our community."
May-10	Bryn Mawr College (Bryn Mawr, PA)	"[n]egative or offensive comments, jokes or suggestions about another employee's gender or sexuality, ethnicity or religion." (Although the language references employees, the policy specifically applies to students as well.)
Jun-10	University of Wisconsin System	Potential examples of racial harassment are "verbal assaults based on ethnicity, such as name calling, racial slurs, or 'jokes' that demean a victim's color, culture or history."
Jul-10	College of the Holy Cross (Worchester, MA)	"unintentionally causing emotional injury through careless or reckless behavior."
Oct-10	Grambling State University (Grambling, LA)	Email policy prohibits "the creation or distribution of any disruptive or offensive messages, including offensive comments about race, gender, hair color, disabilities, age, sexual orientation, pornography, religious beliefs and practice, political beliefs, or national origin."

Month	School	Policy States / Bans
Jan-11	Marshall University (Huntington, WV)	"incivility or disrespect of persons."
Feb-11	Claremont McKenna College (Claremont, CA)	"The College's system must not be used to create or transmit material that is derogatory, defamatory, obscene or offensive. Such material includes, but is not limited to, slurs, epithets or anything that might be construed as harassment or disparagement based on race, color, national origin, sex, sexual orientation, age, disability, or religious or political beliefs."
Mar-11	California State University, Chico (Chico, CA)	Examples of sexual harassment by faculty included use of "stereotypic generalizations" and "[c]ontinual use of generic masculine terms such as to refer to people of both sexes."
Apr-11	University of Florida (Gainesville, FL)	"Organizations or individuals that adversely upset the delicate balance of communal living will be subject to disciplinary action by the University."
Jul-11	Eastern Michigan University (Ypsilanti, MI)	Sexual harassment includes any "inappropriate sexual or gender-based activities, comments or gestures."
Aug-11	Mansfield University of Pennsylvania (Mansfield, PA)	Statement on "freedom from discrimination" prohibits any behavior that would "diminish [another's] self-esteem" or their "striving for competence."
Sep-11	University of Wisconsin–Whitewater (Whitewater, WI)	Prohibition on "obnoxious jerk harassment," including "sexual suggestiveness, jokes, catcalls, whistles, remarks, etc."
Dec-11	St. Olaf College (Northfield, MN)	"Misuse of Computers" policy prohibits "creating or posting of material that is offensive," stating that such actions "are subject to disciplinary review."

Several of the codes we have "honored" as Speech Codes of the Month were changed or reformed not long after being announced, likely due to public embarrassment. But speech codes are often like a multiheaded hydra: cut off one and a new one grows in its place. If there is a will to censor on campus, administrators will find a way.

I occasionally meet people who recognize that such overbroad policies ban a tremendous amount of protected expression, but think this is okay because they trust college administrators to administer these codes fairly. This idea is both naïve and even disingenuous; often, the very same people would be horrified if vague, amorphous laws controlling speech were placed in the hands of, say, Presidents George W. Bush or Barack Obama. And the worst of campus administrators don't even limit themselves to the extraordinarily broad definitions of their codes.

Of course, if campus administrators honestly and consistently applied campus speech codes, they wouldn't last a day, because they sweep in so much protected speech that the overwhelming majority of students could be found guilty. Professors and students wouldn't put up with it and speech codes would end forever. Speech codes can survive only through selective enforcement. What administrators and advocates of restricting free speech want you to forget is that any such restrictive policy sets flawed human beings in charge of deciding what can and cannot be said. As any First Amendment lawyer knows, the first thing to go is any speech that criticizes or annoys those who decide what speech is free. It should therefore come as no surprise that the most frequently censored opinions on campus are those that are unpopular with campus administrators.

What Harassment Is Supposed to Mean

Before I discuss how administrators abuse harassment rationales, it's important to understand what harassment means in the law. Sexual and racial harassment are fairly well-defined legal concepts. Certain examples are easy to identify: *quid pro quo* harassment—that is, if an employer demands sex for a promotion—is universally agreed to be harassment. The vagueness comes in with the concept of "hostile work environment" harassment, especially in the peculiar environment of the university, where you must allow a robust exchange of ideas on concepts including sexuality among young men and women who often can't stop thinking about sex.

While fitting the definition of harassment to the college environment might sound like a puzzle, the good news is that the Supreme Court has *already* provided a definition that balances the protection of students from harassment with the importance of freedom of speech. In *Davis* v. *Monroe County Board of Education*, the Court gave its only ruling on the application of harassment to the educational environment.[27] In that case, the Court dealt with harassment allegations in the K–12 context, but its formula for deciding when to hold an educational institution liable for discrimination is also the correct standard for defining harassment on college campuses. "The *Davis* standard," as I call it, defines harassment as unwelcome discriminatory behavior, directed at a person because of his or her race or gender, that is "so severe, pervasive, and objectively offensive, and that so undermines and detracts from the victims' educational experience, that the victim-students are effectively denied equal access to an institution's resources and opportunities."[28] The *Davis* standard expertly balances legitimate concerns about actual discrimination and harassment with protection of free speech, while not overburdening universities with unrealistic obligations to police every aspect of their students' lives.

The *Davis* standard is a serious answer to a serious problem. Those of us who believe in stopping genuine discriminatory harassment are done no favors by a reinterpretation of harassment that wrongly creates a generalized "right not to be offended." This erosion of the seriousness of sexual harassment became apparent to me during the controversy surrounding Herman Cain, a Republican presidential candidate, in 2011.[29] The media seemed astonished that the initial claims of harassment against Cain were greeted by the public with some ambivalence and skepticism. That ambivalence started to subside as more accusers came forward and the allegations began to sound more like *quid pro quo* harassment and even assault.[30] But I believe that the initial lack of scandal stems largely from the fact that harassment is often invoked too lightly and in contexts where it does not really belong, especially on campuses. Supporters of racial and sexual harassment laws should be striving to bring the campus definition of such harassment back in line with its legal definition—and with free speech.

A Short Selection of Examples of Abuses of Harassment Codes on Campus

Any discussion of campus abuse of harassment codes must start with the example of Keith John Sampson, a middle-aged student and janitor at Indiana University–Purdue University Indianapolis. In 2007, Sampson was working his way through college when he was found guilty of racial harassment for reading a book in public. Some of his coworkers were offended by the cover of the book, *Notre Dame vs. the Klan*, which included a black-and-white picture of a Klan rally.[31] Even though Sampson explained to them that it was a history book *celebrating* the *defeat* of the Klan in a 1924 street fight, the school found Sampson guilty of racial harassment for "openly reading [a] book related to a historically and racially abhorrent subject."[32] Without even giving him a hearing, the administration imposed a death sentence on Sampson's career: any future employer would be likely to assume that a finding of racial harassment meant Sampson was a Klan *member* rather than the reader of a book about their defeat.

A student being punished because his university *literally* falsely judged a book by its cover should have been an irresistible human interest story. But despite the intervention of both the American Civil Liberties Union of Indiana and FIRE, the case received little media attention at the time.[33] Dorothy Rabinowitz published a column about the case in the *Wall Street Journal* over the summer of 2008, but it never approached the iconic infamy of the "water buffalo" case.[34] It seems that most Americans were beginning to take such incidents for granted. I suspect that many view stifling political correctness as a silly, unfortunate, yet mostly harmless part of the collegiate landscape. But as the Sampson case shows, it is far from harmless. Such cases help legitimize knee-jerk reactions to speech that offends, while ingraining a defensive and apologetic attitude about even the most modest exercise of free speech.

Another wild abuse of harassment codes took place at the University of New Hampshire in 2003, when student Tim Garneau was found guilty of harassment, disorderly conduct, and violating the school's affirmative action policy for making a flyer that joked that girls could lose the "freshman 15" by taking the stairs.[35] Garneau posted the flyers because he was angry that some students would take the elevator up just one floor and even *down* one floor, which slowed elevator service for students who, like him, lived on the seventh floor. The flyers, which were torn down within two hours, read in their entirety: "9 out of 10 freshman girls gain 10–15 pounds. But there is something you can do about it. If u live below the 6th floor takes the stairs. [*Image of a slender young woman.*] Not only will u feel better about yourself but you will also be saving us time and wont be sore on the eyes [*sic*]."[36] Even though he apologized to the student body with the intensity of someone who had committed a war crime (rather than a fat joke), Garneau was kicked out of his dormitory and sentenced to mandatory psychological counseling, two years' probation, and a 3,000-word reflection paper. After his appeal was denied, he had to resort to living out of his car in the cold New Hampshire autumn for weeks. FIRE launched a national publicity campaign about the absurdity and patent unconstitutionality of this abuse of power. Shortly afterwards, the school received a phone call from Jon Stewart's *Daily Show*, which wanted to cover the incident. With remarkable speed, the university announced that Garneau would be allowed back into the dorms.[37] Jon Stewart apparently cared more about this abuse of rights than Garneau's fellow students, who largely expressed ambivalence about the school's misuse of power.[38]

In 2007, the same year that Keith John Sampson was being punished, Tufts University found a conservative newspaper guilty of two counts of racial harassment.[39] The paper, called *The Primary Source*, had been criticized in December 2006 for publishing a parody Christmas carol called "Oh Come All Ye Black Folk."[40] The point of the carol was to lampoon the university's aggressive attempts to attract black students. When called out for insensitivity, *The Primary Source* apologized for the joke and the case was forgotten for several months. Later that spring, however, *The Primary Source* published an ad questioning what the writers saw as the overly rosy depiction of Islam during the school's "Islamic Awareness Week."[41] It contained two direct quotes from the Koran, including "'I will cast terror into the hearts of those who disbelieve. Therefore strike off their heads and strike off every fingertip of them.' – The Koran, Sura 8:12." It also pointed out that "In Saudi Arabia, women make up 5 percent of the workforce, the smallest percentage of any nation worldwide. They are not allowed to operate a motor vehicle or go outside without proper covering of their body. (*Country Reports on Human Rights Practices 2001*)," and that "Ibn Al-Ghazzali, the famous Islamic theologian, said, 'The most satisfying and final word on the matter is that marriage is a form of slavery. The woman is man's slave and her duty therefore is absolute obedience to the husband in all that he asks of her person.'" The only factual error I could find in the ad was that it claimed that the seven countries that punish homosexuality by death are all Islamic theocracies. At the time, there were in fact eight Islamic theocracies where homosexuality was a capital offense.

Did this paint Islamic extremism in a nice light? No. Was it one-sided? Yes. But that was the entire point: to present a counterargument to what the paper saw as a one-sided view presented by the university. Too many of us have been conditioned to apologize for words that offend, when open debate is bound to create some offense. Indeed, it *should* happen. Being offended is what happens when you have your deepest beliefs challenged, and if you make it through four years of college without having your deepest beliefs challenged, you should ask for your money back.

If the complaining students had argued that *The Primary Source* got its facts wrong, that could have been a constructive or at least interesting debate. But instead, in predictable fashion, the offended students plowed ahead with a harassment claim. Here, the fact that *The Primary Source* printed largely verifiable information—with citations, no less—was no defense, nor was the fact that the ad concerned contentious issues of dire global importance. Even under U.S. libel law, truth is an absolute defense. Tufts may have made free speech history by being the first institution in the United States to find someone guilty of harassment for stating verifiable facts directed at no one in particular.

I doubt that the Tufts disciplinary board thought through the full ramifications of its actions. If a Muslim student had published these same statements in an article calling for reform in Islam, would that be harassment? An atheist saying religion is bunk? A Protestant railing against Catholicism? Nonetheless, a judicial panel consisting of both faculty and students found the publication guilty.[42] After intense pressure from FIRE, the president of Tufts, Lawrence Bacow, eliminated the sanctions against *The Primary Source* in the fall of 2007, but he left the harassment finding intact.[43] (Tufts would be "awarded" our June 2008 Speech Code of the Month for its policy banning "unwelcomed communications such as phone calls, misuse of message boards, email messages, and other behaviors calculated to annoy, embarrass, or distress.")[44]

Some other notable abuses of harassment rationales include a 2005 case in which the University of Central Florida put a student on trial for creating a group on Facebook that posted "Victor Perez is a jerk and a fool" when Perez was running for student government.[45] In 2004, at Occidental College in California, a student disc jockey was found guilty of harassment on his radio show, not only for making fun of his fellow members of student government, but also for cracking jokes about his own mother. In a classic administrative overreach, the student was charged for disparaging "treatment of the category [of] 'mother.'"[46]

As troubling as such incidents are for students, it may be professors who have the most to fear from the overzealous reinterpretation of harassment codes. I will leave much of this discussion to Chapter 10, but it is worth noting some cases here. In 1999, in one of the first cases I ever worked on, Mercedes Lynn de Uriarte, a professor at the University of Texas at Austin, was investigated for "ethnic harassment" of another professor. Interestingly, both de Uriarte and the accusing professor were Mexican American and the complaint accused her of both *not mentioning* her accuser's ethnicity when it was helpful to do so and also *mentioning* it when it was not helpful.[47] The facts suggested that the ethnic-harassment accusation was an excuse for the university to retaliate against de Uriarte for filing a grievance.

Another incident targeting faculty took place in 2011–2012 at Purdue University Calumet, where nine complaints of harassment or discrimination were filed against a professor for criticizing Islam and Muslims on Facebook and in class. Some of the complainants never took his class, and many of them left unspecified what speech, exactly, they were complaining about.[48] On November 6, 2011, the professor posted a photo on Facebook of "Christians killed by a radical Muslim group" in Nigeria, adding: "Where are the 'moderate' Muslims['] reaction[s] to this? Oh, I forgot they are still looking at the earth as flat according to the idiot Mohammad, may his name be cursed." While I can understand how this speech might have hurt some students' feelings, feeling hurt and being harassed are categorically different things.

In 2011 the University of Denver provided another example of how far the concept of harassment has morphed from its legal origins, when Professor Arthur Gilbert was declared guilty of sexual harassment and sentenced to mandatory "sensitivity training" because the content of his class "The Domestic and International Consequences of the Drug War" was considered too racy.[49] According to the syllabus, one of the themes in the course was "Drugs and Sin in American Life: From Masturbation and Prostitution to Alcohol and Drugs."[50] How, precisely, you can have a meaningful discussion of these topics without offending anybody is beyond me. While Denver faculty, FIRE, and the American Association of University Professors (AAUP) rose to Professor Gilbert's defense, the university refused to reopen the case.[51]

These are just a few of the cases that illustrate how often "harassment" is used as an all-purpose accusation for speech that offends someone. This abuse became so widespread that in 2003 the Office for Civil Rights (OCR) of the U.S. Department of Education—the department that polices the enforcement of federal harassment regulations—issued a letter of clarification to practically every single college in the country recognizing that harassment rationales were being abused.[52] It stated unequivocally that "No OCR regulation should be interpreted to impinge upon rights protected under the First Amendment to the U.S. Constitution or to require recipients to enact or enforce codes that punish the exercise of such rights." The letter further stated, "Harassment, however, to be prohibited by the statutes within OCR's jurisdiction, must include something beyond the mere expression of views, words, symbols or thoughts that some person finds offensive." Nonetheless, most colleges still maintain unconstitutional harassment codes today.

The Department of Education Muddies the Waters

The story of harassment codes on campus is largely one of universities brazenly ignoring the right to free speech and the law concerning harassment as they pass speech codes that, when challenged, are almost laughed out of court. Since 1989, there have been nearly two dozen court cases involving campus speech codes.[53] Almost all of them have challenged a substantially overbroad harassment code, and virtually all of these challenges have been successful.

So there was good reason to hope that the days of speech codes would be numbered, but in April 2011, the Office for Civil Rights of the Department of Education appeared to step back from the strong statement it had made in 2003 in favor of rational harassment codes and free speech. The agency issued a nineteen-page letter dictating to colleges the procedures they must follow in sexual harassment and assault cases.[54] Among its many troubling points is a requirement that sexual misconduct cases be adjudicated using the lowest possible standard of evidence allowable in court (which will be discussed at length in Chapter 6). Moreover, the letter made no mention of the First Amendment or free speech, ignoring the way that vague and broad definitions of harassment have been used to justify campus speech codes and censorship. By mandating many procedural steps that colleges must take to respond to allegations of sexual harassment—while failing to mandate a consistent, limited, and constitutional definition of harassment—OCR has effectively encouraged campus officials to punish speech they simply dislike.

Along with a remarkably broad coalition of groups—including the Tully Center for Free Speech at Syracuse University, the National Coalition Against Censorship, the National Association of Scholars, the Alliance Defense Fund

Center for Academic Freedom, Feminists for Free Expression, Woodhull Sexual Freedom Alliance, the American Booksellers Foundation for Free Expression, Accuracy in Academia, and the American Council of Trustees and Alumni—FIRE wrote to OCR in January 2012 requesting that it publicly affirm the *Davis* standard as the controlling definition for harassment on campus.[55] I also published an article in the *Washington Post* the same day that we mailed the letter, explaining:

> By simply following the Supreme Court's guidance, the OCR would assure that serious harassment is punished on campus while free speech is robustly protected. In one move, OCR could rid campuses of a substantial portion of all speech codes. . . . Most important, by recognizing the *Davis* standard, the OCR would send a message that free speech and free minds are essential to—not incompatible with—the development of creative, critical and innovative thinkers on our nation's campuses.[56]

Thus far, we have received no response from OCR. Of course, OCR can enforce regulations, but it cannot overrule the First Amendment. While the agency's new letter may embolden universities to enforce their speech codes, I'm confident that any attempt to do so will be consistently shot down by the courts.

The Harm of Campus Speech Codes That Are "Just on the Books"

Campus speech codes do, of course, have their defenders. When forced to concede that the codes do not meet First Amendment standards, these defenders often use the same rationalization: "What's the big deal? Those speech codes are never enforced!" As you have seen already, that assertion is wrong. These codes are enforced, often against unambiguously protected speech.

But let's play the game as if it were true. What is the harm of speech codes if they are merely "on the books"? Plenty. The very existence of these codes poses serious problems. First, they create a "chilling effect": if people have any reason to fear that they might be punished for offering an opinion, most people will refrain from doing so. This creates a campus atmosphere in which some students won't talk about important issues, while others share their opinions only around likeminded people. The result is polarization and a failure to develop a deeper understanding of controversial issues.

Speech codes are also harmful in and of themselves, because they miseducate students about free speech, their rights, the rights of others, and what it means to live in a pluralistic democracy. Some scholars, including Robert Post, dean of Yale Law School, see education's role in serving the proper functioning of democracy as the primary reason for the existence of academic freedom and view the academy as a place to instill an understanding of democratic values.[57] It is therefore inexcusable that institutions of higher education, through their unconstitutional speech codes, are teaching students the exact opposite of the lessons they are supposed to be learning about democracy, pluralism, and expression. In other words, by propagating speech codes, universities are lying to their students about what their rights are and misinforming them about how speech relates to the functioning of democracies, thus undermining the very reason for academic freedom.

So what lesson have campus speech codes given to a generation or more of students? That censoring certain viewpoints is both constitutionally and morally correct. Ask students today if they believe in free speech, and I suspect most would answer "yes." But if you dug deeper, you would discover that many students have been so badly misinformed about what it means to live in a free society that they accept selective censorship as a fact of life. They have never learned how crucial hearing a multitude of opinions is to our entire intellectual system. Making the most of free speech is a habit and a discipline that must be taught, and speech codes short-circuit that process.

The "Silent Classroom"

As I mentioned in the introduction, the venerable Association of American Colleges and Universities unveiled a massive study in 2010 called *Engaging Diverse Viewpoints*.[58] The study asked a sample set of 24,000 students about their feelings and views concerning diverse viewpoints on campus. One question asked whether the students thought it was "safe to hold unpopular views on campus." Think about how this statement is worded. It does not ask if students "feel *confident* that they can *express* views that are unpopular on campus," but rather whether it is "safe" to merely "hold" them on campus. The question seems like a whitewash, designed to garner an inaccurately positive response that would allow the AACU to say, "All is fine on campus." Even those who would never make an unpopular argument on campus wouldn't go so far as to say they wouldn't feel "safe" merely believing one, right? Actually, they would. Among the college seniors in the survey sample, only 30.3 percent answered that they strongly agreed that "It is safe to hold unpopular views on campus."[59]

Even more alarmingly, the study showed that students' sense of the safety of expressing unpopular views steadily declines from freshman year (starting at 40.3 percent) to senior year.[60] College seems to be the place where bad ideas about free speech go to get even worse.

But the students were downright optimistic compared to the 9,000 "campus professionals" surveyed, including faculty, student affairs personnel, and academic administrators. Only 18.8 percent strongly agreed that it was safe to have unpopular views on campus.[61] Faculty members, who are often the longest-serving members of the college community and presumably know it best, scored *the lowest of any group*—a miserable 16.7 percent![62]

While it still might strike some readers as unlikely that anything could stop students—especially undergraduates—from expressing their opinions (at all times and in all ways), the fact that the current generation shies away from meaningful debate has been a much-discussed phenomenon in academia for at least a decade now.

My first run-in with the mystery of the "silent classroom" came when I read *New York Times* columnist Michiko Kakutani's March 2002 article "Debate? Defense? Discussion? Oh, Don't Go There!"[63] Kakutani engaged several authors, social critics, university professors, and the dean of students at Princeton to get to the bottom of the "reluctance of today's students to engage in impassioned debate." Amanda Anderson, the author of *The Way We Argue Now* and an English professor at Johns Hopkins University, offered one of the more compelling theories on why students are hesitant to speak their minds: "It's as though there's no distinction between the person and the argument, as though to criticize an argument would be injurious to the person. . . . Because so many forms of scholarly inquiry today foreground people's lived experience, there's this kind of odd overtactfulness. In many ways, it's emanating from a good thing, but it's turned into a disabling thing."

Kakutani went on to discuss other theories that range from the deep and thoughtful—including her argument that relativism and the broad acceptance of the "principle of subjectivity" make meaningful argument seem less important—to the somewhat silly—referencing Oprah Winfrey, 9/11, the popularity of the drug ecstasy, and "the often petty haggling between right and left, Republicans and Democrats, during President Bill Clinton's impeachment hearings and the disputed presidential election of 2000."

Given the range and breadth of what she was willing to consider, it was striking to me that she never mentioned the fact that students and faculty get in trouble for expressing unpopular opinions. Surely even the vaguest fear of being punished for speaking your mind would have a more profound effect on the state of debate on America's campuses than, say, the off-putting "spectacle of liberals and conservatives screaming at each other on television programs like 'Crossfire'"?

Kakutani's piece was one of several that came out around that time bemoaning the disappearance of debate and discussion on college campuses but failing to consider speech codes and campus punishments as contributing factors. For example, months earlier, University of Massachusetts Amherst student Suzanne Feigelson wrote an article in *Amherst Magazine* titled "The Silent Classroom" that gained substantial attention.[64] Feigelson considered many factors that cause students to "stop talking in class about midway through freshman year." She emphasized concerns about sounding stupid or redundant, classmates judging them, being embarrassed, or not being cool. Feigelson neglected, however, to examine the effect of the implicit threat of punishment for badly received statements of opinion. This is especially surprising given that Feigelson attended UMass Amherst, a college that has repeatedly punished students for clearly protected expression. The very same fall that Feigelson wrote "The Silent Classroom," UMass received negative publicity for permitting a rally in opposition to a military response to the 9/11 attacks but refusing to allow students to rally in support of the newly minted "war on terror."[65] The students held a rally anyway, but their materials were reportedly publicly vandalized with no response from the university. Indeed, UMass Amherst maintains unconstitutional speech codes limiting expression both within the classroom and outside of it.[66] Might not the detailed and explicit speech code banning classroom speech that is "clearly disrespectful" have something to do with a classroom environment where students are hesitant to speak their minds?

At the time these articles were published, I was in my first year at FIRE. I was neck deep in hundreds of case submissions dating back to the organization's founding two years before, reading story after story of students and faculty members alike being punished for protected speech, and much of which—far from being "hate speech"—was remarkably tame by the standards of the larger society. If these commentators on student silence had bothered looking, they would have found numerous examples of campus censorship that were going on at that very moment.

In fact, 2001–2002 brought a brief jump in media awareness of campus censorship in the wake of the September 11 attacks. Some cases that received national attention included one at Central Michigan University, where students were told by administrators to take down pictures of American flags, eagles, and a *San Francisco Chronicle* article titled "Bastards" because they all purportedly violated the policy on "hate related items and . . . profanity."[67] At San Diego State University, a student from Ethiopia was threatened with punishment for chastising Saudi students who he said had expressed delight at the 9/11 attacks.[68] The Saudi students apparently didn't know that Zewdalem Kebede also spoke Arabic and could understand them. Despite the fact that Kebede was one student arguing against four, he was the one brought up on charges of being "verbally abusive." Meanwhile, at UC Berkeley, the home of the free speech movement, members of the student government attempted to punish the student newspaper for running a cartoon that showed the 9/11 hijackers surprised to find themselves in hell.[69] I would learn that characterizing speech critical of Islamic terrorism as offensive to all Muslims—which, if you think about it, is pretty offensive in itself—is a common tactic on campus.[70]

Even professors were not safe. A University of New Mexico professor was threatened with punishment for joking on 9/11 that "anyone who can blow up the Pentagon has my vote."[71] The professor's remark caught the attention of mainstream and conservative media alike, and he apologized profusely for his insensitive joke, but the incident led to his early retirement from teaching.[72] Professors at both Duke and Penn were chastised by administrators for posting articles in favor of the war on terrorism, while professors at the City University of New York were threatened with punishment for holding a teach-in opposing a strong American reaction to 9/11.[73]

These were only a handful of the 9/11-related cases that affected faculty and students, right, left, and center. In spite of the media attention these controversies received, no one made the connection between the culture of silence (or, at least, excessive reticence) on campus and the fact that students were increasingly aware that they could get in trouble for simply expressing their opinions. Even the faintest threat of actual punishment is a far more efficient and effective way to stifle debate than the reasons suggested by Kakutani and Feigelson. A silent classroom is a natural—indeed, inevitable—result of an educational atmosphere full of speech restrictions and a culture that teaches students to shy away from controversy.

Speech Codes, Juan Williams, and the Danger of Honest Talk

Too few Americans know that campus speech codes are real and more numerous than they were in their supposed heyday of the early '90s. The fact that students can get in trouble for "politically incorrect" speech is probably more commonly accepted, but is not regarded as a particularly serious problem. At Stanford, I knew many people who would applaud that practice. I also saw this attitude reflected among some of my fellow columnists in their ambivalent or even supportive reaction to NPR's decision to fire the commentator Juan Williams in 2010.[74]

For those of you who didn't follow the case, Williams is an African American civil rights historian and a journalist who had been working for National Public Radio since 1999. In a debate with Bill O'Reilly on Fox News, Williams conceded that he felt nervous getting on a plane when he saw Muslims in traditional garb getting on, as well. Williams explained in his 2011 book *Muzzled*,

> This was not a bigoted statement or a policy position. It was not reasoned opinion. It was simply an honest statement of my fears after the terrorist attacks of 9/11 by radical Muslims who professed that killing Americans was part of their religious duty and would earn them the company of virgins in heaven. I don't think that I'm the only American who feels this way.[75]

Note that Williams made his comment while arguing *against* lumping all Muslims together with terrorists and *against* racial profiling. A major obstacle to getting a handle on both race relations and religious tensions is that people are afraid to be candid about how they really feel towards people of other cultures and faiths. Williams took a rare step and admitted to an all-too-human fear, and for that he was fired from his job. The day after he was fired, NPR's CEO, Vivian Schiller, told an audience at the Atlanta Press Club that Williams should have kept his feelings about Muslims between himself and "his psychiatrist or his publicist."[76] Schiller's words sent a powerful message: "We don't really want to know your real feelings, fears, and emotions. If they might offend, shut up."

It is true that the situation at NPR is distinct from that on campus, because NPR can fire an employee for good or bad reasons, while public colleges may not legally expel students for their opinions. Yet the message sent by NPR is precisely the one that speech codes and viewpoint-based punishments send. And the result is cowed students, silent classrooms, and whispers in cliques rather than serious, meaty, honest talk.

As you will see, the problem goes far beyond the cliché of "PC run amok," to the larger question of what people do when handed the power to shut down speech. Administrators, being people, exercise this power for both good and bad reasons, for higher purposes and selfish ones. Students and even faculty members learn to watch what they say, or to retreat into groups of the likeminded.

CHAPTER 3

The College Road Trip

Y OU ARE A SIXTEEN-YEAR-OLD JUNIOR IN HIGH SCHOOL. It's fall, and you have decided to get an early jump on your college campus visits to see where you want to apply. Your parents are trying to steer you towards a public college, since the prices of the top private colleges are, as your father says, "highway robbery." You think he must be wrong. Your parents need to understand that college is considered mandatory for most jobs these days, and a big-name school holds the key to a stellar career. Besides, everyone else seems to have figured out how to pay for college, right?

While your heart is still set on Harvard and Yale and you have secretly promised yourself you will apply to them, you clamber into your mother's aging Ford Taurus and visit some state colleges. After a seeming eternity in the car, you are now on a guided tour of Big State University, a school so large that there are twice as many students enrolled as people in your home town. Maybe it's the fall chill or just the newness of the whole thing, but you find yourself excited as the good-looking sophomore begins your tour of the campus. It is a vast complex, with a library the size of the hospital where you were born, a cafeteria that seems to go on for days, and lecture halls that could hold your entire high school.

At one point during the tour, you pass a twenty-foot-wide octagonal gazebo. Jason, an irreverent potential classmate, laughs. "Ah, the infamous 'free speech gazebo.'"

"Like 'Speakers Corner' in London?" you ask, showing off your Quiz Bowl knowledge. Jason shrugs, not knowing what you are talking about. "A place where you can always speak your mind no matter what?" you add.

"You wish," he says. "It's the *only* place on campus designated for 'free speech activities' and you have to reserve it days in advance."

You laugh, but then pause. He isn't serious, is he?

Quarantining Free Speech

Trevor Smith was unaware of Texas Tech University's free speech zone before he decided to enroll. But when he began to organize a protest against the war in Iraq in February 2003, he was told that he had to limit his group to the campus's twenty-foot-wide "free speech gazebo."[1] This was the sole area where Texas Tech's 28,000 students could engage in any free speech activities, from handing out flyers, pamphlets, or newspapers, to holding demonstrations. Requests to engage in these time-honored forms of campus expression outside of the gazebo had to be "submitted at least six university working days before the intended use."[2]

The gazebo was much too small to hold all the students who might wish to engage in an average protest. I asked a friend of mine with a math degree from MIT to do a dimensional analysis of the gazebo. What if all the students at Texas Tech wanted to exercise their free speech rights at the same time? My friend calculated that you would have to crush them down to the density of uranium 238 to jam all 28,000 students into the gazebo.

Trevor Smith wondered how he could have an effective protest in a tiny gazebo in a tiny corner of the huge campus. If no one can hear or see your protest, what's the point? So Trevor appealed to FIRE for help. By that time, I had been at the organization for two years and was learning that every time I thought I'd seen it all, I would confront something like the free speech gazebo. I wrote to the university:

Texas Tech's nearly 28,000 students deserve more than 20 feet of freedom (approximately 1 foot of freedom per 1,400 students). This caricature of constitutional law should be anathema to any institution committed to intellectual rigor, robust debate, and a free and vibrant community. We call on you to tear down the barriers to speech and declare all of Texas Tech University a "free speech area."[3]

The tone may have been melodramatic, but I meant every word. With pressure from FIRE and unfavorable press coverage, the university decided to let Trevor's protests proceed as planned and expanded the free speech zone. Merely expanding the zone, however, was not good enough, especially since Texas Tech also maintained a broad speech code. So in June 2003, the Alliance Defense Fund, a Christian litigation organization, launched a lawsuit against Texas Tech in coordination with FIRE. The resulting 2004 decision in *Roberts v. Haragan* overturned Texas Tech's remarkably restrictive free speech zone policy, declaring that all open areas on campus are presumed to be available for free speech activities.[4] The decision also overturned the campus speech codes that banned, among other things, "insults" and "ridicule."[5]

One might think that restricting free speech to tiny areas of campus is an eccentricity unique to Texas Tech that ended after a defeat in court. Sadly, restrictive and out-of-the-way free speech zones have been around for a long time and show little sign of disappearing.

I have never been able to determine the precise genesis of campus "free speech zones." Many such zones popped up during the campus free speech movement of the 1960s and '70s, but it isn't clear when they were transmogrified from an additional area on campus where one could always engage in free speech, to a method of restricting free speech to as small a space as possible. I suspect this change took place in the late 1980s and through the '90s, during the accelerated bureaucratization of campuses that I address later in this chapter. In *The Shadow University*, Kors and Silverglate recount efforts to fight back against free speech quarantines, starting with a successful battle at Tufts University in 1989.[6] Other attempts to impose tiny zones had been defeated at Oklahoma State University, the University of South Florida, and the University of Wisconsin–Whitewater.[7] I had been at FIRE for only a few weeks before I started running into these zones.

The first case that I encountered was at West Virginia University, where Professor Daniel Shapiro and students Matthew Poe and Michael Bomford were leading the fight against the school's two tiny zones, bringing together groups like the College Democrats, the College Republicans, and the West Virginia Animal Rights Coalition to protest the policy.[8] Even added together, the two zones limited free speech to less than 1 percent of the total campus. It took nearly a year and a half, and a dozen detailed letters, to get the zones opened up and the policy liberalized. When a libertarian litigation group called the Rutherford Institute filed suit, it was the final straw—the university finally abandoned the zones. Over the course of the following years, fighting absurd free speech zones became a staple of my work. We challenged these zones at scores of schools, including the University of North Texas, the University of Central Florida, the University of Nevada at Reno, Clemson University, Citrus College in California, Florida State University, the University of North Carolina at Greensboro, California State University at Chico, Tarrant County College in Texas, and Appalachian State University.[9]

Many campuses that imposed free speech zones were not content with limiting free speech to a tiny fraction of campus, but also applied onerous rules within those zones. At Western Illinois University, for example, you had to apply forty-eight hours in advance to use a zone that was smaller than a classroom.[10] It took student and faculty protests, along with bad publicity, to get the school to expand the zone in 2003. At Valdosta State University, the same school that kicked out Hayden Barnes for his Facebook collage, the free speech zone consisted of one small stone stage, which also required forty-eight hours' notice to reserve. Furthermore, it was available for only two hours a day, from the "hours of NOON to 1 PM and/or 5 PM to 6 PM." It was not until FIRE took out a full-page ad in *U.S. News and World Report*'s college ranking edition in 2008 that Valdosta backed down from this unconstitutional policy.[11]

Speech zone policies have won our Speech Code of the Month title many times. Our July 2007 SCOTM (yes, the acronym sounds a little gross to us too) went to McNeese State University for limiting demonstrations to two small free speech zones and allowing them to demonstrate only "once during each Fall, Spring, and summer [sic] session in the assigned demonstration zone only."[12] Applications to use the zones had to be received at least seventy-two hours in advance, and the zones could only be used from Monday through Friday. Our August 2010 SCOTM went to Front Range Community College for its free speech zone policy, which according to Samantha Harris, the attorney who evaluates these codes for constitutionality, "contain[ed] a perfect blend of unintentional hilarity and horrendous unconstitutionality."[13] It included a waiver that you had to sign binding yourself along with your "heirs, successors, [and] executors" to indemnify the college if you were harmed, even due to the negligence of the college, while exercising your free speech rights. It also forbade handing out any literature, pamphlets, or material within the zone unless a passerby actually went up and asked for it. In addition, it banned "[p]ictures, displays, graphics, etc. . . . if they promote hate, harm, violence, or the threat of these to others," and even "[d]e minimus [*sic*] speech (speech that amounts to nothing and has no purpose)." The idea of campus administrators giving themselves the power to decide which speech has value and which doesn't is almost as comical as it is unconstitutional. Our September 2010 "honor" went to UMass Amherst, which maintained a policy on "Controversial Rallies" stating that "[s]pace for controversial rallies must be requested 5 working days prior to the scheduled date" and that "[s]pace may only be reserved from 12 noon to 1 PM."[14] The policy also required the student organization sponsoring the controversial rally to "designate at least 6 members to act as a security team" (thereby putting these students at risk of physical harm). And our March 2012 SCOTM went to the University of Missouri–St. Louis, where "students wishing to hold a rally or demonstration on campus must provide the university with six weeks' notice and may not do anything to 'discredit the student body or UM–St. Louis.'"[15]

Our December 2007 SCOTM—the University of Cincinnati's "free speech area," which amounts to just 0.1 percent of the school's 137-acre campus—was challenged in a February 2012 lawsuit.[16] In addition to quarantining "demonstrations, pickets, and rallies" to the zone, the policy requires that all expressive activity in the zone be registered with the university a full ten working days in advance and threatens students that "[a]nyone violating this policy may be charged with trespassing." And the university has been true to its word. When the campus chapter of Young Americans for Liberty asked for permission to gather signatures and talk to students across campus in support of a time-sensitive ballot initiative, they were told in an email that they were not even "permitted to walk around," and that "if we are informed that you are, Public Safety will be contacted." The student group filed suit, challenging the policy's constitutionality on First Amendment grounds.[17]

So, why free speech zones? How can they be defended when they dramatically restrict speech at institutions that should be the preeminent free speech zones of our whole society? One reason is that the courts, unfortunately, have been too permissive with unreasonable "reasonable time, place, and manner restrictions." Courts have permitted, for example, creating crude and tiny free speech zones (sometimes rightfully called "free speech cages") to prevent protestors from getting too close to the Republican or Democratic national conventions. As a principle, allowing for the reasonable regulation of the "time, place, and manner" of speech makes sense; putting a reasonable cap on the volume of any concert in a densely populated neighborhood, for instance, is understandable. But on campus, the excuse that university administrators are only regulating the "time, place, and manner" of speech has been twisted out of recognition.

"Time, place, and manner" has become the censor's mantra—literally, in the depressing case of Northern Arizona University. On September 11, 2011, two students who wanted to hand out small American flags in the student center to commemorate the tenth anniversary of 9/11 were not only ordered to stop but also charged with a disciplinary offense.[18] NAU's response to the flags involved no fewer than four administrators and a police officer. Three of these administrators cited "time, place, and manner" restrictions as the justification for demanding that the students stop their action, and one chanted the phrase over and over again when the students claimed that their minimal form of expression should be allowed. (The campus police officer, for her part, looked like she'd rather be doing just about anything besides stopping students from passing out American flags.) Watching the strange ordeal on video, I was struck by how important it was to these administrators to shut these students down, and how they believed the incantation of "time, place, and manner" conferred upon them the unquestionable power to silence the students.

What these administrators probably did not know is that the Supreme Court had anticipated that "time, place, and manner" restrictions could be abused to stop speech disfavored by those in power, and therefore the Court imposed a number of requirements for their use.[19] To be constitutional, the regulations must be "content-neutral"; they cannot be directed at the content or viewpoint of the speech. In addition, they must be "reasonable"— related to an important university interest (like preventing the disruption of classes). They also must leave ample alternative options for free speech. The zones discussed in this chapter come nowhere near the legal definition of constitutionality, nor do they stand up to public scrutiny. FIRE has had great success defeating free speech zones by pointing out to the public that "there is nothing reasonable about transforming 99% of a public campus into a censorship zone."

But while campaigns against speech zones are usually successful, the zones persist for a simple reason: while everyone claims to love free speech, we are quick to leap on any exception pliable enough to target opinions we dislike. Those of us who defend freedom of speech watch this happen with incredible speed and predictability. The reason we have such strong protections for freedom of speech as part of our constitution is because the urge to censor opinions we don't like is so powerful. In fact, Steven Pinker—a Harvard psychology professor, bestselling author, and FIRE Board of Advisors member—believes that we may be hardwired to suppress ideas that make us uncomfortable. Pinker has linked this instinct to a deep "psychology of taboo," which he speculates may incline us to surround ourselves with people who feel that even thinking certain "bad" thoughts is evil.[20]

Free speech champion Nat Hentoff nicely summed up the universality of this censorship urge in his book *Free Speech for Me—But Not for Thee: How the American Left and Right Relentlessly Censor Each Other*. Hentoff argued that "censorship—throughout this sweet land of liberty—remains the strongest drive in human nature, with sex a weak second. In that respect, men and women, white and of color, liberals and Jesse Helms, are brothers and sisters under the skin."[21]

Four Factors That Work against Campus Free Speech

Over the years, I have observed four primary factors that explain the creation of speech zones, the tenacity of speech codes, and the pervasiveness of campus censorship: ideology, bureaucracy, liability, and ignorance.

IGNORANCE: After years of speaking at conferences of university administrators and in front of students, I realized something that First Amendment attorneys can easily forget: the value of free speech is not obvious or intuitive. What is obvious to people is that some ideas are hurtful and we should try to get along with each other. It is far harder to understand that we should commit ourselves to discussion that is often painful, for the good of all. You have to be taught the profound rationales that undergird free speech, and you have to learn the value of debate by experiencing it.

Students cannot be expected to understand the liberating power of new and challenging ideas when the administrators who run campuses have not themselves learned an appreciation for the practice of free speech. Those in charge are also slow to acknowledge that their good intentions may get confused with self-interest, and that they may be censoring people simply for having critical or contrasting opinions. Administrators must be willing to "tie their own hands" and guard themselves from the temptation to punish opinions they dislike.

IDEOLOGY: "Political correctness" has become the butt of many jokes, yet a PC morality still thrives on campus. It emphasizes the prevention of "hurtful speech" at all costs, with special protection for "historically underrepresented groups," including gay students, racial minorities, and women. But the justification for campus speech codes and the reality of campus censorship are entirely different things.

Defenders of speech codes will invoke nightmare scenarios of students being chased off campus by mobs of bigots shouting racial epithets. These hypothetical examples usually involve speech that is not constitutionally protected, such as true threats, stalking, or vandalism. In reality, the way speech codes are implemented often bears no resemblance to such horror stories; many cases involve nothing more serious than mockery of the university or the administration. Conjuring up scary scenarios to justify speech codes allows administrators to manipulate the emotions of goodhearted students, professors, and other administrators to support speech limitations that often have nothing to do with "hate speech."

While I was speaking at a conference of administrators several years ago, one of them angrily asked me, "So there is nothing that can be done to prevent a student from calling another the n-word?" This administrator actually saw anything short of punishment as doing nothing. My response was that political correctness as a cultural phenomenon has been incredibly successful; even back when I graduated from Stanford in 2000, anyone who used a racial epithet would have been rightly vilified as a bigot (and, notably, I can't think of a single incident where anyone did). And that is how change should come about in a free society—through cultural shifts, not coercion or enforced silence.

As for the idea of "underrepresented groups" that need special protection from offense, it is based on an outdated concept of a dominant campus majority. It has been a long time since white Protestant males have dominated college campuses. Women now constitute the majority at most colleges. Since 2000, women have represented around 57 percent of college enrollments, and in some colleges they make up as much as two-thirds of students.[22] In my own city, Hunter College and Lehman College, both CUNY schools, hover at around 70 percent women.[23] Much of the rhetoric around free speech issues seems oblivious to this seismic campus shift.

Nevertheless, PC ideology with its focus on "underrepresented groups" still endures, in part because it invokes values like politeness, fairness, tolerance, and respect. Simply put, political correctness seems "nice." In practice, though, it often promotes intolerance, often for those who are culturally right of center, or for anything that mocks or satirizes a university itself. Most troublingly, it provides a convenient excuse for those in authority to marginalize criticism and nonconformity.

One predictable result of working so hard to prevent offense is that students quickly learn that claiming to be offended is the ultimate trump card in any argument. After all, if you knew you could immediately win an argument by calling the other person's position offensive, wouldn't you be tempted to use that tactic? Jonathan Rauch refers to this as an "offendedness sweepstakes." Being offended is an emotional state, not a substantive argument; we cannot afford to give it the power to stifle debate.

LIABILITY: This is the least known and least understood factor in the expansion of campus speech policies into the lives of students. Universities are afraid of being sued even for frivolous claims of harassment and discrimination by students or employees. Currently, the logic seems to be that a free speech lawsuit is comparatively rare and will not cost much in court, while lawsuits for harassment and discrimination are far more common and costly. Therefore, university attorneys conclude that it is best to have broad speech-restrictive policies that you can point to during litigation to show you were proactive against "offensive speech," and that protecting speech must be secondary.

Andrew Hacker and Claudia Dreifus examined universities' fear of liability and the link between legal fees and out-of-control tuition in their book *Higher Education?* (2010). They concluded that "[a] big slice of the tuition pie ends up with lawyers and their clients. After hospitals, colleges may be our society's most sued institutions."[24] While some legal threats to universities are valid (say, a lawsuit for the denial of free speech), many others contribute to an overly cautious, overly regulated atmosphere that's hostile to free speech.

BUREAUCRACY: The dramatic expansion of the administrative class on campus may be *the* most important factor in the growth of campus intrusions into free speech and thought. While FIRE has long been concerned about the harmful results of swelling campus bureaucracy, Professor Benjamin Ginsberg of Johns Hopkins University made the case in detail in his stinging 2011 book, *The Fall of the Faculty: The Rise of the All-Administrative University and Why It Matters.*[25] Ginsberg exposed the dizzying growth of the administrative class at universities, the usurpation of powers that once belonged strictly to the faculty, the surprising lack of qualifications of many administrators, the unseemly rise in the salaries of administrators (especially university presidents), and how a burgeoning bureaucracy jacks up costs while diluting educational quality. This ever-expanding bureaucracy creates and enforces an environment of censorship on campus.

The Price of Bureaucracy and Hyperregulation

From the 1981–1982 school year to the 2011–2012 school year, the cost of tuition and fees at private, nonprofit four-year colleges almost tripled, even adjusting for inflation, according to the College Board, a nonprofit collegiate testing organization. During the same period, the cost of attending a four-year public college almost quadrupled.[26] Meanwhile, between 1980 and 2010, the "average family income declined by 7% ($1,160 in constant 2010 dollars) for the poorest 20% of families," while it rose by only "14% ($7,249) for the middle 20% of families." The increase in college costs even outstripped the 78 percent ($136,923) growth for the wealthiest 5 percent.[27] In other words, the cost of higher education at both public and private colleges has skyrocketed relative to all income levels.

Bringing this gap into stark relief, for the 2011–2012 school year, tuition at the one hundred most expensive schools in the country ranged from $59,170 (#1, Sarah Lawrence) to $51,182 (#100, University of Miami) per year.[28] These top hundred colleges include New York University, Johns Hopkins, Georgetown, Boston College, Duke, the University of Chicago, Tufts, MIT, Brown University, Notre Dame, Pepperdine, Yale, and my alma maters American and Stanford.[29] Meanwhile, median family income in the U.S. hovers around $50,000 a year.[30]

As the cost of college has distanced itself from what all but the richest Americans actually make, students and parents have relied more and more on debt. In 2010, student loans overtook credit cards as the largest category of American personal debt. It will soon total over a *trillion* dollars, and it has increased by 25 percent just since the start of the Great Recession.[31] Average student loan debt is around $25,000, and it is not uncommon for college grad-uates to owe more than $100,000.[32] Unsurprisingly, default rates are rising.[33]

The result is what Peter Thiel, founder of PayPal, has called the "higher education bubble." Thiel sees the rising costs in higher education as similar to the tech and housing bubbles of the last two decades: in each case, an asset suddenly skyrockets in value, far outstripping any normal expansion of price. Today, education is "basically extremely overpriced," writes Thiel:

> People are not getting their money's worth, objectively, when you do the math. . . . It is, to my mind, in some ways worse than the housing bubble. There are a few things that make it worse. One is that when people make a mistake in taking on an education loan, they're legally much more difficult to get out of than housing loans.[34]

Critics, especially those who work for or run colleges, have scoffed at Thiel's notion of a higher ed bubble. But Standard & Poor's issued a report in February 2012 agreeing that "[s]tudent-loan debt has ballooned and may turn into a bubble" and that defaults and downgrades of student-loan-backed securities are on the rise.[35]

The rise in cost is related to the decline in rights on campuses in important ways. Most importantly, the increase in tuition and overall cost is disproportionately funding an increase in both the cost and the size of campus bureaucracy, and this expanding bureaucracy has primary respon-sibility for writing and enforcing speech codes, creating speech zones, and policing students' lives in ways that students from the 1960s would never have accepted.

The most conspicuous component of rising costs in higher education has been the soaring salaries of top administrators. According to Andrew Hacker and Claudia Dreifus, "[b]etween 1992 and 2008—that's only sixteen years—the salaries of most of the college presidents we looked at more than doubled in constant-value dollars. Some rose closer to threefold. (For a comparison, overall American earnings rose by 6 percent during this period.)"[36] Their book provides specific examples of staggering pay hikes:

> The pay of Stanford's president increased from $256,111 to $731,614 in con-stant dollars, while that of NYU's president burgeoned from $443,000 to

$1,366,878. The trend was similar at smaller schools. At Wellesley, Carleton, and Grinnell, presidential compensation rose from the low $200,000s to over $500,000.

In 2008, the most recent reports available show a dozen presidents receiving more than $1 million. Among them were the heads of Northwestern, Emory, Johns Hopkins, and the University of Pennsylvania.[37]

Keep in mind that all of these university presidents are the heads of *nonprofits*.

These inflated salaries help create a disconnect between the administrations of universities and both their students and the public. Take Johns Hopkins University in Baltimore, for example, where President William Brody served for thirteen years pulling in a salary of close to a million dollars. In 2007, a fraternity member posted a Facebook invite to a "Halloween in the Hood" party that relied on urban slang as well as Dave Chappelle- and Chris Rock-esque humor. (The fraternity had already hosted a self-consciously politically incorrect party called the "White Trash Bash" and suffered no consequence for it.)[38] Justin Park, the student who sent the invitation, was an eighteen-year-old, first-generation Korean American student who was admitted to Hopkins at the age of fifteen. He believed he was making a hip joke, and he profusely apologized after students complained about the invitation's racial insensitivity. The issue should have ended there, but President Brody's administration went after Park aggressively. He was found guilty of "harassment," "intimidation," and "failing to respect the rights of others."[39] Although Park's sentence was later reduced in the face of public pressure (he also agreed not to talk further about his case in order to get leniency), his original punishment included a lengthy suspension from the university, completion of three hundred hours of community service, an assignment to read twelve books and write a reflection paper on each, and mandatory attendance at a workshop on diversity and race relations.[40] Brody made matters worse shortly after Park's suspension by introducing a new and almost laughably broad "civility" code prohibiting "rude, disrespectful behavior" at the university. He also stated in an article in the December 11, 2006, issue of the *JHU Gazette* that Johns Hopkins would not allow speech that is "tasteless" or that breaches standards of "civility."[41]

FIRE usually succeeds in getting universities to back down from their decisions to punish students for freedom of speech, but not at Johns Hopkins. I believe this is, at least in part, because President Brody was paid such a high salary that he had little incentive to care about public opinion. When Brody retired in 2009, while the country was still deep in recession, he received a $3.8 million compensation package.[42]

The problem is not just the rise in cost per administrator, but also the startling growth in size of the administrative class. In 2005, with little public fanfare, an important milestone in the transformation of higher education was reached: for the first time, the number of full-time faculty was outstripped by the number of administrators on campus.[43] This trend has only accelerated since then. In 2010, the National Center for Education Statistics (NCES), a branch of the U.S. Department of Education, reported that, as of 2009, only 46 percent of the approximately 1.6 million professionals employed full-time by our nation's colleges were faculty.[44] As Benjamin Ginsberg explains:

> The fact is that over the past thirty years, administrative and staff growth has outstripped by a considerable margin virtually all other dimensions of the expansion of American higher education. Between 1975 and 2005, the number of colleges, professors, students, and BA degrees granted all increased in the neighborhood of 50 percent. During the same time period, as we saw earlier, the number of administrators increased 85 percent, and the number of administrative staffers employed by America's schools increased by a whopping 240 percent.[45]

In August 2010, the Goldwater Institute published a report titled *Administrative Bloat at American Universities: The Real Reason for High Costs in Higher Education*, which found that spending on administration per student grew by 61 percent between 1993 and 2007, a rate that far exceeded the growth in cost for instruction.[46] Among the universities examined, two dozen had "more than *doubled* their spending on administration for each student enrolled, adjusted for inflation. For example, at Wake Forest University, administrative spending per student has increased by more than 600 percent in real terms."[47] Illustrating how this bureaucratic expansion has come at the expense of instruction, the report points to Arizona State University, where the number of administrators per one hundred students grew by 94 percent, even while the university was "reducing the number of employees engaged in instruction, research and service by 2 percent."[48]

Students are not paying for an exponential increase in the quality of their education, but rather for a massive increase in campus bureaucracy. This includes an expansion in the number of residence life officials (who are in charge of dormitories), student judicial affairs personnel (who administer campus discipline), and university attorneys. The administrative class is largely responsible for the hyperregulation of students' lives, the lowering of due process standards for students accused of offenses, the extension of administrative jurisdiction far off campus, the proliferation of speech codes, and outright attempts to impose ideological conformity (like the ones you will see in Chapter 5). Parents and students are paying tens—even hundreds—of thousands of dollars for the privilege of being censored!

Tuition and budget concerns have collided in earnest with campus over-regulation during the Great Recession. In 2009, three professors at South-western College in California were placed on immediate administrative leave just hours after they took their protest over budget cuts outside the college's absurdly small "free speech patio." FIRE got involved and the professors were reinstated within two days, thanks also to public outrage. But getting the college to reform its absurd limitations of free speech took the help of the ACLU of San Diego and years of work.[49]

More recently, on July 20, 2011, members of the Nassau Community College Federation of Teachers were forced behind metal barricades by the college's public safety office and warned that their "right to remain on campus may be forfeited" if they protested outside of those barricades. Faculty members tried to protest again, and the administration took its power trip one step further by deciding that the teachers could not take handheld signs into the protest area. Once again, after FIRE became involved, the college publicly claimed that professors would no longer be required to stay behind metal barricades if they chose to protest.[50]

Meanwhile, over the course of the last several years, student protests over tuition hikes have exploded across the country, especially in California, where students have particularly felt the shifting cost burden. Many of these protests have involved unprotected civil disobedience (simply put, things you can be expected to be punished for, like taking over an administrative building) as opposed to protected speech, but others that were perfectly constitutional were also prevented, punished, or censored. One brazen example took place in December 2011 at Arizona State University, where the university blocked students' access to a petition advocating lower tuition on the progressive web-site Change.org. It was only after the media reform group Free Press brought the university's action to public attention that the university restored access to the petition in February 2012.[51]

These are just a handful of the cases that are occurring all over the country, pitting students and faculty members against their overbureaucratized universities. The students are right to be angry, but professors, particularly those who have been on campus for a long time, should take a moment to think about how we got here in the first place. Not nearly enough professors have taken a stance against the massive expansion in administrative staff and the explosion of tuition costs over the last thirty years.

An Opportunity for Free Speech on Campus?

The confinement of free speech on campus to tiny designated areas, the passage of speech codes, the expansion of the bureaucratic class, skyrocketing tuition, rising student debt, and the ongoing attack on student rights have together provoked a major and sustained pushback by students. In the fall of 2011, I visited the original Occupy Wall Street movement in Zuccotti Park in lower Manhattan several times and spoke with many of the protestors there. I was impressed by how many of them were focused on college tuition and student debt. In particular, they were rightfully outraged that the federal government has made it almost impossible for students to declare bankruptcy on their student debt, thereby imposing a difficult burden on students who reasonably believe that a college education is the key to a good job. Many in the Occupy movement understand that universities are wealthy megacorporations; when last I checked, higher education was a half-a-trillion-dollar industry in revenue alone. The worst of university administrators are showing their true colors by requiring (often selectively) that protests be confined to tiny zones far away from the eyes and ears of university presidents who often fit comfortably within the "1 percent." Students have been bamboozled for too long to go along with free speech zones and speech codes imposed by administrators who present themselves as benign philosopher-kings.

There is both good news and bad news about the current situation. The bad news is that the cost of college is now at levels that most Americans would've thought absurd only a generation ago, and that most colleges still restrict speech in practice or on the books, or both. The good news is that the solution to the problem of cost may bring with it an improvement in the state of free speech on campus. If we care about both the quality and the accessibility of higher education, we must cut costs, and a great place to start is slashing the administrative bureaucracy. This would not only help bring university prices back towards sanity, but also leave fewer administrators who might attempt to justify their salaries by policing student speech. Lowering the cost of college and restoring rights may be different sides of the same coin.

CHAPTER 4

Harvard and Yale

IT'S 5 P.M. ON MARCH 29, AND YOUR HEART IS POUNDING as you sit staring at your computer screen. Any minute now, you should receive the email that tells you whether or not you've been accepted to Harvard. Your parents thought your desire to apply was unrealistic and that attending would be much too expensive, so you slaved over your application in secret, paid for the filing fee yourself, and told only a handful of friends. After all, if you got in, how could your parents possibly say no? Any minute now, according to the Harvard admissions officer you called a few too many times, those decisions will be zipping through the Internet on the way to your email account. With every click of the refresh button, you grow more excited. Admission to Harvard would change everything. Everyone knows that. There is no college more iconic or revered in the world, and if you could just . . .

Finally, the email arrives.

All Is Not Well at Harvard and Yale

Probably the worst argument that I run into—with surprising frequency— when talking about campus abuses of student rights is that our shocking cases at schools like Valdosta State University (Hayden Barnes) and Indiana University–Purdue University Indianapolis (Keith John Sampson) don't really matter; all that really matters is what happens at *elite* colleges. And those places, the Yales and Harvards, are too smart and sophisticated (so goes the "logic") to violate student rights the way a less prestigious college might do. But this reasoning is not only snobbish, it's also dead wrong. Yale and Harvard have demonstrated just as much, if not more, discomfort with free speech in the last decade as other colleges across the country.

Of course, that Harvard and Yale enjoy iconic status among universities almost goes without saying. Every single current Supreme Court justice attended one of these two universities, and every U.S. president after Ronald Reagan has attended either or *both* schools. Yale and Harvard are not only internationally regarded as two of the finest educational institutions in the world, but they have also permeated popular culture. Hollywood has chosen Harvard—America's first college, founded only sixteen years after the Pilgrims landed at Plymouth Rock—for particular veneration. Harvard-based films range from classics, like *The Paper Chase*, to box office hits, like *Legally Blonde* and *The Social Network*, to the purely forgettable (anyone remember *Stealing Harvard* or the dreadful drama *With Honors*?).

So how do these twin titans of American higher education fare when it comes to respecting student rights, especially free speech?

Yale's About-Face on Free Speech

While free speech controversies at Harvard were comparatively common during the last eleven years, Yale University seemed inclined to protect free speech. Perhaps the stirring language of the university's vaunted "Woodward Report" was inspiring administrators to follow the righteous path.[1] This 1975 report by a committee on free expression, chaired by the historian C. Vann Woodward, argued that students should be free to "think the unthinkable, discuss the unmentionable, and challenge the unchallengeable." The committee correctly understood that such an environment helps people overcome their comfortable certainties and experiment with ideas. For this freedom to work, it has to be cultivated as part of the campus culture from top to bottom.

My first experience with a problem at Yale, however, came at the very beginning of my career in student rights, in that crazy fall of 2001 when campuses all across the country were responding to 9/11 with censorship. In some cases, they disciplined professors deemed unpatriotic, but more often they targeted students and faculty who were angry and upset about the attacks and wanted the United States to go after the terrorists.

Many weeks after the attacks, a few Yale students put a banner in their dorm window with a quote that might be familiar to you: "Kill 'em all, Let God sort 'em out." According to the unidentified male students who put it up, "it was meant as a joke to counter pro-peace banners."[2] One student further explained, "It was quoting a redneck bumper sticker slapped on the back of a pickup truck driving down Broadway with a gun rack—then we knew it was an ultraconservative. . . . [It said] 'Kill 'em all, let God sort 'em out.'"[3] Thus, the intent of the poster was to make fun of the supposedly backwards nature of two favored targets for PC derision on college campuses: "rednecks" and "ultraconservatives."

The expression has been used as an informal slogan for special forces, as well as a popular T-shirt and bumper sticker design. It can be traced back to the early thirteenth century and the so-called Albigensian Crusade, in which (as any fan of *The Da Vinci Code* can tell you) the French wiped out the legendary order of the Cathars. Lore has it that Arnaud Amaury, Abbot of Citeaux, was asked how to tell the supposedly heretical Cathars from innocent Catholics, and he replied, "Kill them all, God will know his own."[4]

To me, the expression was the name of the legendary rock band Metallica's debut album (shortened to "Kill 'Em All"), which was everywhere when I was a kid. (My best friend made me sit through *hours* of bootleg concert videos.) The quote was usually meant to be ironic, even among the metal heads I knew. For those who either don't know or don't remember, college students tend to use multiple levels of irony and sarcasm. "It's funny because I'm saying what a stupid person would say" is a staple of college humor. (Likewise, Eric Cartman from the TV show *South Park* is considered a funny character not because his anti-Semitic, self-obsessed worldview is correct, but because it's hysterically, awfully wrong.)

The prevalence of ironic jokes on college campuses should present a valuable lesson in freedom of speech: because the actual meaning of someone's words is often very hard to guess, it's a bad idea to police jokes. Nevertheless, some students saw the "Kill 'em all" banner as an opportunity to strike out against what they somehow viewed as a threat against "Muslims and South Asians" on campus.[5] Freshman counselors came into the students' room and removed the banner, while others warned of campus-wide protests. According to the *Yale Daily News*, "Ethnic counselor Edward Teng '02 said he believed that although everyone has the right to free speech, the banner might create a hostile environment for some ethnic minorities."[6]

Re-enacting a pattern that I have seen time and time again, a student attempt at irony and humor was met with the powerful "will to be offended" that distorts discussion on campus. It's hard to imagine how any rational person could believe that this joking pop-culture reference was a threat, and it's even more bizarre to label it an explicit threat to Muslims or South Asians. But where there's a will, there's a way.

Eventually, the controversy became national news and the university rethought its original actions. A prominent administrator stated to the *Yale Daily News*:

> When we allow the suppression of speech in cases when it is found objectionable, we implicitly authorize restrictions that could harm free expression on other occasions. . . . The right thing would have been to explain why the banner was objectionable and to leave its author to decide: in other words, to have made this an occasion for persuasion and education, not for censorship however well-intended.[7]

That this prominent administrator was Richard Brodhead, the person who would later, as president of Duke University, disgrace himself with his handling of the "Duke Lacrosse" case (discussed in Chapter 6) may have been ironic, but his point was right on. In other words, it was silly to throw away Yale's proud tradition of free speech over a joke that people simply didn't get. For years after this incident, Yale was conspicuous by its absence in censorship cases, and I was often happy to tell friends of the school's good behavior.

Unfortunately, Yale's positive streak came to an abrupt end in 2009. One example of Yale's failure is somewhat comic, the other more sinister, but each is illustrative of different trends in campus censorship.

The less serious case arose from the fabled Yale-Harvard football rivalry. Every year, each university's student body pulls together to find creative ways of insulting the other before the clash known simply as "The Game." Past slogans have included such high-minded rhetoric as "You can't spell Harvard without V.D." and "Harvard Sucks. But So Will I for Crack." In 2009, Yale's Freshman Class Council took the very Ivy League approach of quoting F. Scott Fitzgerald's semi-autobiographical novel *This Side of Paradise* for their T-shirts. In the novel, one character says, "I want to go to Princeton. . . . I don't know why, but I think of all Harvard men as sissies, like I used to be." The Yale freshmen decided to print "I think of all Harvard men as sissies" on the front of the T-shirt and "WE AGREE" on the back.

The case then fell into a familiar pattern. Offense was taken and official threats of censorship soon followed. After the design was announced, a few students claimed that "sissies" was an anti-gay slur. It didn't matter that to most people under the age of forty, "sissy" is considered anachronistic and is primarily used ironically. In my experience, anyone calling someone a "sissy" is making fun of himself as much as he's mocking the other person. Nor did it matter that the line was from one of America's greatest authors, who never meant to imply homosexuality (the character was not describing himself as formerly gay). All that mattered was that someone said it was offensive. That was enough.

Shortly after receiving complaints, the dean of Yale College, Mary Miller, announced that the shirts were "not acceptable" and pulled the design.[8] So much for Yale's promised rights to "think the unthinkable" and "discuss the unmentionable." Apparently, quoting Fitzgerald is a bridge too far. In the face of media mockery, led again by FIRE, Miller and Yale's president, Richard C. Levin, eventually admitted their "regret" for their role in what students called "Sissygate."[9]

The most recent kerfuffle over T-shirts about The Game involved a design with the slogan "How to Be Successful at Harvard. Step One: Drop out." Below this was the familiar Facebook image of that statement being "liked" by famous Harvard dropouts: "Bill Gates, Mark Zuckerberg, Matt Damon and 69 others." But when the freshman class consulted with the "Yale University Licensing Program," they were told they would have to get permission from Harvard to use its name—in order to make fun of it.[10] You don't need to be a lawyer to know that you don't have to get the permission of those you plan to mock before making fun of them. Unsurprisingly, Harvard refused to give its permission, and Yale students were forced to water down their T-shirts again, this time as part of a tag-team effort between both schools.

Yale's history of censorship is not always so lighthearted. The school still steadfastly refuses to admit its mistake and reverse its far more troubling decision in 2009 to censor images of the prophet Mohammed in Jytte Klausen's book *The Cartoons That Shook the World*.[11]

The book—an exploration of the controversy and violence that followed the publication of cartoons of Mohammed in a Danish newspaper in 2005—

was to contain the cartoons and other images of Mohammed. In fact, when submitting her manuscript, Klausen made inclusion of the cartoons a pre-requisite for publication. Yale University Press accepted Klausen's terms and vetted the manuscript, a process that included a thorough legal review. The manuscript won the unanimous approval of the press's University Publications Committee.

However, Yale University soon intervened. The school subjected Klausen's manuscript to an unusual second review due to its controversial nature and a fear that its publication would spark fresh violence. In an unprecedented step, the school submitted the images in the manuscript—just the images, not the text—to a group of anonymous consultants. Yale then yanked the images from the book on account of what Yale's vice president and secretary, Linda Lorimer, admitted to be an unspecified fear of retaliatory violence.[12] Yale even went so far as to eliminate some depictions of Mohammed that had never triggered a violent reaction.

Klausen characterized herself as "stunned" by Yale's decision, and she wasn't alone. A storm of criticism followed from all corners. Yale was blasted in an open letter signed by Joan Bertin, the head of the National Coalition Against Censorship, along with FIRE, the American Civil Liberties Union, the American Association of University Professors, the American Booksellers Foundation for Free Expression, the Middle East Studies Association, and others, which pointed out that "the failure to stand up for free expression emboldens those who would attack and undermine it."[13] To this day, however, Yale defends its unprecedented maneuver to protect Islamic sensibilities.

Yale did not display a similar concern for Jewish sensibilities in 2011 when it suddenly decided to close down the Yale Initiative for the Interdisciplinary Study of Antisemitism (YIISA). By most accounts, the reasons for the abrupt move were confused and apparently rushed. Critics of the decision believed it had to do with YIISA's August 2010 conference on "Global Anti-Semitism: A Crisis of Modernity," which addressed, among many other topics, anti-Semitism within Islam. Walter Reich, a George Washington University professor and a member of YIISA's advisory committee, wrote an op-ed in the *Washington Post* stating that "Yale administrators and faculty quickly turned on the institute. It was accused of being too critical of the Arab and Iranian anti-Semitism and of being racist and right-wing."[14] An article by Ron Rosenbaum published in *Slate* on July 1, 2011, highlighted the controversy and reported a related theory of why YIISA was shut down: "There has been talk—though no proof—of fear of offending potentially lucrative donors from the Middle East."[15]

While it is within the power of a university to open or close a department or center, the relationship between the anti-Semitism conference and the decision to shut down YIISA is exceptionally troubling, and may demonstrate an increasingly selective tolerance for dissent and discussion of serious issues at one of the world's preeminent colleges.

Fraternities at Yale Make Matters Worse for Free Speech

In one area, Yale is no different from other colleges; if any group can be accused of engaging in speech that purposefully offends for the sake of offending, it is our nation's fraternities. Fraternities consistently produce some of the least sympathetic cases for campus free speech advocates. Incidents like dressing in blackface and Klan robes for a Halloween party, as Tau Kappa Epsilon at the University of Louisville did in 2001, do little to endear fraternities to the public.[16]

In the fall of 2010, Yale's chapter of Delta Kappa Epsilon (DKE) followed this ignominious tradition by requiring pledges to march around campus blindfolded, chanting slogans like "My name is Jack, I'm a necrophiliac, I fuck dead women" and "No means yes, yes means anal." Now, be sure to take a deep breath. Yes, the statements are obnoxious, but that was the point—it's difficult to think of a more perfectly wrong thing to say at Yale. The fraternity's goal was to embarrass the pledges and shock the campus by invoking one of the sacred cows that men could never, ever mock: "No means no." Anyone who wants to eradicate offensive speech needs to understand this: there will always be some subset of society that will purposefully mock everything society holds dear. In the world of entertainment, these people include our most beloved comedians. But when this happens on campus (and especially when the joke isn't particularly funny), students and administrators alike act as if they've never heard a Chris Rock or George Carlin comedy routine and treat the speakers like the embodiment of human evil.

In my experience, fraternity free speech cases often follow this pattern:

1. Fraternity members do something specifically intended to offend, but the frat brothers overshoot their mark. The campus erupts in calls to punish the fraternity.

2. The fraternity members and the fraternity itself apologize, and the students throw themselves at the mercy of the college and their superiors within the frat. Often, the fraternity or its national organization will launch an investigation resulting in the punishment of individual members, if not the whole fraternity.

3. Occasionally, instead of apologizing, a member of the fraternity decides to stand up for himself. Time and time again, his fellow members will not support him and the student ends up being both punished by the fraternity and rendered defenseless against the university.

4. In the rare case that the entire campus fraternity chapter is united in its desire to fight for its First Amendment rights to provoke and offend, its national organization does not have its back and either pressures the fraternity to back down or punishes it outright.

One of the ironic things about this pattern is that when a fraternity chooses to stand up for its First Amendment rights, it often wins.[17] Meanwhile, the downside of the "offend, capitulate, offend, capitulate, repeat" pattern is that it provides an excuse for speech codes and other crackdowns on student speech. The DKE case at Yale is perhaps the most spectacular example of this. At first, the case followed the familiar pattern: The fraternity made its pledges say obnoxious chants specifically to offend the community, the campus predictably became angry and offended, the fraternity members apologized, the national fraternity promised an investigation and punishment, and Yale condemned the fraternity speech but didn't express a clear interest in punishing the fraternity because it had agreed to discipline its own members.[18] Fraternities, by the way, have every right to punish their own members for breaking their rules or for ungentlemanly behavior. Furthermore, you have just as much of a free speech right to apologize for offensive speech, if you so choose, as you do to engage in it.

However, the combination of the DKE case and Yale's allegedly weak action in other cases (including the serious charge that Yale did not adequately punish students who had been found guilty of sexual assault) angered students enough to prompt complaints to the Department of Education's Office for Civil Rights (OCR), which launched an investigation of Yale.[19] OCR has the power to ensure that universities enforce antidiscrimination laws, and can punish them for their inaction on such issues by taking away all of their Department of Education funding. At Yale, this means a potential loss of hundreds of millions of dollars per year.

In the face of this huge financial threat, Yale rushed to announce that it was individually punishing the students involved in the incident on charges of intimidation and harassment and had suspended the campus chapter of DKE for five years, an effective death sentence for any fraternity.[20] Despite the severity of these punishments, the national DKE organization chose not to fight the ruling, although it stressed that "Equating this behavior to illegal harassment is an unjust overreaching by an administration looking to shift campus anger away from real issues of harassment."[21] True, by making pledges embarrass themselves publicly, the fraternity may have been guilty of hazing, but allowing the university to define what is merely highly offensive as harassment gave strength to the misperception that harassment laws create a generalized "right not to be offended." The failure of the students or the fraternity to fight back has troubling ramifications for student free speech at colleges and universities across the country. If colleges know that they can be subjected to an onerous OCR investigation and face a ruinous financial hit if they do not punish "offensive" speech on campus—even if that speech would've been protected by the First Amendment outside university walls—they have every incentive to overreact. And as I've seen over the years, some campus administrators hardly need an excuse to punish students who dissent, offend, or provoke, or those whom they simply dislike.

The Yale DKE case and the intervention of the newly assertive OCR had repercussions for virtually every college across the country, most importantly with regard to due process, which I'll be discussing in Chapter 6.

One somewhat ironic outcome of Yale's subsequent investigation of its "sexual climate" was that it imperiled Yale's always-controversial Sex Week, which over the years had included a heavy focus on sex workers and pornography that earned the scorn of conservatives across the country. After a formal committee argued for ending Sex Week in its traditional form, the president of Yale decided to go ahead with Sex Week as long as the event changed its content; but the entire incident points out how the same forces that claim to be progressive defenders of women can look a great deal like Victorian moralizers in other circumstances.[22]

Taken as a whole, the last decade or so should make Yale students and professors a little nervous about discussing everything from sex to bumper stickers to anti-Semitism and radical Islam—and even about making fun of their rivals at Harvard. And the examples I've spotlighted only represent the incidents that have been made public; many others have not, since students at elite colleges, in my experience, are particularly disinclined to fight back against their universities. I hope that Yale will recommit itself to the lofty ideals expressed in the Woodward Report. But if you asked me even a handful of years ago whether Harvard or Yale had a worse record regarding free speech, I would have said Harvard hands down. While Harvard still earns that dubious distinction, Yale in recent years almost seems to be trying to make up for lost time.

Harvard's Surprising Cluelessness about Free Speech and Free Minds

Despite its reputation as a center of rigorous intellectual jousting, Harvard University has generated some terrible censorship cases over the past ten years. Many of my experiences with cases at Harvard never made it to the public eye; students contacted FIRE after getting in trouble for campus speech, but didn't want to come forward and take on their school. I have found an unusually strong unwillingness among Harvard students to challenge their hallowed institution.

I have discussed this "Harvard Effect" with many friends who attended the institution, and according to one friend, the wife of FIRE's senior vice president, it is a very real phenomenon. She remembered that students feared Harvard's mysterious "Ad Board" (short for Administrative Board, which enforces Harvard's regulations on student behavior) because their actions were shrouded in secrecy: "No one had any idea what actually happened at Ad Board hearings, but we all knew at least one person who'd been expelled after tangling with them, and we suspected we'd be considered guilty until proven innocent if we crossed them." The secretive nature of Ad Board charges and proceedings—ostensibly to protect student confidentiality—leaves students uncertain about what kind of behavior could end their Harvard careers and unwilling to take any action that could make them a target of the administration.

Harvey Silverglate is a Harvard Law School alum who lives in Cambridge, and in 2012 his assistant Daniel R. Schwartz wrote an extensive piece on Harvard's history of censorship for FIRE's online magazine *The Lantern.* Daniel examined the history of censorship at Harvard going as far back as the 1950s, when Professors Robert N. Bellah and Leon Kamin lost appointments at Harvard due to the university's support of the House Committee on Un-American Activities.[23] But 1992 brought a new level of rights violations to Harvard: speech codes. A tasteless *Harvard Law Review* parody mocked a recently murdered professor's work on feminist legal philosophy (naming her "Rigor Mortis Professor of Law"), which sparked widespread anger on campus. One faculty member went so far as to claim that female students who received the parody in their student boxes viewed it "as a direct threat of personal violence."[24] Unable to punish the students because it had no rule forbidding this kind of expression, Harvard Law then enacted a code restricting the creation of an "offensive environment."[25]

In 2002, Harvard Law School faced another controversy, this time over race. A student's email in which he referred to a controversy involving the notorious "n-word" ignited outrage. After the student apologized, Professor Charles Nesson tried to salvage the situation by turning it into a learning experience. He suggested using the incident as the basis for a mock trial, arguing that the event would give students "a chance for ideas to be articulated, hard questions asked and deliberated on, some meeting of minds and, conceivably, a solution."[26] The student body responded by turning its ire on Nesson, with the Black Law Student Association calling for him to be publicly censured and banned from teaching first-year students. Nesson stepped down for the rest of the semester. As Daniel Schwartz put it, "there was to be no teaching in response to the incident at Harvard Law, in order that learning could continue."[27]

My first public tussle with Harvard came early in my career, when Harvard Business School (HBS) threatened a student newspaper and its cartoonist with punishment for making fun of the administration. In the fall of 2002, the HBS computer network started going on the fritz during the week when most students were interviewing for jobs. Interview week at business schools is intense and nerve-wracking, especially at high-powered institutions like Harvard. When I heard about this case, I was surprised that the students didn't mount a full-scale riot—after all, would you want to tell a Harvard Business School student he lost his dream job to a student from Wharton because the computers were down?

Instead of a riot, there was a mildly satirical cartoon referencing the incident in *The Harbus*, HBS's student newspaper.[28] The cartoon shows a number of computer pop-up windows, each spoofing the IT department's various excuses for the poorly timed glitches. One of the pop-up windows, behind many others, reads, "incompetent morons." For this, the editor of *The Harbus* and the cartoonists were called into the office of Steve Nelson, the director of the MBA program, who reportedly threatened them with punishment for violating Harvard's "community standards." The potential sanctions for such a violation are amorphous, running from admonition to expulsion. Nelson justified his outrage by claiming that publishing the cartoon showed insensitivity towards Harvard's IT staff.

Nelson's approach is instructive, because it shows how a call for sensitivity and respect can be used as a tool to prevent students from publicly criticizing the administration or the university itself. Whatever Nelson's motivation, he threatened his students' careers for pointing out that the business school had screwed up something important—a fact that he clearly did not want the larger community and alumni to know. Rather than risk expulsion, Nick Will, the editor of *The Harbus*, resigned.

In the November 12, 2002, issue of the *Harvard Crimson*, Nick's close friend, a second-year student at HBS, explained his thoughts on the case: "I know that Nick is very scared, and I know that the *Harbus* staff is very scared. . . . Nick didn't resign because he felt like it, but because he thought he might get kicked out of school. He's had some people tell him that these guys play hardball and you're not necessarily safe."[29]

Even after this case came out in the *Boston Globe*, the dean of HBS stood by the school's treatment of *The Harbus*. Under intense pressure from both FIRE and some alumni, however, the dean changed course and apologized for running roughshod over student rights.[30] But the warning had been sent. The business school may have backed down in this case, but future editors of *The Harbus* are now on notice that criticizing Harvard is unwise.

Another case that has always fascinated me took place in 2006, when Harvard Law School students tried to restrict "offensive speech" even further. In that year, there were a number of forums that dealt with concerns over the "Law School Musical," an annual satirical event that is pretty typical at law schools around the country (we had one at Stanford, too). According to the *Harvard Law Record*, it was repeatedly suggested during a town hall meeting that students be given a chance to opt out of being parodied.[31] A Ph.D. student at the meeting even "expressed disgust at the concept of parodying real people, posing the question, 'Why not make fun of yourselves?'" It may be that these students were not unfamiliar with satire or parody, but rather, like so many students, had the ability to turn their "I'm offended" switches on when it was useful and turn them back off when they sat down to watch TV, have a drink, or otherwise live.

The professional schools are not alone in their excessive administrative control over Harvard student life. In 2008, two Harvard undergraduate student groups—the Latino Men's Collective (LMC) and Fuerza Latina—sought permission to hold a dance party in the dining hall of the school's Adams House residence. The request was approved; student groups have held all kinds of events in the Adams dining hall, including "Erotica Night" and "S&M bingo." A dance would be tame by comparison. But when the LMC and Fuerza Latina started advertising the party around campus under the name "Barely Legal"—as in "so crazy it should be illegal"—Adams House administrators abruptly revoked their approval.[32] Even though they publicly apologized for any offense and explained the name's mild intent, the party planners were told that the event would be canceled unless they changed its name. Under pressure, the student groups acceded.

The phrase "barely legal" is hardly some kind of obscenity in today's collegiate lexicon; it's more of a cliché these days. A quick Internet search of the expression brings up a legal blog run by two recent law school grads, a radio show dealing with legal topics, the name of an art show by the British graffiti artist Banksy, and, yes (as so many searches do), some pornography. The students were using a mildly edgy name, and advertisements for the party indicated that it would be almost laughably tame. Irony, though, is not usually a midlevel administrator's strong suit.

FIRE wrote to Harvard to remind the school of its stated and contractually binding commitments to free speech.[33] The response from the Harvard attorney was a head-scratcher. Bradley A. Abruzzi argued that threatening to cancel the party was justifiable because permission to hold an event at Adams House "necessarily carries an endorsement" of the event.[34] This makes zero sense. People at Harvard say all sorts of contradictory things. If an Israeli student group hosts an event celebrating Israeli settlements at Adams House one week, and a pro-Palestinian student group hosts a meeting on the same issue there the next, does Harvard then definitively endorse both viewpoints? Abruzzi's response represents a deliberate misunderstanding not only of free expression, but also of Harvard's supposed role as the "marketplace of ideas"—a marketplace being where things are exchanged, not necessarily endorsed. For Harvard to endorse all ideas spouted during campus events would be incompatible with the idea of a university, and frankly impossible.

While the "Barely Legal" is a minor and funny case, it is a testament to an environment in which administrators see their role as preventing any form of offense, even if their responses are petty and unreasonable. An incident with more serious implications for free speech was the firing of Subramanian Swamy, an economics professor at the Harvard Summer School, over an article he wrote in a publication on the other side of the world.

On July 16, 2011, Swamy, who is also a politician in India, published a piece in the Indian newspaper *Daily News and Analysis* in response to a series of terrorist bombings in Mumbai on July 13 that killed 26 and injured 130 people.[35] The column focused on how to "negate the political goals of Islamic terrorism in India," advocating that India "enact a national law prohibiting conversion from Hinduism to any other religion," "remove the masjid [mosque] in Kashi Vishwanath temple and the 300 masjids at other temple sites," and "declare India a Hindu Rashtra [nation] in which non-Hindus can vote only if they proudly acknowledge that their ancestors were Hindus." Doubtless, this is a passionately nationalist agenda. Unsurprisingly, when word got out about the column, Harvard students started a petition against Swamy, demanding that Harvard "repudiate Swamy's remarks and terminate his association with the University" on the grounds that he was "a bigoted promoter of communalism in India."[36]

We wrote to Harvard's president, Drew Gilpin Faust, on July 27, and though she did not respond directly, Harvard issued a strong statement on August 1, 2011, defending freedom of speech.[37] But this admirable sentiment was not to last. In December 2011, the Harvard Faculty of Arts and Sciences effectively fired Swamy by canceling all of his classes.[38] In doing so, it specifically referenced the op-ed. The leader of the movement to oust Swamy was Professor Diana C. Eck, who claimed, in a sentence I still have not been able to figure out, "There is a distinction between unpopular and unwelcome political views."[39]

This is hardly the first time that Harvard faculty members have voiced controversial opinions in impassioned terms, but more importantly: what did his op-ed have to do with Swamy's ability to teach economics? Nobody has offered any compelling argument that his views on strife in his home country affected his teaching. Some of the most revered thinkers in history have held opinions that would curl the toes of modern academia. Should colleges really be policing an economics professor's views on how his country should respond to terrorism? Was Professor Eck's enigmatic statement an implication that Harvard knows best what political views people should have? At around the same time this controversy was taking place, Harvard was making it very clear to its freshmen that the answer to that question was, "Well, yeah."

Pledging Yourself to Oversimplifying
Moral Philosophy at Harvard

Freshmen arriving at Harvard in the fall of 2011 made history: For the first time in Harvard's multicentury existence, students were asked to sign a pledge to specific ideological values.[40] They were asked to pledge "to sustain a community characterized by inclusiveness and civility" and to affirm that "the exercise of kindness holds a place on a par with intellectual attainment."[41]

Who could possibly object to such a warm and fuzzy pledge? Well, for starters, Harvard's former dean Harry Lewis. In an eloquent blog post on August 30, 2011, Lewis explained why pressuring students to sign loyalty oaths to seemingly unobjectionable values goes completely against what Harvard has always represented.[42] He argued that "Harvard should not condone the sacrifice of rights to speech and thought simply because they can be inconvenient in a residential college." He also debunked the claim that the pledge was voluntary in any meaningful sense: freshmen were approached by resident advisors with disciplinary powers when they first arrived on campus and were "encouraged" to sign the pledge, and if they did so, their names were added to a list of signatories that was posted on dormitory entryways. Students not signing the agreement were therefore subject to "public shaming." Lewis went on to add, "Few students, in their first week at Harvard, would have the courage to refuse this invitation. I am not sure I would advise any student to do so."

Still, students and some commentators didn't see what the fuss was all about, or what made the pledge so objectionable. The title of my September 7, 2011 *Huffington Post* article about the pledge effectively sums up the heart of my objection: "Does Harvard Want Bold Thinkers or Good Little Boys and Girls?"[43] To me, nothing better exemplifies the problem of cultivating in students a mindless certainty about serious issues than such an oath.

The comparative merits of civility, kindness, industry, etc. versus intellectual attainment is a great topic for debate, but here Harvard basically said, "Oh screw it, it's much too hard to actually discuss the relative merits of all these competing values. Just sign this damn pledge." This is intellectual laziness, and it teaches terrible lessons about the way an intellectual community is supposed to work, as it places conformity above deep and meaningful questioning. It's as if Harvard suddenly came to believe, after hundreds of years of existence, that it could take a shortcut to solving profound questions of ethics and moral philosophy. Trying to sidestep the ethical questions and simply inject a set of qualities through a piece of paper is a glowing path to groupthink. As John Stuart Mill well knew, those in power often invoke civility to punish speech they dislike, but overlook the equally acid-tongued statements that are in agreement with their own assumptions.

Furthermore, the claim that Harvard values "inclusiveness" is an exercise in cognitive dissonance: Harvard *defines* and celebrates elitism. This is an institution that rejects the overwhelming majority of people who apply, heaps glory upon those who succeed with particular distinction, and takes credit for the accomplishments of its elite-among-the-elite graduates.

In the face of Harry Lewis's criticism, the freshman dean decided to stop engaging in the public shaming of students who didn't sign the pledge, but the pledge had already achieved its goal. Students had been warned that they were not entering a smorgasbord of critical thought, and they had better keep themselves in line or keep their thoughts to themselves.

Ironically, Ralph Waldo Emerson's seminal text "Self-Reliance" was once required reading for incoming Harvard freshmen. As he states in the essay, "Whoso would be a man must be a nonconformist. He who would gather immortal palms must not be hindered by the name of goodness, but must explore if it be goodness. Nothing is at last sacred but the integrity of your own mind."[44] Emerson understood the danger of uncritical thinking and coerced pledges.

Larry Summers, and How Playing with Ideas Teaches Us to Talk Like Grownups

No discussion of free speech at Harvard would be complete without examining the incident that led to the resignation of Larry Summers as president of Harvard. The controversy began when Summers spoke in January 2005 at the National Bureau of Economic Research's conference on "Diversifying the Science and Engineering Workforce." He had been asked by the bureau to discuss the comparative lack of female faculty members "in tenured positions in science and engineering at top universities and research institutions." In the introduction to his speech, Summers emphasized that his specific intention was to provoke discussion, and that he felt it was important to "think about and offer some hypotheses as to why we observe what we observe without seeing this through the kind of judgmental tendency that inevitably is connected with all our common goals of equality."[45] In other words, he hoped that a vigorous exchange of ideas, free of knee-jerk responses to provocative concepts, would lead to a solution to this puzzle.

In my experience, the number of people who have strong opinions about what Summers said and the number of those who have actually read the speech are wildly out of whack. The text of the speech is available online, and I encourage you to read it and reach your own conclusions about Summers' intent.[46] For now, here is a quick summary.

Summers began by presenting three hypotheses. The first was that women might not be attracted to the eighty-hour work weeks required by these positions, perhaps preferring more flexibility in order to raise a family. He also explored the continuing role of gender discrimination in hiring. But what started the national firestorm was his suggestion that some of the underrepresentation might stem from small differences in IQ between men and women at the highest end of the intellectual spectrum, which some research supports.[47] Keep in mind that this proposition was never anything more than a speculation that Summers thought might provoke discussion, and that it only applied to the tiny subset of people whose IQs would put them in the one-out-of-5,000 or one-out-of-10,000 ranges. He explained:

> So my best guess, to provoke you, of what's behind all of this is that the largest phenomenon, by far, is the general clash between people's legitimate family desires and employers' current desire for high power and high intensity, that in the special case of science and engineering, there are issues of intrinsic aptitude, and particularly of the variability of aptitude, and that those considerations are reinforced by what are in fact lesser factors involving socialization and continuing discrimination. I would like nothing better than to be proved wrong, because I would like nothing better than for these problems to be addressable simply by everybody understanding what they are, and working very hard to address them.[48]

The speech bears little resemblance to the caricature it has become in the general culture and even among the Harvard faculty. But merely suggesting the possibility that there might be some minor differences in IQ in a *minuscule* subset of the population was apparently unacceptable—even as part of a deliberate "attempt at provocation." So the speech became an immediate scandal.

The Faculty of Arts and Sciences gave Summers a vote of "no confidence," and about a year later he announced that he was resigning.[49] While it is true that tension already existed between Summers and the faculty, this incident was the "but-for" cause of his resignation.

Of course, not every Harvard faculty member was willing to join the attack on Summers. The famous Harvard psychologist Steven Pinker stated in an interview with the *Harvard Crimson*, "Good grief, shouldn't everything be within the pale of legitimate academic discourse, as long as it is presented with some degree of rigor? That's the difference between a university and a madrassa."[50] Pinker knows full well the dangers of tackling taboos, as he has done through his linguistic exploration of the nature-versus-nurture debate. In his bestseller *The Blank Slate: The Modern Denial of Human Nature*, Pinker explained that for decades it was deemed a heresy to veer in the slightest from the view that all human characteristics arise from environment and upbringing. This dogma even plagued scientists as revered as E. O. Wilson, who was vilified in the 1970s as a "genetic determinist" because he argued that our genes influence the way people behave socially.[51] It is now commonly accepted that genetics plays a role in many human traits, yet this concept is often received with horror on campus. And if there is any place where we should be able to talk about something so fundamental to biology and society, it's in our universities. Harvard's decision to use Summers' intentionally provocative comment as an excuse to run its president out of town on a rail paints a bleak picture of the state of inquiry in higher education. After all, if the president of Harvard can't start a meaty, thought-provoking, challenging discussion, who on earth can?

It may seem paradoxical, but in order to have a serious intellectual environment you have to allow space and encouragement for your scholars and students alike to play with ideas. If you want people to be creative, out-of-the-box thinkers, you can't tell them never to step outside a tiny corner of the box. Yale and Harvard could be providing a model of how a lively, dynamic society of diverse ideas can work. But rather than showing that debate and thought experimentation can be fun pursuits, Yale and Harvard have mastered the art of selective and strategically deployed intellectual uptightness. It's a great way to shut down debate you don't like, but it also closes down the intellectual curiosity, creativity, and critical thinking our society needs.

Chapter 5

Welcome to Campus!

Y<small>OU HAVE JUST TURNED EIGHTEEN</small>. For the first time in your life, you can legally vote, serve in the military, and even buy cigarettes if you want to. That email from Harvard was a huge disappointment, but your parents couldn't be happier you made it into Big State U.

It's orientation week in late August, and swelteringly hot outside, but you are cold in your air-conditioned new dorm room as you unpack. Your roommate, whom you have not met yet, has already put up some posters of bands that you liked when you were in grade school but thought most people would have grown out of. You wonder if you should bring that up.

Suddenly, your RA is at your open door. As you have just learned, each floor of the dormitory is more or less run by a resident assistant, better known as an RA. They are usually graduate students or other undergraduates who are employed by the university and work under the Office of Residence Life—a campus office that seems to be everywhere you look.

Your RA doesn't look any older than you, but he holds himself with authority. He checks to see if you've received your orientation handbook. Yes, you have the schedule: five packed days of seminars, speeches, tours, social activities, and other events. Your RA also lets you know that in addition to the required floor meeting at the end of the week, you've been slotted for a mandatory "one-on-one" meeting with him tomorrow. This sounds a little strange, but you say "fine" and he leaves to talk to other students on your floor.

The next two days are a bit of a blur. Speeches by the president of the university, lunch on the quad with your parents and your classmates, and a tour of the computer labs and the library. By the second day, your parents have left and your sessions are more focused, including subsessions with the dean of the College of Education, where you're considering majoring. That afternoon, you attend three meetings, one on the perils of binge drinking, another on the many different services available to gay and minority students, and the third featuring a strange play put on by Residence Life about date rape. You didn't really think you needed to be told that you shouldn't binge drink or sexually assault anyone. Do your fellow students not know this?

You head back to your dorm room, your head swimming with everything you've heard that day, and you find your RA waiting at your door for your "one-on-one" session. You go with him to his room, he closes the door, and then he hands you a questionnaire. You start looking at the questions and your face contorts with puzzlement. It only gets weirder. Your RA says: "This is part of a new program to take full advantage of the educational opportunities available in the dormitories about life, respect, and tolerance. So, in order to start, I need to ask you some questions. First, let's talk about when you discovered your sexual identity."

You wait for him to laugh, or at least titter. He doesn't.

Disorientation

In my experience, the two most polarizing issues when it comes to student rights on campus are the right to due process for those accused of sexual offenses, including assault (which I will be dealing with in the next chapter), and ideologically geared orientation programs. Conservatives see ideological orientation programs (as opposed to merely instructional ones, like "how to use the computer lab" and "what to do in case of fire") as the heart of darkness. Meanwhile, we liberals tend not to see what all the fuss is about.

My personal experiences with orientation programs were not particularly troubling. For pretty much every job I had at American University, I had to attend something called a "pride and sensitivity" seminar in which students who were gay, African American, or Latino talked about what it's like to be different on campus. It was an open discussion, and while conservatives might argue that it reinforced the university's excessive emphasis on identity politics, it seemed harmless to me.

So when I started working at FIRE, I was somewhat skeptical of what Alan Charles Kors had dubbed "thought reform"—the mandatory, noncurricular university programs designed to get students to adopt particular ideological and political beliefs. Kors recommended I read his article "Thought Reform 101," published in *Reason* magazine in 2000. In the article, Kors provided an overview of the orientation industry and cited numerous examples that surprised me, including one at Swarthmore where students were asked to line up according to skin color, from lightest to darkest, to demonstrate how oppression disfavors the darker-skinned in the United States.[1]

Harvey Silverglate later related a time when he was on a public radio show in Minnesota with a host who was skeptical that the Swarthmore orientation program had taken place. But while he was on the air, a student from Hamline University in Saint Paul called in to describe his experience with an orientation program where sexual preference was the topic of choice.[2] This time, students were asked to line up according to how gay or straight they felt, with students who were unsure standing in between. While the spirit of the program was to make students more comfortable discussing their sexuality, asking people to reveal the secrets of their sexual identity brings up profound issues of privacy and conscience.

Meanwhile, I heard friends describe mandatory orientation programs that do the same, except with social class as the distinguishing mark. (It's not shocking to report that students tend to lie about their economic backgrounds when economic privilege is vilified.) According to one friend, her daughter, who is a Latina, rated herself as a "10" on the "empowerment scale" in a version of this event, but was told that she couldn't possibly be so empowered because she was both a woman and a Latina, and therefore systemically oppressed. The fact that she is also half Jewish was met with confusion: they couldn't figure out if that made her more or less oppressed.

The sharply different focus of the various orientation programs demonstrates that even among the diversity trainers there is disagreement about which aspect of identity is destiny.

You might be wondering what is troubling about any of these programs. I believe that people should be aware of the continuing legacy of racism, homophobia, and classism in daily life. But liberal ends do not justify illiberal means. There are some places where people in power have no right to forcibly delve, including our individual, private conscience. If we wish to remain free people, we cannot tolerate the use of authority to conduct mandatory inquisitions into the deepest beliefs of our citizenry or the use of coercive tactics to browbeat citizens into adopting specific ideological points of view. Seminars on race, culture, sexual identity, and class can be useful. Mandatory orientation programs that presume to tell students not only what they mustn't say but also what they must say and *think* in order to be decent people are in violation of the law, and they put the leaders of these programs in the position of all-knowing arbiters of moral truth. It is arrogant for anyone to assume such a position. It's also incompatible with academic freedom to tell students what their *conclusions* must be on issues as crucial to our society as race, culture, class, and identity, before they have even begun the process of sustained critical examination for themselves. Programs that do this are aggressive promoters of lazy thinking, unwarranted certainty, and manipulative tactics for shutting down discussion.

Residence Life: From Hall Monitors to Morality Police

Over the years, FIRE has documented many overreaching orientation-type programs, almost all of them arising out of the ever-growing world of "residence life," which has increasingly assumed the role of educating students outside the classroom.[3] Many of the policies and programs that come from residence life offices have received FIRE's Speech Code of the Month "honor." These include our September 2005 SCOTM at the University of Nevada at Reno, which stated that "Lack of civility, any behavior or action, physical or verbal, that is meant to devalue, demean, or incite an individual or group, directly or implied, is prohibited" in the residence halls. Our February 2008 SCOTM at the University of Utah banned "any information that is deemed to be racist, sexist, indecent, scandalous . . . or in any way oppressive in nature" from the residence halls. The January 2009 SCOTM at the State University of New York at Buffalo included a Statement of Civility requiring those in the residence halls "to be courteous and polite or, simply put, to be mannerly."[4] The Buffalo policy also provided that "[a]cts of incivility . . . will not be tolerated by the Residential Life community."

Much of the residence hall overreach comes in the form of "bias related incident" programs, in which university administrators would walk the dormitory halls looking for offensive material written on students' dry erase boards (which students still use to leave messages for each other on their doors). Our April 2010 SCOTM at the Claremont University Consortium in California targeted "expressions of hostility against another person (or group) because of that person's (or group's) race, color, religion, ancestry, age, national origin, disability, gender or sexual orientation, or because the perpetrator perceives that the other person (or group) has one or more of those characteristics."[5] When I spoke at Claremont in 2011, I was told by students that the policy had become something of a joke among students, who would chuckle when administrators sent grave-sounding emails announcing that someone had called a friend a "foxy lesbian" on her dry erase board, or explaining in excruciating detail a reference to a joke from *South Park*. (The joke, for those of you who know the show, was "Scissor me, Xerxes.")

Meanwhile, the University of Georgia's residence hall program required resident assistants to call the police to address violations of UGA's "Acts of Intolerance" policy. According to documents from the University of Georgia Police Department, between August 1 and September 27, 2010, eight police reports were filed for "acts of intolerance," including the words "Dick and Sideboob" and "Fire Crotch" written on the dry erase board of a student's door.[6] It is downright strange to read a police report that explains with solemnity that a student had changed a sign that read "WELCOME TO BOGGS 3RD FLOOR" to "WELCOME TO BOOBS 3RD FLOOR."[7]

Such incidents capture the absurdity of residence life officials taking on the role of morality police. Most universities, however, were smart enough not to post too many details of their orientation and residence life programs online for the world to see. Therefore, it was frustratingly difficult to uncover what was really going on other than through secondhand reports from students and parents. But then, in part by luck, we got a look inside the University of Delaware Residence Life program—and the reality was astounding.

The University of Delaware "Treatment"

I first learned about the University of Delaware Residence Life program in the fall of 2007 after a student's parent contacted FIRE about sessions that his son described as "ugly, hateful, and extremely divisive." (The son would later leave the university.) The fact that all students participating in this mandatory program had to return all of its printed materials after the sessions ended set off red flags: Residence Life was making sure that the program did not get out to the wider public. Fortunately, with the help of two University of Delaware professors in the School of Education, Jan Blits and Linda S. Gottfredson, we were able to obtain over five hundred pages of documents describing the Delaware program.[8]

What we discovered was a four-year process of "orientation" by Residence Life officials that equaled nothing less than a mandatory ideological training program for all seven thousand students who lived in the University of Delaware dormitories. The program was so expansive that it defies an easy summary. It took Adam Kissel, my colleague at FIRE, six thousand words to catalogue the deep and numerous problems with the program, in an article titled "Please Report to Your Resident Assistant to Discuss Your Sexual Identity—It's Mandatory! Thought Reform at the University of Delaware."[9] While much of the media either ignored or were ambivalent about the program at the time, the National Education Writers Association recognized Kissel's article with a 2008 EWA award.

It is crucial to understand that the University of Delaware program was not an aberration. It was designed over the course of many years by officials at the university and had received an award from the American College Personnel Association (ACPA), a leading association of university administrators. UD's program was held up as a model by the ACPA both before and *after* the public discovered its full scope.

It should come as no surprise that the UD Residence Life office also imposed a speech code that classified "any instance that is *perceived* by those involved as being racist, sexist, anti-Semitic, homophobic, or otherwise oppressive" as an emergency of equal urgency to fire, suicide attempts, and alcohol overdose.[10] But the orientation program went well beyond a restrictive speech code; its goal was the interior transformation of the beliefs of all seven thousand students in the University of Delaware dormitories on issues as varied as moral philosophy, environmentalism, tolerance, human rights, and social policy, to make those beliefs conform to a specific political agenda.

The program differed from similar undertakings at colleges around the country in that it explicitly did not follow the "voluntary" model, but imposed its "curriculum" on the entire student body (except for a small percentage who lived at home) in every aspect of their lives in the dormitories. According to Sendy Guerrier, a UD administrator, students "should be confronted with this information at every turn."[11] Guerrier also wrote that the program should "leave a mental footprint on their consciousness," apparently missing the echo of the villain from George Orwell's *1984*.[12]

The program included an aggressive series of mandatory floor meetings where students would engage in exercises. In one such activity, they had to stand along one wall if they supported various social causes, including the right to gay marriage or abortion, and along the other wall if they didn't. Students were not allowed to say they hadn't made up their minds—it was explained to them that in the real world there is no middle ground. (I wonder how proponents of the "No Labels" movement would feel about that claim.)[13] One student reportedly asked to be excused from the activity when the choice was whether eating disorders were caused by society or the person's own mental state. Her request was denied; she was forced to pick a side even after revealing that she had struggled with an eating disorder and had not yet made up her mind. This event functioned as a state-sponsored public shaming of students with the "wrong" beliefs.

Another mandatory floor activity used similar shame tactics to get freshmen to sign on to a preapproved political and social agenda. It opened with an exercise called "Surrounded by Stereotypes." Students were presented with thirteen pieces of paper, each listing a social identity including categories like poor, Jewish, Asian, lesbian/gay, African American, obese, Latino/Latina/Hispanic, etc. Students were then required to quickly come up with as many stereotypes as they could think of for each group and write them down on the walls around the room. (The hapless boss Michael Scott came up with a similar program in the NBC sitcom *The Office*. I will return to that episode, titled "Diversity Day," at the end of the chapter.) Then came the "Day In, Day Out Deluge," in which students were assigned to teams to act out how life would be if everyone always accused them of fulfilling these stereotypes. Next was the "Fishbowl Discussion," during which individual students had to sit in the middle of the room and discuss their feelings of being stereotyped. The goal was to get students to sign a "commitment to diversity statement." RAs were instructed to follow up with students in one-on-one sessions to see how they were doing in fulfilling their commitment.

These and other exercises were actually referred to as "treatment" by Residence Life officials. While a voluntary exercise discussing racial stereotypes in a classroom setting could be productive for students, the Delaware exercises worked from the presumption that all students harbor gross racial prejudices that corrupt them at the deepest psychological levels.[14] Furthermore, they assumed that the source of this racism is a corrupt American culture that can be beaten out of students through high-pressure guilt and shame tactics. This may or may not be true, and it might make an interesting topic for research, but going a radical step further and appointing Residence Life officials to be the healers of America's presumed cultural sickness is beyond arrogant and a perfect formula for promoting uncritical thinking. One UD student, Kelsey Lanan, said it was as if ResLife were shouting at them, "You guys are so racist! Don't be racist! Don't be racist!"[15]

The mandatory "one-on-one" sessions with the RAs were, to me, the creepiest aspect of the whole program. During the sessions, students were asked to fill out surveys while an RA watched. Here is a sampling of some of the questions:

2. Would you be comfortable being close friends with any of the following persons? Mark YES or NO

African American/Black . . . . Y   N
A heterosexual man. . . . . Y   N
An international student. . . . . Y   N
An openly gay or bisexual woman . . . . Y   N

3. Would you be comfortable dating any of the following persons? (Assume that you are single)

Middle Eastern . . . . Y   N
A heterosexual woman . . . . Y   N
A person with different religious beliefs than yours. . . . Y   N
An openly gay or bisexual man . . . . Y   N [16]

Prying into students' sexual identities, dating habits, and preferences is something state employees have no business doing. When they do so with the stated goal of changing students' attitudes about sexuality and dating practices, they cross lines that even parents are often unwilling to cross. Yet this unconstitutional, mandatory interrogation of personal sexual practices seems to have been tolerated by most students at UD.

In the five hundred pages of documentation, there was only one clear example of a student who resisted these bizarre invasions of privacy. According to a report from her RA, this girl had fun with one of the questionnaires, answering the question "When was a time you felt oppressed?" by saying, "I am oppressed every day [because of my] feelings for the opera. Regularly [people] throw stones at me and jeer me with cruel names. . . . Unbearable adversity. But I will overcome, hear me, you rock loving majority."[17] The female freshman—apparently alone in her male RA's dorm room—had the guts to deflect such creepy questions through humor. But when the questionnaire asked, "When did you discover your sexual identity?" she responded, "That is none of your damn business."[18]

For challenging an unlawful intrusion into her private life by a state employee, this student was listed by name and room number in the report as one of the "worst" examples of students resisting the program (yes, it does start to sound a bit like the Borg), and the resident assistant even noted that he had filed an incident report against *her*. It would not have surprised me if the student had been found guilty of harassing the RA.

Like junior professors but with vastly greater power over students' everyday lives, Delaware's Residence Life program directors even listed learning outcomes, cryptically called "competencies," that all dormitory students should achieve—and by what year. For example, in their sophomore year, the goal was that "Each student will recognize that systemic oppression exists in our society" and that "Each student will recognize the benefits of dismantling systems of oppression." Two of the goals for junior year were that "Each student will be able to utilize their knowledge of sustainability to change their daily habits and consumer mentality" and "[l]earn the skills necessary to be a change agent" for social, economic, and environmental justice. Finally, by senior year, students were expected to have fully become the activists the program envisioned and to "Demonstrate civic engagement toward the development of a sustainable society."[19]

I was shocked to discover that some students could see nothing wrong with a mandatory residence hall program having such specific political and ideological goals. There is a major distinction between teaching people *facts and methods* they must know and mandating *philosophies* they must believe; teaching a student in a classroom about the philosophy of Stoicism, for example, is not the same as requiring that your students all become classical Stoics. Providing a student with information and requiring them to demonstrate that they understand it is acceptable pedagogy. Creating a 24-hour-a-day environment with the goal of getting students to subscribe to specific ideological and political conclusions (many of which are hotly debated) is rightfully scorned as "indoctrination." It also trains students to follow uncritical, visceral reactions on crucial societal issues over reasoned debate.

Wanting students to "recognize that systemic oppression exists in our society" is fundamentally a political and ideological aim. Scholars, critics, pundits, and citizens in general disagree on whether racism is systemic, or a cultural phenomenon, a unique historical problem, a specific national issue, a fact of human nature, an evolutionary defect, an idiosyncratic trend, or some combination of all. The entire University of Delaware program was designed to sidestep any debate on this and other questions, and to impose definitive, university-sponsored conclusions through repetition, immersion, and browbeating.

Professor Blits discovered a practice by Residence Life that epitomizes my concern for the effects that such programs have on the larger society. RAs at Delaware were actually trained to shut down debate and discussion:

> One of my students described how, if an RA heard students discussing politics or religion (and some other topics), the RA would intervene and take control. The RA would give each student the chance to state his or her opinion and then tell the students to disperse. There were to be no questions, no answers, no back and forth. Discussion meant no exchange, no probing, no explanations. It meant not being held accountable or holding anyone accountable for what one says or thinks. When I asked some RAs about this, they said that they had been trained to quash such discussions as being uncivil. They were trained to run floor meetings in the same way, they said. Radically diminished intellectual inquiry characterized the program as a whole.[20]

The quite literal shutting down of discussion should come as no surprise when you consider the role that Residence Life had assumed. To impose this aggressive program, you have to have absolute certainty that you are the holder of unique and essential truths; and once you reveal those truths, what's the point in debating anything?

Given how laden with politics such programs are, criticism of them stirs up the worst aspects of the culture wars. We on the left side of the spectrum are too quick to defend any project that promises to promote diversity, tolerance, and multiculturalism. Thankfully, most people who sift through the hundreds of pages of documentation on the University of Delaware program conclude that it goes much too far. Unsurprisingly, however, the program has its defenders even outside the American College Personnel Association.

Some argue that dorm administrators have academic freedom and the right to express their beliefs, so the University of Delaware program was defensible as a genuine expression of the beliefs of the RAs.[21] This is wrong from stem to stern. College staff, when they are acting as employees of the university, are not considered to have academic freedom as faculty do in their classrooms. (With the deployment of this heavy-handed program, Delaware proved the wisdom of that distinction.) And even if staff did have such freedom, the academic freedom of students is violated by programs that rely on pure indoctrination.

Moreover, this argument is premised on the incorrect idea that the resident assistants came up with the program themselves and happily carried it out. This was a program that was *imposed* on the RAs from above, after an intensive screening process and through a long summer training period in which they learned techniques like "confrontation training" for students who resisted the "treatment." In fact, we received multiple reports from RAs that they had objected to the heavy-handedness of the program and the invasiveness of the questions that students were required to answer. When these RAs dissented, they were met with hostility, intimidation, and outright threats from the administration.[22]

Another disingenuous argument about the Delaware program relies on a counterfactual claim that the program wasn't really mandatory. This argument is refuted again and again in the materials, which specifically point out the program as being distinct precisely because it did not follow the "voluntary" model. For those who don't believe the plain language of the policy itself, an RA put it quite clearly in an email to her students: "Not to scare anyone or anything, but these are MANDATORY!!"[23]

FIRE took weeks to go through the hundreds of pages of materials that Professor Blits obtained. We took our opposition to the program public on October 30, 2007. The media response was quick but both disappointing and predictable. The conservative blogosphere and Fox News paid attention because they saw a case of PC run amok. Local newspapers and the *Chronicle of Higher Education* covered it, but presented the program mainly as a well-intentioned diversity program, not the insulting and unconstitutional program it actually was.[24]

The first response from the University of Delaware was by the vice president, Michael Gilbert, who defended the program. But a day later the president, Patrick Harker, returned from a trip to China and immediately suspended it.[25] To the public, it looked as though the fight had ended in a matter of days, but the administrators in charge were not fired or removed. Kathleen Kerr and Jim Tweedy, the director and associate director of Residence Life, made many attempts over the following months and years to get the program reinstated. At the same time, the ACPA lauded the program vigorously and continued fighting for its return. In March 2012, the ACPA elected Kerr as its vice president, a role that comes with a three-year term, first as vice president, then as president, and then as past-president of the association.[26] Far from punishing her for this wildly unconstitutional program, the forces of residence life have made her one of their leaders.

The ACPA hosted a conference in January 2008, a few months after the Delaware program had been suspended. Once again, secrecy was maintained and outside parties were not allowed to attend. A member of the National Association of Scholars did manage to make it into the meeting and reported facts that made the ACPA seem more like a cult than an umbrella organization of administrators. According to the NAS report, the conference opened

> with a presentation by a senior residence life official from a large private university in the northeast. She lit one large candle "to represent the knowledge and responsibility that we have as student affairs and residence life professionals." The large candle was next to a plate of many smaller candles, which she explained were the students, to whom "we pass on that light." . . . Suddenly, she blew out the large candle. She dramatically looked at the audience and said that in fall 2007, "Our light went out," and it was "hate, fear, ignorance, and stupidity" that caused it to go out. She did not name the source of these candle-snuffing iniquities, perhaps because the name FIRE would have damaged her metaphor. She then . . . declared, "With this conference, we relight the candle . . . and hate, fear, ignorance, and stupidity will not snuff it out [again]." She relit the candle, and continued in this vein, concluding, "Journey with me towards our revolution of the future."[27]

A closed meeting in which candles are used to symbolize the truth and enlightenment that only select people understand, and which culminates in a call for a revolution? An exclusive gathering in which leaders paint themselves as the light that will combat the darkness of evil? I don't think it's a coincidence that the program seemed more like a mystery cult than a dormitory orientation program. Its authors believed they were saving American society from moral sickness, decay, and ignorance—a messianic duty that public officials are neither qualified nor allowed to assume.

The advocates of programs like the University of Delaware's rely on a powerful combination of guilt and shame to break down resistance to their agenda. Almost no college-age students want to be accused of opposing diversity, multiculturalism, or sustainability, so those in power use these terms to justify programs that go far beyond what respect for individual conscience would ever allow.

While I believe it is immoral to place residence life officials in the position of enlightened priests fighting inborn American evil, and I am certain the programs that do so are unconstitutional, it is fair to ask: Do they at least work? Do they teach students tolerance, respect for each other, and open-mindedness?

Professor John L. Jackson's book *Racial Paranoia: The Unintended Consequences of Political Correctness* (2008) provides part of the answer.[28] Jackson is a well-respected African American scholar of anthropology and communications at the University of Pennsylvania. While never directly addressing speech codes or programs like Delaware's, Jackson argues that America's aggressive attempts to root out overt expressions of racism have resulted in a society where racism remains *de cardio* (in the heart), but is not discussed. This fosters a kind of "racial paranoia," where the knowledge that racism still exists but the inability to talk frankly about it leads many people to see racism as the hidden motivator of everything, correctly or not. Jackson argues that allowing space for frank and open dialogue about the realities of race, racial distrust, and race-related feelings in this country is preferable to a society where people have learned never to talk about it.

I've seen firsthand the serious impact that programs like Delaware's have on the ability of students to think critically and discuss openly. Just a few weeks after the university suspended the Residence Life program, I spoke to an audience of about a hundred students at the school. With the exception of a panel I once was on concerning the Mohammed cartoons, it was the angriest reception I have ever received. The students who showed up were overwhelmingly opposed to the University of Delaware program, but the minority who supported it shouted the loudest. The factions broke into three parts in a large theater-like classroom. In the front half of the classroom were students who found the program an insulting invasion of privacy. In the upper right corner were students who were more uncertain but admitted that the program went too far. In the upper left corner were representatives of Residence Life who were furious. The question-and-answer period devolved into yelling, with the Residence Life supporters shouting down and pointing fingers while accusing other students, as well as me, of a hidden racist agenda. Interestingly, it was usually white students making these accusations, and the African American students who did speak usually opened by saying that they fully agreed that the program went too far, but that it was difficult being black on an overwhelmingly white campus.

I kept repeating that I denied nothing about their difficulties and only objected to the methods used to impose the program. I also tried to explain that a comprehensive program designed to determine students' sexual identity would have been used just a few decades ago to root out homosexuals, not to support them. In earlier times and other forms, such a program probably would've been used to identify communist sympathizers, anarchists, or "radicals" of any stripe. Therefore, even if we think we are on the side of all that is good and right, it is both illegal and unwise to have such thought reform programs. But this seemed to mean nothing to the Residence Life supporters. Their goals were correct; therefore, their tactics were correct. What I saw that night in that angry room was a student body divided and a community unable to discuss serious issues rationally.

The more I learned about the ideology behind the University of Delaware program, the more I realized that the ideas behind it could never promote understanding or tolerance. It relied on gross oversimplifications of serious societal tensions around race, class, and gender that are often used to justify aggressive attempts to silence or indoctrinate students. Take, for example, the mandatory training session for all University of Delaware RAs in which the university invited Shakti Butler to teach about race and racism. The materials for her presentation included this definition:

> A RACIST: A racist is one who is both privileged and socialized on the basis of race by a white supremacist (racist) system. The term applies to all white people (i.e., people of European descent) living in the United States, regardless of class, gender, religion, culture or sexuality. By this definition, people of color cannot be racists, because as peoples within the U.S. system, they do not have the power to back up their prejudices, hostilities, or acts of discrimination.[29]

This definition is not unique to the University of Delaware. Although it clashes with any standard understanding of racism, it was a very popular theory when I was at Stanford. Butler anticipated the objection that this definition of racism was itself racist. If anyone tried to argue that other groups besides whites in the United States can be racist, Butler offered this definition:

REVERSE RACISM: A term created and used by white people to deny their white privilege. Those in denial use the term reverse racism to refer to hostile behavior by people of color toward whites, and to affirmative action policies, which allegedly give "preferential treatment" to people of color over whites. In the U.S., there is no such thing as "reverse racism."[30]

So, you're automatically a racist if you are white; you cannot be racist if you are from any other group; and if you try to disagree, you are relying on a theory that has already been ruled out as categorically impossible? It's a tidy way for people to evade any questioning of their own premises.

And what would you expect from students who have experienced such heavy-handed ideology and negative repercussions for disagreeing? I think you would expect to see an awful lot of educated people who clam up when serious and heated political issues come up, and another set who demand total compliance with their political beliefs and don't feel they need to explain the reasoning behind them, either because they think any disagreement is morally unacceptable or because they have never really been taught the reasoning behind their now fiercely held beliefs. I suspect this sounds familiar to some of you.

It certainly sounds familiar to Rachel Cheeseman, a summer 2011 FIRE intern who confirmed that programs like the one at Delaware are still operating. Rachel served as an RA at DePauw University during her sophomore and junior years, from 2009 to 2011. Before she met a single one of her residents, she endured a weeklong RA training session where she and her peers "were lectured repeatedly about white privilege, racism, sexism, and every other 'ism.'" In Rachel's words, any "who questioned the information were silenced immediately or heckled for their refusal to accept [these] dogmatic views." As the training week wore on, many of the RAs began refusing to participate in the endless discussions of race, gender, sexuality, and religion, frustrated by the message that they were all bigots who needed retraining. But when she finally began working with her students, Rachel realized that she would be expected to aggressively spread this unquestioning ideology to all of them.

As soon as the residents arrived, Rachel was required to escort them through a mandatory "Tunnel of Oppression," walking through the halls of a house and interacting with various live performances in different rooms. What kinds of lessons did these performances teach? One room helped students discover that "religious parents hate their gay children." A different room taught them that "Muslims will find no friends on a predominantly white campus," while another revealed that "white people believe all black women are 'welfare mamas.'" One room warned gay students that they might be "'outed' by their partners if they leave an abusive relationship." Rachel watched her students' reactions, and saw hopelessness and shame on their faces.

After this depressing spectacle came the daily work of monitoring and reporting any issues that might be related to an RA's mission of promoting "egalitarianism." Students were encouraged to tell Rachel about any behavior that could be considered "hate speech," and Rachel then had to file an incident report to her superior. This "hate speech" was not the hurling of epithets, but rather snarky humor or emotional debates that happened to offend someone. Punishments ranged from sensitivity counseling to probation. Rachel described the resulting atmosphere as "a remarkable level of self-censorship. Aware that they are always watched, heard, and potentially reported, students act and speak accordingly." This environment, Rachel realized, produced "a lack of the intellectual engagement necessary for productive discourse. Not only do students not want to talk for fear they will be punished, they just don't want to talk at all."

Unwilling to be part of that system anymore, Rachel left the RA program and spent her senior year questioning this kind of thought reform as a student activist and the managing editor of the campus newspaper. Her experiences are far from unique; colleges including Georgetown University, Clemson University, Washington State University, the University of North Carolina at Chapel Hill, Florida State University, Michigan State University, and Ohio State University, just to name a few, proudly display their Tunnel of Oppression programs on their websites.[31] At the Illinois State University tunnel, students have the opportunity to "witness societal atrocities against under-represented groups" and can view "Matthew Shepard hang[ing] lifelessly from a post."[32]

But the larger question about the Tunnels of Oppression is whether they reflect an educated view of the world. Do they promote sophisticated and critical thinking about tough questions? Activities like the Tunnel of Oppression put simple answers on top of complex questions, which is precisely the opposite of what critical thinking is all about.

"Us versus Them": The Culture War as Hero Narrative

If programs like the one at Delaware stunt serious discussion, create further tension, and impede progress, why do they appeal to anyone? As a mirror to the absurd in modern American life, the hit American TV show *The Office* provides some insight. Back in 2005, in only the second episode, the writers lampooned "sensitivity" or "diversity" training at work in an award-nominated episode called "Diversity Day." In the episode, clueless boss Michael Scott gets in trouble for repeating a famous, totally un-PC Chris Rock routine. Once corporate finds out, they send a sensitivity trainer to help rectify the situation. The sensitivity trainer is played by the always brilliant Larry Wilmore (of *Daily Show* fame), who begins by challenging the audience to be a "HERO," an acronym that stands for "honesty, empathy, respect, and open-mindedness." In fact, the notion of a heroic diversity advocate lies behind much of the censorship on campus.

I find that many heavy-handed orientation and training programs, like the one at Delaware and countless other colleges around the country, promote something that I refer to as "the hero narrative" (to borrow a term from Joseph Campbell). That is, they teach students the romantic notion that they are not flawed human beings, but rather heroes put on this earth to crusade against intolerance, insensitivity, and ignorance. While this idea may sound pleasant, it creates crusaders, not scholars. A scholar is trained to evaluate facts and arguments on the basis of their merits, and recognizes that you must constantly battle against your own biases to inch ever closer to the truth. It's a disciplined, rational approach that requires people to distinguish the world as it is from the world as they wish it would be. A crusader, in contrast, is a "romantic" (by which I mean "antirationalist") figure, someone who is tasked by passion to battle evil, undaunted by opposing evidence. Crusaders and heroes feel entitled to follow their emotions and instincts because they are among the select few privy to secret truths about the world. They do not need to explain themselves, and they expect to be forgiven their excesses (like punishing a student for reading a book or kicking a student out of the dorms for a fat joke) because of the presumed purity of their motives. In the end, however, the crusaders are stunting real progress by preventing students from thinking critically about serious issues. While societies need both crusaders and scholars, I am much more frightened of putting the crusaders in charge, since they don't see their own beliefs as things that must be critically evaluated, but rather as representations of moral truth around which the world must be transformed to fit.

I felt the call of the crusader mentality myself in my third year of law school, when I took a class in "Cause Lawyering," which was mandatory for anyone doing an internship with an ideological nonprofit (I was interning at the ACLU of Northern California). The class was an unabashedly liberal advocacy class about how to be an effective lawyer for a cause. In one session, we focused on the legendary "Powell Memo," which supposedly proved that special interest groups and conservatives were conspiring with the Chamber of Commerce to improve the public perception of capitalism. You can still see liberal websites that credit the memo as the blueprint of modern conservatism, but an article in *The American Prospect,* a liberal publication, cast serious doubt on the memo's relevance to the movement.[33] Nonetheless, I was told by my professor that this memo was outrageous, and so, responding to the call of the crusader and not entirely understanding why, I left class outraged. I ran into a friend who had devoted his prelaw career to public interest work and would go on to a career in civil liberties. I was so riled up that I said, "This just makes me want to go out and change things 'by any means necessary.'" He replied, "We have a word for people like that. We call them 'Generalissimo.'"

With these words, my friend talked me down and reminded me that self-righteous rage is not always conducive to clear thinking. He also exemplified something I have seen time and time again. The most unthinkingly radical people I have met are sometimes those who do the least actual work for the causes they claim to believe in, whereas my friends who have worked in, say, the refugee camps of Afghanistan are less prone to oversimplifying and are far more practical. And we should remember, just because we all may have some crusader-like urge to improve the world, we don't all agree on what that means or how it should be implemented. That's the value of open inquiry and free discussion. Once we are able to determine our own opinions, free from ideological indoctrination, we are able to debate their merits, refine their power, and put them into action. Programs like the one at Delaware short-circuit this essential process.

In the grand incentive structure that cultivates uncritical thinking, group polarization, and unjustified certainty, the "hero narrative" is the carrot, while fear of punishment or social ostracism is the stick. Together they cause some students to adopt the "us versus them" mentality of champions battling a world of villains, while others feel alienated and inclined to tune out and reject anything the administrators say. After all, nobody likes being considered a villain or hearing calls for stamping out his or her own moral or religious beliefs. And if our colleges and universities are cultivating such an oversimplified story of the good educated class versus the evil American masses, how can we possibly expect to have a healthy, constructive national dialogue?

You don't have to look far to find traces of the "hero narrative" in American debate. We are increasingly using loaded words to brand our opponents as evil. Even the vice president accused Tea Partiers of being like "terrorists" in the budget debate during the summer of 2011, after Fox News commentators had earlier referred to Barack Obama's fist bump with his wife as a "terrorist fist jab."[34] And as you can see in the image on the following page, it took nothing more than a Google search to make a collage of depictions of both President Bush and President Obama as Hitler.

(People who lightly accuse people who disagree with them of Nazism should watch the *Daily Show* segment from June 16, 2005, linked in the notes.)[35]

We should expect better from a society that's more educated (or, at least, better credentialed) than it has ever been, but campus programs that oversimplify our country's political and philosophical disagreements only make matters worse. After all, if you see yourself as a specially appointed messenger of divine truths, anyone who opposes you must be on "the Dark Side." If colleges want to be a force for enriching the great national discussion, they must reject programs that attempt to replace dialogue with coerced beliefs and replace the complexity of everyday life with uncritical sloganeering.

Source: *Greg Lukianoff*

CHAPTER 6

Now You've Done it!
The Campus Judiciary

IT'S ONLY YOUR THIRD DAY OF ORIENTATION and you are terrified that you might have blown the whole thing already. It all happened so quickly. Your one-on-one session with your RA spiraled out of control. When he presented you with the questionnaire about what races and sexes you would date, you got angry. Here was this (by all appearances) rich kid who was talking down to you, who apparently thought you were some hick from the sticks who had never met—let alone dated—someone from a different ethnic background. It was too much. "This is all none of your damn business!" you snapped.

Your RA snatched the questionnaire from your hand. "That's it, I'm writing you up. Report to the student judiciary—I mean the student conduct office, tomorrow."

It's only been three days and you're already in trouble. The day is a panicked blur. Is there any way you can keep your parents from finding out? According to the student handbook, punishments for violations of the student conduct code range from a warning to expulsion. You don't even know what you're being charged with, but given how angry the RA was, you're not optimistic.

The student conduct office tells you that you've been charged with "flagrant disrespect" and informs you that you must report to Student Accountability Training. It is a four-step "early intervention." Failure to complete all four sessions will result in expulsion. The training will also cost you $50, but you don't care. You will do anything to get this behind you.

By four o'clock you're at accountability training. When you show up, you are surprised that the session isn't a class or seminar but a one-on-one meeting between you and a twenty-something man who describes himself as an "accountability facilitator." The two of you sit down across the table from each other and he asks, "Why are you here? Tell me in your own words." You gush, "I am so sorry. I shouldn't have been rude to my RA. It's not like me. It will never happen again."

Silence. The facilitator shakes his head. "You are not taking accountability for your actions. Fill this out." He hands you a worksheet. You study it. It's a series of blank lines where you are asked to write what you did over and over again. You thought this was going to be some kind of psychological counseling or anger management class, but now you're completely confused. Then the facilitator shows you another piece of paper: "Now, take a look at this. It's very important. We call it the Power and Control Wheel."

The Student Judiciary
and the Criminalization of Everything

The scenario I just presented may seem like the most far-fetched example I've used so far, but it is based on a "Student Accountability in Community" program that ran for years at Michigan State University. (The "flagrant disrespect" charge is also a real charge that nearly ruined a student's career, which I'll discuss in the next chapter.)

In some mythical time in ages past, the primary concerns of collegiate judiciaries were issues of academic misconduct: did a student cheat on his exam, plagiarize a paper, or otherwise fail to uphold standards of academic integrity? Of course, colleges also had procedures to deal with more serious disciplinary infractions, but over the past several decades these judiciaries have grown in size and scope, extending their reach far beyond the borders of campus and into areas once reserved for criminal courts. They have also begun to investigate and punish students for conduct and speech that few would consider unusual, let alone a crime—including "bad attitudes."

This expansion of the campus judiciary plays a crucial role in miseducating students about what it means to live in a free society. While some campus judiciaries are run much better than others, many teach students that clear policies, fair hearings, and due process simply get in the way of justice. Lost in all this, a generation has come of age unaware that our legal system is based on the simple belief that we need open procedures and clear, specific rules to prevent the natural human tendency to rush to judgment, punish those we dislike, and decide things on the basis of our hunches and inclinations.

Furthermore, a lack of commitment to due process is one of the most disturbing symptoms of uncritical thinking and unscholarly certainty. These problems are most manifest in how universities deal with the very real and very serious problem of sexual assault on campus. University administrators now seem to believe such a serious problem demands that we reduce the safeguards that make the process more legitimate and accurate. But it isn't clear how making it easier to find someone guilty of assault will make the system better. Advocates of diminishing due process rights try to bridge the logical gap with outrage, but little more. As you will see in the following sections, the result can be a bizarre, unfair, and frightening experience for students who get caught up in the university judiciary.

Violations of Due Process and Free Speech Often Go Hand in Hand

It's important to note that most of the cases in this book involve due process issues. Hayden Barnes at Valdosta State University was given no meaningful due process before he was kicked out of school for posting a collage on Facebook. Keith John Sampson, the student who was punished for reading a book, received no due process before being declared guilty of racial harassment. All of the cases involving Syracuse University that will be discussed in the coming pages include serious violations of the university's promises of due process.

One particularly egregious case was the unceremonious suspension and later firing of Professor Thomas Klocek from DePaul University in 2004. Klocek got into an argument about Palestinians, Islam, and terrorism with students from two groups, Students for Justice in Palestine (SJP) and United Muslims Moving Ahead (UMMA). By all accounts it was heated, but nothing beyond expression (including a hand gesture of debated meaning) was alleged. Nine days later, Klocek was suspended—without ever receiving a copy of the complaint letters, a hearing, or any other chance to face his accusers.[1] The story made it around the blogosphere primarily because it involved a conflict about Israel and Islam, but the most galling part of the case was the lack of due process shown in ending a professor's fifteen-year career. Instead of using due process as an effective way to discover what had really happened, DePaul University treated it like an inconvenience.[2]

The students and faculty whose stories I discuss in this book often received little or no procedural protections before the university passed judgment on them. The issue of due process may seem tangential, but it is intrinsically linked to the protection of free speech, as this chapter illustrates.

Michigan State University's Surreal Inquisition Program

In 2002, I attended the innocuously titled seminar "How to Increase Student Accountability in Your Campus Community" at the annual conference of the Association for Student Conduct Administration (ASCA, formerly the Association for Student Judicial Affairs), the lead umbrella group for administrators involved in student discipline. I had been sent there because FIRE's founders had noticed that many of the bad policies we encountered seemed to arise from this conference, and they wanted me to investigate. At the session, three officials from Michigan State University, Richard Shafer, Holly Rosen, and Peter Hovmand, presented a "model program" for dealing with troublesome students, euphemistically called the Student Accountability in Community seminar (SAC). SAC was described as an "early intervention" session that could be imposed as a mandatory sanction for many actions that fell far short of what has traditionally been covered by student conduct codes.[3]

I'm not sure I would have believed it if I hadn't been there. Before the session started, the presenters placed a graph on the whiteboard. At the bottom of the graph was listed "practical jokes" and at the top was "assault" and "rape." I thought to myself, "Please tell me they aren't going to say that people who commit assault and rape often start with practical jokes, so we should sentence practical jokers to 'accountability training' as early as possible."

Lo and behold, that was pretty much what they said. It is also true that if you lock up every male from the ages of sixteen to thirty, crime would drop, but that doesn't make the plan fair or even efficient. The session only went downhill from there.

The SAC program was essentially this: if you were caught speaking or behaving in a way that was not otherwise punishable but was deemed "aggressive" by a university administrator, you could be sentenced to treatment. You then had to sit in a room with an administrator for four sessions—for which you had to pay—in order to learn to take "accountability" for what you did. First, you wrote down what you thought you did wrong. By the looks of it, you could never come up with the right answer. Like the famous scene in *1984* where Winston is forced to say he sees five fingers when his interrogator is holding up four, you would complete the program only when you described your behavior using the exact (strained and strange) language the program wanted you to use.

The SAC program was started in August 1998 out of "a desire to intervene with male students who were being abusive toward other members of the university community."[4] The seminar and the materials admit that it was originally intended to deal *only* with male students and issues like "male/white privilege." MSU's Judicial Affairs Office and the MSU Safe Place Program collaboratively developed the model, drawing primarily from approaches used to deal with perpetrators of domestic violence. As the ASCA handout made clear, "The basic philosophy of SAC is rooted in batterer intervention groups using an accountability model."[5] In other words, the program was designed to treat things like practical jokes in the same way you would treat spousal abuse.

According to the SAC brochure, "Examples of situations that would generally be appropriate for SAC" included, among other things, "[h]umiliating a boyfriend or girlfriend," "[i]nsulting instructors or teaching assistants," "making sexist, homophobic, or racist remarks at a meeting," and, with regard to student organizations, "failing to understand how members' actions affects [*sic*] others."[6] The SAC program not only established a subjective, vague, and flatly unconstitutional speech code, but also set up an invasive system for enforcing it. This is especially striking because Michigan colleges have repeatedly been told by courts that speech codes are unconstitutional, from the *first* legal challenge of such codes in 1989 to a later Court of Appeals decision in 1995.[7]

Examples that were given of behavior that might get a student sentenced to mandatory SAC seminars included a girl slamming a door after a fight with her boyfriend, a student being rude to a dormitory receptionist, or telling an administrator that he's acting like a Nazi. For these offenses, students had to pay $50 out of their own pockets to attend four SAC sessions. Failure to attend resulted in a hold on the student's account, which in effect was an indefinite suspension from the university, as the student would no longer be able to register for classes.

Once in the program, students were instructed to answer a series of written questionnaires. In their answers, they were to describe their "full responsibility" for their offensive behavior, using language that the director of the session deemed acceptable. Students were asked to fill out this same questionnaire multiple times, inching closer to what administrators deemed "correct" responses. The student who had been sentenced for being rude to a dormitory receptionist, for example, initially explained "I should've been more polite." The leaders of the ASCA session informed him that this was not an adequate response; the "correct" answer was "I feel entitled to be in the residence hall and that's wrong." Of course, given how much students have to pay to stay in dormitories at most colleges, he *was* entitled to be there.

After filling out the first two forms and recounting what happened in their own words, students were given the "Power and Control Wheel," a chart that categorizes negative behaviors and equates them with forms of violence.

These "behaviors" include things as innocuous as "putting someone down," "making someone afraid by using looks, actions, gestures," and, mystifyingly, "using others to relay messages."[8] The Power and Control Wheel was developed jointly by the Domestic Abuse Project and the Alternatives to Domestic Aggression, a program of Catholic Social Services of Washtenaw County. When someone is convicted of domestic abuse, it may or may not be useful for therapeutic purposes to examine if they also "put people down" or "use others to relay messages," but investigating such behavior in a student who slammed a door during a fight with her boyfriend is as misguided as it is invasive. Never mind that even a domestic violence perpetrator would be allowed to mount a formal legal defense before being sentenced to mandatory counseling.

Participants were shown the wheel and the list of definitions of negative behaviors, which included "using" one's "white privilege" or "heterosexual privilege," "any action that is perceived as having racial meaning," or "obfuscation," defined as "[a]ny action of obscuring, concealing, or changing people's perceptions that result [sic] in your advantage and/or another's disadvantage." Then they had to confess the negative types of power and control they exhibited during the reported incident.

POWER-AND-CONTROL WHEEL

Original Power-and-Control Wheel developed by:
Domestic Abuse Project, 206 West Fourth Street, Duluth, MN 55806 (218) 772-4143

Revised and adapted by:
Alternatives to Domestic Aggression (ADA) Catholic Social Services of Wastenaw County,
4925 Packard Rd., Ann Arbor, MI 48108 (313) 971-9781

MSU Safe Place
G-55 Wilson Hall, Michigan State University, East Lansing, MI 48824 (517) 353-1100

Source: *Catholic Social Services of Washtenaw County*

Students could not deny or justify their behavior; rather, they were asked to identify specific alternative behaviors that would have been more desirable, using the "Equality Wheel." This chart was a mirror of the Power and Control Wheel, but categorized acceptable ways of dealing with conflict. The list of "nonviolent" approaches included "economic partnership," defined as "making money decisions together, making sure both partners benefit from financial and academic arrangements," and "respect," defined as "listening to someone non-judgmentally," "being emotionally affirming," and "being a positive role model for children." Surely, some of these are "positive" attitudes, but it is not the role of a state institution to enforce its own idea of correct living on everyone.

One of the most unsettling moments in the presentation occurred when an audience member asked if it was appropriate to suspend a student for being unwilling to take part in this kind of thought reform. Richard Shafer objected to the implication that the SAC program was something students *had to* do. He reasoned that because the goal of the program was to increase accountability, students should recognize that they had the *choice* of taking part or being, for all practical purposes, expelled. I was stunned: under no standard of fair dealing or law would this be considered a free choice. Shafer's answer to the question was the best demonstration of "obfuscation" the ASCA audience would see that day.

A second glimpse of the program's true nature came when an audience member asked, "How do I deal with people with religious beliefs that 'justify' their anger?" Holly Rosen responded that "religious beliefs may be a form of obfuscation." This was just one of many responses that revealed that no outright expression of anger could ever be justified under the program. Taken at face value, this concept outlaws nonviolent protest.

Students' responses in SAC sessions were not confidential, and confessions could be reported to the school's disciplinary body for further punishment. The SAC program unconstitutionally compelled students to express opinions and beliefs that they might fundamentally disagree with, and generally showed an appalling lack of respect for the individual autonomy and private conscience of MSU students.

The SAC program also broke MSU's contractual promises of free speech and fair procedures, unlawfully forced students to self-incriminate under threat of permanent suspension, and violated both state and federal privacy laws. Legal claims against MSU for operating such a program could include federal and state claims for having and enforcing an unconstitutional speech code, for compelling people to speak against their will, for basic denial of due process, and even—given the statements of the hosts of the ASCA seminar and the specific assumptions required by the "power wheels"—for violating both the constitutionally protected freedom of religion and the establishment clause. All in all, the SAC program was a legal minefield.

Over the following years, FIRE was so overwhelmed with requests that any deeper examination of these legal problems ended up on the back burner. In fact, I assumed that the SAC program could not survive at a public college without outraging the students forced into it or garnering a lawsuit. So when I heard nothing about it for a few years, I figured the program must have ended. In the summer of 2006, however, I had an intern look into it. Not only did we confirm that it was still running, but the director of the program was proud enough of its work to send us updated materials that showed little change since 2002. We wrote to MSU, and when the university did not adequately respond, we took our objections to the program public.[9]

After several Michigan newspapers covered the program, and additional letters were sent making clear that it could not survive a lawsuit, MSU finally suspended the program in April 2007.[10]

The fact that the program ran for at least five years and no student came forward to object to it speaks volumes about how badly students understand their own rights, how hesitant students are to challenge rights violations, and the incredible power that colleges and universities have in keeping most of these violations private. (Universities are empowered by a deeply problematic law called the Family Rights and Privacy Act, or FERPA. Craig Brandon makes a powerful case for its repeal in his book *The Five-Year Party: How Colleges Have Given Up on Educating Your Child and What You Can Do About It.*)[11] The SAC program also shows what lengths some administrators are willing to go in order to fight what they see as social evils—forgetting that higher education's larger aim is not to browbeat "bad" thoughts or attitudes out of students, but rather to enable them to make up their own minds through scholarship and research.

Campus Justice and Sexual Assault

For the Student Accountability in Community program at Michigan State University, the "social evil" to be fought was aggression, in whatever form, justified or not. Many other college administrators have tried to deal with the far more serious evil of sexual assault and date rape through similar means, thereby restricting speech, violating rights, and ignoring due process.

Rape is one of the most dehumanizing acts that one person can commit against another. It is a human rights violation of the first order, and attempts to draw greater attention to this once overlooked and underreported crime are a necessary step to a better and more just society. The idea of rape should and does fill us with rage and disgust. But crimes that produce such anger and outrage are precisely those where due process becomes most important. Our righteous hatred of a societal evil can cloud our judgment and lead to a mentality in which an accusation is as bad as a conviction and where innocence itself is no defense.

"Due process" and "fair procedure" represent two essential democratic concepts. First is what is called procedural due process; that is, we put in place procedures to help us fairly and accurately adjudicate the guilt or innocence of the accused. These include the right to cross-examine, the presumption of innocence, and the right to know who is charging you and why. Second is substantive due process, which refers to the fairness of the substance of the rules themselves. Most of the examples in this chapter deal with violations of both of these concepts.

What constitutes due process has evolved over hundreds of years and is rooted in both pragmatism and deep philosophy. It recognizes several truths about human nature: people can be mistaken in what they remember or believe; people do falsely accuse their neighbors; people can even convince themselves that false things are true if they desire to punish someone they hate or feel has wronged them; and we must limit people in power to enforcing clear laws fairly to avoid abuse of the system. Judges and juries have their own biases, blind spots, areas of expertise, and areas of ignorance, all of which need to be systemically balanced out (through processes for appeal, for example) to minimize the likelihood that people are unfairly punished.

The premises underlying the need for due process are in many regards the same premises that undergird the principle of freedom of speech. The idea, again, is that no one is omniscient, so we need procedures that prevent us from throwing someone in jail just because our guts tell us we should. Due process is why we have concepts like "innocent until proven guilty" and standards of proof like "beyond a reasonable doubt" and "clear and convincing evidence."

Over the decades, however, campus judiciaries have been pressured to lower due process standards for those accused of sexual assault and to broaden the definition of sexual misconduct. Given that occurrences like date rape can be difficult to prove, I do not blame advocates for their frustration. No one wants a rapist to go free. But the crucial problem with lowering due process protections to make it easier to find someone guilty of sexual assault is that it impairs the accuracy of the justice system. Due process exists not simply to protect the innocent, but also to accurately identify the guilty. Once too much subjectivity is allowed into the system, guilt or innocence determinations are unduly influenced by less rational factors, like whether or not the administrator in charge likes or dislikes the accused.

In my years at FIRE, I have seen students who I am quite convinced committed sexual assault be let off by the campus judiciary *precisely because* due process at that university had been so badly eroded as to allow for favoritism. On the other hand, I have seen students I am quite confident did nothing wrong found guilty of rape because the school's policies and practices gave too much discretion to the hunches of administrators. Due process is not a problem that must be done away with to make administrators' work easier; it is a crucial prerequisite to justice. Not only have many schools turned away from these essential principles, but many have also expanded the definition of sexual assault so broadly that they have made basic human interaction a crime.

Step One of Doing Away with Due Process in Sex Cases: Redefine Normal Human Interaction as an Offense

Just as with speech codes, campus administrators have been broadening the definition of offenses as serious as sexual assault to a point where it bears no resemblance to what these terms mean in everyday society. Defining a crime so broadly that all students are guilty of violating it gives administrators what one campus "risk management" expert calls "wiggle room" to easily find students guilty if administrators suspect they are guilty. The system relies on campus administrators being preternaturally skilled at divining others' guilt, and it assumes that they wouldn't use this power to ruin a student's life. As readers may recognize by now, such trust is misplaced.

The most famous college sexual misconduct policy in history was passed in the 1990s at Antioch College in Ohio. Here is its definition of consent to sex, in full:

> Consent: Consent is defined as the act of willingly and verbally agreeing to engage in specific sexual conduct. The following are clarifying points:
> ❏ Consent is required each and every time there is sexual activity.
> ❏ All parties must have a clear and accurate understanding of the sexual activity.
> ❏ The person(s) who initiate(s) the sexual activity is responsible for asking for consent.
> ❏ The person(s) who are asked are responsible for verbally responding.
> ❏ Each new level of sexual activity requires consent.
> ❏ Use of agreed upon forms of communication such as gestures or safe words is acceptable, but must be discussed and verbally agreed to by all parties before sexual activity occurs.

❏ Consent is required regardless of the parties' relationship, prior sexual history, or current activity (e.g. grinding on the dance floor is not consent for further sexual activity).

❏ At any and all times when consent is withdrawn or not verbally agreed to, the sexual activity must stop immediately.

❏ Silence is not consent.

❏ Body movements and non-verbal responses such as moans are not consent.

❏ A person can not give consent while sleeping.

❏ All parties must have unimpaired judgment (examples that may cause impairment include but are not limited to alcohol, drugs, mental health conditions, physical health conditions).

❏ All parties must use safer sex practices.

❏ All parties must disclose personal risk factors and any known STIs. Individuals are responsible for maintaining awareness of their sexual health.

These requirements for consent do not restrict with whom the sexual activity may occur, the type of sexual activity that occurs, the props/toys/tools that are used, the number of persons involved, the gender(s) or gender expressions of persons involved.[12]

Did you get all that? So at Antioch, unless you verbally asked your wife, husband, girlfriend, or boyfriend at each step of a sexual encounter and received a verbal affirmation to proceed, you would have committed "non-consensual sex," more commonly known as rape. You also violated the policy if you were drinking, smoking pot, or not using "safer sex" practices, or if the person you were having sex with was depressed. I would venture that every non-virgin on the planet has violated this policy, possibly on a daily basis.

The code at Gettysburg College in Pennsylvania, though less known, had an even broader definition of "sexual misconduct." Gettysburg's policy defined consent to sexual interaction as "the act of willingly and verbally agreeing to engage in specific sexual conduct." The policy's broad definition of sexual interaction included not only sex acts but also "touching," "hugging," and "kissing."[13]

Does anyone get verbal consent to hug their friends and then continue to ask for it during the entire hug? Should tapping someone on the shoulder be a violation of a university policy? This rule effectively makes every student—man, woman, married, or single—guilty of sexual misconduct.

When FIRE first asked the Gettysburg administration how it could defend such a policy in 2006, it answered that the policy existed and was enforced, but had not been enforced against people for merely hugging.[14] In other words, the university was saying, "Yes, we do retain the power to find virtually every single Gettysburg student guilty of sexual misconduct at any time, but trust us—we'll only use it when we think someone has done something really bad." It's lunacy to give people the power to punish whomever they want based on their promise that they won't abuse it.

I know people who rush to the defense of the Antioch and Gettysburg policies, saying that the codes were just aspirational—a positive model of sexual behavior that one should aspire to. This is wrong for two important reasons. First, it was a *rule*, not a "statement of ideal sexual encounters." It was written as a rule and incorporated into the rules, and you could be punished under it. Second, is this how anybody really aspires to live? As Cathy Young wrote in her *Boston Globe* column,

> Forget spontaneity, passion, the thrill of discovery. Forget letting go. At the time of the Antioch policy debate, one sexual assault counselor primly condemned "the blind give-and-take of sexual negotiations," arguing that it should be replaced by clear communication. The worthy goal of rape prevention has been twisted into a utopian attempt to remake human sexuality—in an image that is not particularly attractive.[15]

After a surprisingly amicable back-and-forth with Gettysburg (schools do not always take kindly to FIRE questioning their sexual misconduct policies), the school decided to change its policy in 2007 to one that only banned things that most people would consider sexual misconduct.[16] The current policy at Antioch College still requires explicit verbal consent, although "consent" is now defined in a way that isn't so byzantine.

Unfortunately, the move to fight the very real problem of sexual assault by redefining sexual assault to include extraordinary amounts of normal behavior did not die with Antioch. The most recent high-profile example popped up at Duke University in 2010, when it passed a sexual misconduct policy almost as broad as those at Antioch and Gettysburg.

What made the policy so shocking was that if any college in the country should know the importance of not rushing to judgment and know that accused students may actually be innocent, it's Duke. In March 2006, three members of the Duke University lacrosse team were falsely accused of rape by Crystal Mangum, a stripper who had been hired to perform at a party hosted by members of the team. The case against the students was weak from the start. Mangum gave the Durham Police Department several conflicting accounts of the events of that night, including a denial that any rape took place.[17] Reade Seligmann, one of the accused students, had a strong alibi that included cell phone calls, ATM records, and an affidavit from a taxi driver who drove him to several places—all during the time of the alleged assault.[18] Yet Mike Nifong, the Durham County district attorney, rushed to charge the students with rape, fighting to convict them through a series of shocking due process violations.

Launching a media frenzy in which he accused the students of "gang-like rape," Nifong withheld the mounting evidence of the students' innocence from both the public and the defense team, including a physical examination of Mangum that revealed no indication of rape.[19] And when the DNA report from a rape kit administered within hours of the alleged assault found no DNA matching a single member of the Duke lacrosse team—but, rather, the DNA of multiple other males—Nifong decided to conceal that evidence, as well.[20]

As the trial progressed and due process played its critical role, Nifong was forced to turn over all of the records and evidence he had suppressed while attempting to try the accused students in the court of public opinion. The facts that Nifong had buried spoke for themselves, and the North Carolina Attorney General's Office dropped all charges against the students on April 11, 2007.

Don't imagine that Duke had remained silent during this fiasco. In an exceptional example of the dangers of groupthink, eighty-eight Duke professors had signed a manifesto condemning the students before any of the facts were known, presuming that the lacrosse players had to be guilty.[21] Shockingly, none of those eighty-eight professors have publicly disavowed the statement in light of the students' exoneration.[22] The president of Duke, Richard Brodhead, said he hoped that the lacrosse players would be "proved innocent" at trial—a statement betraying such a profound misunderstanding of due process that it inspired the title of the definitive book on the debacle, Stuart Taylor and KC Johnson's *Until Proven Innocent*. With Duke ultimately forced into a multimillion-dollar settlement with the students for its involvement, one might think that no school had a better, deeper understanding of the importance of due process.[23] But when it came to its own sexual assault policy, Duke somehow decided that due process was unimportant.

Duke's new sexual misconduct policy was introduced with some fanfare in the beginning of the 2009–2010 school year. The director of the Duke Women's Center, Ada Gregory, told the school's paper, *The Chronicle*, that an expansive policy was necessary at Duke because "The higher [the] IQ, the more manipulative they are, the more cunning they are . . . imagine the sex offenders we have here at Duke—cream of the crop."[24] (Gregory later published a self-contradictory letter to *The Chronicle* saying that while the quote wasn't exactly right, Duke did in fact harbor smarter-than-average rapists.)[25]

The policy explained that some students are prone to *unintentionally* coercing others into sex due to "perceived power differentials," meaning that, according to the plain language of the code, a liaison between a revered Duke basketball player and practically anyone else could constitute misconduct, even if both parties thought it was consensual.[26] The university also changed the composition of the hearing panel for sexual misconduct accusations. For these accusations, unlike any other charges, a majority of the panel is composed of faculty members, not students, putting the administration of justice in the hands of those paid by Duke rather than a jury composed mostly of a student's peers.

The policy also stated that students could not give consent when "intoxicated" in any way, a provision that would reclassify an enormous amount of sexual activity on any campus as nonconsensual. This part of the policy was quietly changed more than a year later after FIRE pointed out that problem, but we have seen similar policies in schools across the country.

There is no doubt that we need to educate students about the threat of sexual violence and coercion, we must prosecute those found guilty, and we must encourage victims to report assaults. But it is not a solution to declare everyone presumptively guilty and work backwards from there, as schools like Duke or Antioch have done. It is precisely because rape is such a horrible and serious crime that we must approach the issue with careful policies that protect the rights of victims and the accused and do not criminalize normal human interaction.

Step Two: Lower Due Process Protections (or, How the Federal Government Isn't Helping)

While some colleges are redefining sexual assault to the point where it can no longer be recognized, many others, as we've already seen, have redefined harassment to include the broadest possible range of everyday activities. To cite a few more examples, UC Berkeley lists "humor and jokes about sex in general that make someone feel uncomfortable" as harassment.[27] Alabama State University forbids "behavior that causes discomfort, embarrassment or emotional distress" in its harassment codes.[28] Iowa State University maintains that harassment "can range from unwelcome sexual flirtations and inappropriate put-downs of individual persons or classes of people to serious physical abuses such as sexual assault."[29] Considering the extent to which people have been bombarded with policies like this in the workplace or on campus, it can seem like heresy to remind people that, at some point or another, we have all made someone else feel uncomfortable or distressed, intentionally or not. It's even likely that we have flirted with someone who wasn't interested, and it's unusual to make it through life without making an innuendo here and there.

Given that these definitions make us all guilty of harassment—and that by the Antioch and Gettysburg College definitions we have all committed assault—is there any way to make these policies worse? Indeed there is: you could decrease the protections to which those who are accused of violating them are entitled when trying to defend themselves. And this is exactly what the Office for Civil Rights of the Department of Education began to require of every college receiving federal money (virtually all of them) in its "Dear Colleague" letter of April 4, 2011, mentioned in Chapter 2.[30]

The letter contended that in order to properly address the problem of sexual *assault* on campus, universities had to bring their sexual *harassment* policies in line with OCR demands. The reason for this circuitous route is simple: OCR was not originally intended to have the power to directly enforce laws against sexual assault. But since at least 1999, sexual assault has been defined by the courts as an extreme form of harassment—which empowers OCR to police it through civil rights laws, including Title IX.

While some of the nineteen-page OCR letter, which was sent to virtually every college in the country, provided helpful clarification, its most noteworthy requirements included two things that make the situation for due process on campus far worse. First, it required universities to lower their standard of evidence for those accused of harassment to a "preponderance of evidence." This standard is the lowest judicial standard available. It has been described by campus judicial officers as merely "50 percent plus a feather." In other words, if you find the accuser's story just barely (mathematically, by 50.0001 percent) more credible than that of the accused, you are required to find the accused guilty.

The logic underlying the adoption of this standard turns our normal conception of due process on its head. Supporters of using this low standard to determine whether a student is guilty of sexual assault—one of the most heinous possible crimes—claim that we need the low standard *because* sexual assault on campuses is such a serious problem and such a serious offense. Generally, the rule in English and American law has been that the more grave the offense or charge, the *greater* the due process needs to be, but the federal government has apparently decided that sexual assault is such a serious problem that we need to mandate that universities should be less careful about whom they find guilty.

Taken together with the incredibly broad definitions of sexual misconduct, assault, and harassment that appear on campus after campus, the OCR's April 4 letter is a formula for due process disaster. The nation's top schools used to recognize this too. Data collected by FIRE show that before the letter was issued, nine of America's top eleven colleges (as rated by *U.S. News and World Report*) had a standard of evidence for campus crimes that was higher than "preponderance of the evidence."[31] But the April 4 letter effectively forced them to adopt the lower standard. Generally, the lower a college sat on the *U.S. News and World Report* list, the more likely it would be to use the preponderance standard. (Sadly, preponderance was the most common standard when all colleges were considered, which I believe represents over a decade of work by the university "risk management" industry.)

The threat this lower standard of evidence poses for the accused isn't imaginary, either. At the University of North Dakota, which used the preponderance standard even before OCR's letter arrived in college mailboxes, Caleb Warner was kicked out of school and banned from every North Dakota state campus for three years after he was found guilty by a campus tribunal of sexually assaulting another student.[32] Unfortunately for him, this was about three months before the police, who were also investigating, filed their charges . . . *against his accuser, for filing a false police report about the assault.* Warner asked twice for a rehearing and was denied twice. Only after FIRE's chairman Harvey Silverglate exposed UND's actions in the *Wall Street Journal* did UND "vacate" Warner's punishment.[33] His accuser remains wanted by the state of North Dakota.

This personal disaster for Caleb Warner and institutional humiliation for the University of North Dakota were brought to you directly as a result of the preponderance of the evidence standard. Using a higher standard, such as "clear and convincing evidence" (75–80 percent confidence) or "beyond a reasonable doubt" (99 percent confidence), UND likely could not have "convicted" Warner of sexual assault with the same evidence the police used to charge his accuser with lying to them. But when you only have to be 50.01 percent sure someone is guilty, there can be a 49.99 percent chance that he isn't. When it comes to branding someone a rapist, we should be a little more sure than that.

The second objectionable part of OCR's April 4 letter from a due process standpoint is that it requires universities to offer the accuser the right to appeal if they provide that right to the accused. That sounds fair until you realize what it means for the judicial process. If the student has been found innocent of rape by the hearing body tasked to evaluate the evidence, he (and it is almost always a "he") can nevertheless be found guilty by whoever's in charge of the appeal—often an intermediate dean, or some other midlevel official at the college.

In the criminal justice system, allowing accusers the chance to appeal a properly reached finding of innocence—in other words, trying the same person twice for the same crime—is called "double jeopardy," and the Fifth Amendment prohibits it. This is a smart safeguard, protecting those accused of criminal activity against abuses by police and prosecutors. Our constitutional system allows a guilty verdict reached in an unfair or arbitrary way to be challenged by the accused and overturned on appeal, but the authors of the Bill of Rights recognized that allowing that same appellate body to essentially rehear the case and declare someone guilty invites injustice. As Wendy Kaminer, a FIRE Board of Advisors member, observed in *The Atlantic,*

> Of course, campus disciplinary proceedings are not formal criminal trials governed by the 5th and 6th Amendments. But you'd have to regard the protection against double jeopardy as a mere constitutional technicality to believe that schools should dispense with it. Or you'd have to assume that, as a general rule, fairness requires convictions and provides multiple opportunities to obtain them.[34]

In other words, double jeopardy is inappropriate for campus courts for the same reasons that our nation's founders banned it under the Bill of Rights.

What's at Stake:
A Due Process Cautionary Tale out of Ohio

When you think about the extensive industries and apparatuses that have sprung up to deal with serious campus crimes, you have to ask: are universities panels really equipped to handle felonies? Do we think a college disciplinary board is competent, for example, to handle a murder trial?

And make no mistake about it, the stakes in campus tribunals can be extremely high. A story out of the University of Akron paints a sad picture. We know about it only because the *Akron Beacon Journal* got wind of it, and covered it in depth in 2006.

In December 2005, Charles Plinton, an African American student at the University of Akron, took his life after being kicked out of school on drug charges. When you look at the evidence, Plinton's innocence is clear; he was tried in criminal court and acquitted in only forty minutes. In fact, his accuser was a felon and a paid informant who had a financial incentive to declare him a criminal. (The University of Akron paid the informant $50 "for each alleged drug deal he struck with the student" that he reported to the administration.)[35] This glaring conflict of interest and the weakness of the case were immediately apparent to a criminal court, but a campus judiciary decided that the flimsy evidence was enough to ruin a student's life. Since Plinton didn't have the funds to hire an attorney and appeal his expulsion, he returned home to New Jersey and ultimately committed suicide.

We can only guess how many Charles Plintons may be out there, but we would be naïve to think it's an isolated case. University tribunals often require secrecy and hide their processes from peering eyes with the help of federal laws (primarily the Family Rights and Privacy Act) and can therefore violate students' due process rights in a rush to find them guilty. We live in a time that demands serious reform of higher education, and one of the places to start is the campus judiciary system. Perhaps it would be better if wholly independent systems were developed to take these offenses out of the hands of interested deans and biased students who may know the accusers or the accused and who provide paper-thin due process with zero transparency. In any case, all options for reform should be on the table.

Campus Justice and Unlearning the "Spirit of Liberty"

In 1944, as victory in World War II finally seemed on the horizon for the United States, Learned Hand, one of the country's most famous jurists, made a speech in Central Park about the meaning of liberty. The short speech electrified the crowd, was reproduced across the country, and is often quoted to this day. Of all the wonderful lines in that short speech, the one that is probably most quoted is, "The spirit of liberty is the spirit which is not too sure that it is right."[36] I suspect that line might appear confusing and alien to audiences today. Self-doubt, lack of certainty, and recognizing your own fallibility have seemed to pass out of fashion. We live in an age of certainty and snap judgments. For all its other benefits, social media has also helped us rush to judgment. The judicious are decried as passionless, and those who believe there may be a middle way are dismissed as either naïve or traitors by the true believers (as happened when I spoke about the Residence Life program at the University of Delaware). The root of this trend lies in the gradual breakdown of our understanding of liberty. In that same speech, Hand said,

> I often wonder whether we do not rest our hopes too much upon constitutions, upon laws and upon courts. These are false hopes; believe me, these are false hopes. Liberty lies in the hearts of men and women; when it dies there, no constitution, no law, no court can save it; no constitution, no law, no court can even do much to help it.[37]

Due process and fair procedure are nothing less than manifestations of the systems and structures we have developed in order to live as a free people. Just like free speech and the scientific method, they require recognition of human fallibility, and they involve the establishment of processes that make it easier for the truth to come out. The process isn't perfect, and it can't be, but it replaced systems based on raw power, superstition, and gut instinct. The refusal of universities to reflect the values of due process and fair procedure can only teach students the wrong lessons about what it means to live in a free society. Fair and judicious systems make an impression on people, but so does arbitrary power, which is what universities exercise when they deny students their rights. Due process and fair procedure, much like free speech, are also habits of mind that need to be taught and trained, and if we don't cultivate them we cannot expect them to survive.

No human being needs to be taught to rush to judgment; it's unfortunately something we just tend to do. The Duke lacrosse case, the quickness of the media to declare Richard Jewell guilty of the bombings at Centennial Olympic Park in Atlanta in 1996, the hurry to pass judgment in the trial of Amanda Knox, and even the haste to confirm the allegations of rape against Dominique Strauss-Kahn in 2011—all these should have shown us that human beings do not need to be taught how to be *less* judicious in deciding guilt or innocence. Higher education is supposed to help us overcome this shortcoming, but if it instead reinforces our tendency to make snap decisions on matters as important as guilt or innocence, we cannot expect the ideal of "innocent until proven guilty" to mean very much.

CHAPTER 7

Don't Question Authority

I<small>T'S THE NIGHT AFTER YOUR FIRST MEETING</small> with Student Accountability Training and you just want to get some sleep. If you could only figure out how to say what the coordinator wanted you to say in the right way. But what's the right language?

Then you hear a noise from the hallway and recognize your friend Jason's voice. You poke your head outside your door and see two campus police officers talking to Jason. Jason looks freaked out and the campus police are looming ever closer to him.

A girl on your floor edges next to you.

"Any idea what's going on?" you ask.

"I think so. Jason posted a long complaint about the school on Facebook. He also, umm, quoted that . . . you know, umm . . . 'F-bomb tha Police' song by that guy from *Daddy Day Care.*"

"You mean NWA?" you say, pondering the stupidity of the term "F-bomb" while hoping nobody will ask you what those initials stand for. "What was he complaining about?"

"Well, something called the Student Accountability Training program?" she suggests with a puzzled frown.

And then it dawns on you. This is your fault. You told Jason about the program but you didn't figure he'd go off and start ranting on Facebook about it. But you should have known better—of course he would. This is all your fault.

Oh Yeah, We Actually Meant DON'T Question Authority

As Alan Charles Kors has pointed out, one of the great ironies of contemporary censorship on campus is that it constitutes a "great generational swindle": the same baby boomers who fought so hard for free speech on campus under the banner of "Question Authority" turned around and imposed speech codes and free speech zones when it was their turn to be in charge of the academy. This change can be seen in the excesses of campus police, some of which have been caught on video and circulated around the planet. Whether it's the infamous "Don't tase me, bro!" incident at the University of Florida in 2007 or the more recent video of campus security officers at UC Davis casually spraying a dozen or more peacefully protesting students in the face with an industrial-sized can of pepper spray, the public is becoming aware that universities are getting increasingly aggressive with students who get out of line.[1]

It's undeniably true that in some cases—particularly the ones you'll see in Chapter 11—it's important to stop students from disrupting the campus and infringing on the free speech of others, but many of the cases you will see in this chapter come down to censorship in its rawest, most primal form. Increasingly, students are getting in trouble for simply criticizing the administration. It's hard to teach students the intellectual value of questioning authority when they are, in fact, being punished for questioning authority.

It should come as no surprise that administrators have gone from acting as political correctness police to punishing students and faculty who criticize them. When you start to delegitimize and forget the principles behind freedom of speech, it creates easy opportunities for those with power to shut down speech that is critical of *them*. The desire to silence your enemies or detractors has to be the most fundamental motive in the history of censorship—and in many of the cases discussed in this book, it's disguised by appeals to ideals like tolerance, diversity, civility, or equality. As we look at the following cases, you will see administrators make feeble (at best) attempts to vindicate actions that, at heart, come down to one simple sentiment: "Hey, I believe in free speech and all, but not when you're criticizing me."

Campus Authoritarianism versus Sci-Fi Fans

The example I chose to open this section is close to my heart because it involves a university's attempt to punish a professor for quoting a science fiction show that I (and an extremely rabid core of fans) adore: Joss Whedon's short-lived sci-fi Western *Firefly*. On September 12, 2011, James Miller, a theater professor at the University of Wisconsin–Stout who had recently become a fan of the show, posted this tribute to the captain of the starboat *Serenity*, Malcolm "Mal" Reynolds, outside his door:

You don't know me, son, so let me explain this to you once: If I ever kill you, you'll be awake. You'll be facing me. And you'll be armed.

Source: *James Miller*

If you take a moment to think about what this quote means, it's pretty obvious that it is the character's way of saying, "Hey, I play fair." The quote is from the pilot episode of *Firefly*, during which the new ship's doctor asked Mal, "How do I know you won't kill me in my sleep?" The answer is macho, over-the-top, and very "Mal," but its point is, "You don't have to watch your back with me."

Rather than simply asking what the poster meant, the campus police stepped in. Lisa A. Walter, the chief of police and director of parking services, removed the poster and informed Miller that "it is unacceptable to have postings such as this that refer to killing."[2] She also warned the astounded professor that any future posts would be removed and would cause him to be charged with "disorderly conduct." Disorderly conduct, by the way, has been catching up with harassment as one of the most abused legal terms on campus; its name is vague enough to punish just about anything. Recall that

Tim Garneau at the University of New Hampshire was also found guilty of disorderly conduct for his "Freshman 15" joke.

A brief tour of campus would have dispelled any doubt that Miller was being singled out unfairly. A nearby wall featured a Dilbert cartoon in which one character punches right through another's head. Pictures of a campus rally on Governor Scott Walker's stance on union rights reveal posters with Uma Thurman brandishing a blood-tinged samurai sword and the words "Kill the Bill" written via blade slashes.

Source: *Amy Fichter*

All of these images are and should be protected. Adults, and especially drama professors (anybody read Shakespeare lately?), use violent imagery to convey serious or humorous points all the time. Adult life includes adult content.

Miller rightly deduced that this was both selective enforcement and a wild overreaction. The Constitution protects speech far, far harsher than a quip from *Firefly*. It seemed that someone at the college either had an axe to grind or was just power tripping at Miller's expense. So, on September 16, he posted this:

⚠ **WARNING**

FASCISM

FASCISM CAN CAUSE BLUNT TRAUMA AND/OR VIOLENT DEATH. KEEP FASCISM AWAY FROM CHILDREN AND PETS.

Source: *James Miller*

In a feat of intentional misunderstanding of the kind that is all too common on campus, the university interpreted Professor Miller's protest as being pro-fascist and advocating violence. The police tore down this poster too, with Chief Walter claiming this time that the problem was that the poster "depicts violence and mentions violence or death." She wrote, "[I]t is believed that this posting also has a reasonable expectation that it will cause a material and/or substantial disruption of school activities and/or be constituted as a threat." Walter also told Miller he had been reported to the "threat assessment team."[3]

Walter had transmogrified a post intended to poke fun at her into a pro-fascist threat against the university. This is as absurd an interpretation as it is self-serving. No one was threatened by the *Firefly* poster, and no reasonable person would understand the second poster to be anything other than a rebuke of Walter's heavy-handed actions. The university overreacted to a poster and then doubled down rather than admit error when Miller mocked that overreaction.

At that point, it dawned on Miller that he was in serious trouble, and he contacted FIRE. When we wrote the university to protest, I assumed the chancellor of UW–Stout would realize that this was an overreaction on their part, which made the school look unable to accept criticism—and also that it could place the college on the losing end of a First Amendment lawsuit.[4] We took the case public, and everyone from *Gawker*, *The Onion*'s A.V. Club, and *Reason*, to the *Firefly* star Adam Baldwin and even Nathan Fillion, the actor who played Mal, publicly pointed out the absurdity of the case.[5] I was even more certain then that the chancellor would apologize and rectify the situation. But I was wrong.

On the evening of September 27, the UW–Stout chancellor, Charles W. Sorensen, the provost, Julie Furst-Bowe, and the vice chancellor, Ed Nieskes, issued a statement to all faculty and staff passionately standing by their decision.[6] They claimed that the posters were removed because their top lawyers believed they "constituted an implied threat of violence." The email concluded, "This was not an act of censorship. This was an act of sensitivity to and care for our shared community, and was intended to maintain a campus climate in which everyone can feel welcome, safe and secure."

On the contrary, tearing down harmless posters and threatening the professor who put them up with criminal punishment is the essence of censorship. Rather than admit a mistake, the chancellor had doubled down again, invoking the safety and security of the community as an excuse.

Meanwhile, hundreds if not thousands of *Firefly* fans across the country wrote to express their anger about the university's mistreatment of the professor over a quote from their beloved television show. On October 4, 2011, UW–Stout publicly announced it was backing off and would even hold First Amendment seminars at the university.[7] The irony, of course, was that nobody but the administration itself had demonstrated they needed lessons in the First Amendment.

While it looked as though free speech had won, my reaction to this victory was somewhat bittersweet. First of all, Miller never received a word of apology (or even his posters back). Second, if it had not been for the devoted *Firefly* fans around the globe, I'm not sure the university would ever have admitted its error. The administrators gave every indication that they planned to fight this one until the end. It was only because the case outraged a built-in constituency that Professor Miller was able to find such powerful allies, including the legendary sci-fi, fantasy, and comic book author Neil Gaiman and his 1.6 million Twitter followers. I only wish that the constituency for free speech on campus were as tuned in and committed as my fellow Browncoats (fans of *Firefly*; seriously, watch the show).

Facebook and the Risks of Online Dissent

As we saw earlier, complaining about administrators online can be a risky endeavor. Back in 2006, when I barely knew what Facebook was, four students at Syracuse University (a school that will come up repeatedly for its policing of online speech) were expelled from a course and placed on "disciplinary reprimand" for graphically complaining about a writing instructor on Facebook. (The four were "officers" of a sixteen-member group—all female, according to *Inside Higher Ed*—and apparently they were among hundreds of students who complained about instructors.)[8] That same year, two students at Cowley College in Kansas were banned from participating in theater department activities after they complained about the department on MySpace.[9]

These cases were the first hints (to me at least) that a new realm of speech was subject to suppression: social media, especially this young upstart Facebook. Facebook is now an unwitting part of the campus censorship ecosystem, with administrators policing what students say in a realm that students often assume to be semiprivate or, at the very least, off-limits to official punishment. Campus administrators keep proving this assumption wrong.

This trend continued in two particularly notable cases in 2011. One occurred at Saint Augustine's College in Raleigh, North Carolina, when the campus was recovering from a tornado that had thrashed the area, leaving tens of thousands without power, including many Saint Augustine's students. On April 18, two days after being hit, the college announced that it would reopen the next day, even though some students were literally still in the dark and, in the words of Saint Augustine's own press release, the campus had been "ravaged" by the storm. This placed those students without electricity or otherwise harmed by the storm in the position of having to explain why they could not make it to class or get assignments done. After receiving complaints about the decision, the Saint Augustine's administration announced a public meeting to discuss the reopening with concerned students, along with representatives from the local electric company. In response, Roman Caple, a senior who was just about to graduate and who was frustrated with the situation, wrote on the college's Facebook page, "Here it go!!!!! Students come correct, be prepared, and have supporting documents to back up your arguments bcuz SAC will come hard!!!! That is all."[10] This is essentially a run-of-the-mill complaint that some administrators are sticklers for paperwork. For this, Caple was called into the office of Eric W. Jackson, Saint Augustine's vice president for student development and services, and received a letter notifying him that he would not be allowed to participate in his own graduation ceremony. The only reason the college gave was Caple's "negative social media exchange during the institution's recovery from the tornado."[11] The letter from Jackson also admonished that "[a]ll students enrolled at Saint Augustine's College are responsible for protecting the reputation of the college and supporting its mission."[12] On April 29, the college issued a public statement claiming that Caple's Facebook post and other alleged (yet never revealed) comments by other students were an "attempt to create chaos."[13]

FIRE became involved, but the university refused to back down, stating through an outside law firm that Saint Augustine's had "legitimate reasons" to bar Caple—the first in his family to complete college—from attending his graduation ceremony.[14] Caple filed a lawsuit against Saint Augustine's College for violating its very clear and strong contractual promises of freedom of speech.[15] According to the complaint, for his mild comment on Facebook, Caple not only was banned from graduation, but was also forced to receive his cap and gown from campus police.[16] Saint Augustine's later extended its spiteful punishment even further, preventing Caple from attending the college's homecoming celebration.[17] Caple and Saint Augustine's College eventually settled the lawsuit in late 2011, and Caple is reportedly happy with the deal they reached. Still, a university that so harshly punishes the slightest criticism of its own bureaucracy seems incapable of creating a bold environment for questioning, thought experimentation, or critical thinking.

Just two months later, another student, Marc Bechtol at Catawba Valley Community College (CVCC, also in North Carolina), was pulled out of his class and banned from campus after he complained on CVCC's Facebook page about the college's aggressive marketing of the creepily named Higher One debit card company to its students. (Higher One, based in New Haven, reportedly has deals with about seven hundred campuses around the country to provide bank cards and accounts to students who receive financial aid.)[18] The Higher One debit card also served as a student's ID at CVCC, making it essential that students sign up with the company. In order to activate his card, Bechtol had to provide information to the company that included his student identification number, date of birth, and Social Security number. Bechtol found the whole process unseemly. And the fees were hardly nominal; students were charged $2.50 for any non–Higher One ATM they used and $.50 for debit purchases they made using their card's PIN instead of their signature, and could be charged up to $19 per month if their accounts remained inactive for nine months or more.[19] Bechtol believed that his attendance at college should not be contingent upon signing up for a debit card and revealing personal and commercial information about himself to a private company.[20] According to Bechtol, the college and the company barraged students with ads and emails advertising that they would receive their Pell grants and tuition refunds sooner if they opened Higher One checking accounts. And after Bechtol gave in and signed up for everything, he started receiving marketing calls from other credit card companies, leading him to believe that Higher One had sold his information. (Higher One denies that claim.)

Aggravated, Bechtol began regularly criticizing what he saw as the troubling coziness between the college and the company, and on September 28 he wrote on CVCC's Facebook page, "Did anyone else get a bunch of credit card spam in their CVCC inbox today? So, did CVCC sell our names to banks, or did Higher One? I think we should register CVCC's address with every porn site known to man. Anyone know any good viruses to send them?" He immediately followed up with, "OK, maybe that would be a slight overreaction."[21]

Taking this in context, and especially with the last disclaimer, no reasonable person could assume that this comment was anything other than an exasperated response to a months-long problem that only seemed to be getting worse—not an attempt to mount a cyber attack. Nonetheless, Bechtol was pulled out of his classroom on October 4 and was told by the executive officer of student services, Cynthia L. Coulter, in the presence of a county sheriff's deputy, that he could not return to campus. The next day, Coulter sent Bechtol a letter suspending him from CVCC and banning him from the campus for two semesters, stating that his Facebook post was "disturbing and indicates possible malicious action against the college," all without offering Bechtol a proper opportunity to explain or defend himself.[22]

Once again, FIRE became involved. With some interest generated by the ongoing Occupy Wall Street protests in New York City's Zuccotti Park, the case received substantial media attention, even inspiring a rally by dozens of students against Higher One all the way across the country at Western Washington University. Students also created a Facebook page of their own: "Students Against Higher One."[23] In the face of public pushback, CVCC dropped all charges against Bechtol.

War at Peace College and the Spamification of Dissent

One of the classic cases of my career involved a student who got into trouble for trying to do nothing more than have a sensible discussion about a university decision that affected both curriculum and costs. In 2008, Kara Spencer, a student government leader at Michigan State University (the same school that had the crazy brainwashing program discussed in Chapter 6) was found guilty of violating the university's spam policy for emailing a number of professors about the university's plan to shorten the academic calendar and orientation schedule while not offering students a discount for the reduced service.[24]

This was a serious and legitimate campus issue worthy of discussion among MSU students and faculty, and Spencer wrote the email in her capacity as a student member of the University Committee on Student Affairs. UCSA—which consisted of several student government members, faculty members, and administrators—had previously met and exchanged emails to discuss the matter and to construct a formal response to the university. Spencer then took the initiative to inform UCSA that she would send a personal version of this formal response to faculty members. None of the professors or administrators in the group gave any indication that MSU would frown upon the email or accuse her of violating university policy, and one of the faculty members on the committee encouraged her to proceed.

Spencer carefully selected the 391 professors, representing approximately 8 percent of MSU's faculty, to receive the email. It was a polite and thoughtful message, bringing up numerous issues about academic quality, cost, and the process that was followed in making the decision.[25] One MSU faculty member, however, complained about receiving the email, leading MSU's network administrator to accuse Spencer of a slew of conduct violations for sending unauthorized "spam."[26] Despite the fact she wasn't sending out an advertisement for a kegger or a chain-mail letter, she was found guilty of violating MSU's Network Acceptable Use policy for her "unauthorized" use of the MSU network.[27] Spencer had a formal "Warning" placed in her file, a red flag to future schools or employers. She was also warned that if she were ever to do such a thing again she would face serious punishment.

The spam policy in question was so broad that it made virtually every student using university email guilty of violating it at some point. FIRE, along with the Electronic Frontier Foundation (EFF) and eleven other civil liberties organizations, wrote to Michigan State University protesting both the absurdly broad policy and the treatment of Spencer.[28] Happily, the university decided in the face of this public pressure to withdraw its punishment. But MSU refused to revise its spam policy to meet constitutional standards, and instead actually made the policy worse. Whereas the old version of the policy prohibited the sending of an unsolicited email to more than "20–30" recipients over two days without prior permission, the current version of the policy defines "Bulk e-mail" as "The transmission of an identical or substantially identical e-mail message within a 48-hour period from an internal user to more than 10 other internal users who have not elected to receive such e-mail."[29] Also preposterous is the policy's declaration that "The University's e-mail services are not intended as a forum for the expression of personal opinions." Yes, that's right: No personal opinions in email. Once again, the guiding principle is to define a rule in such absurdly broad terms that all students are guilty, then work backwards from there when someone is charged.

In the fall of 2011, yet another North Carolina school, the somewhat ironically named Peace College, went to war with alumni who had signed a petition. The petition protested the decision of the all-female college to go coed and lodged numerous complaints against the college's president, Debra Townsley.[30] Rather than demonstrate what it means to be a deliberative institution devoted to rational debate and discussion by taking on the petition's claims, Peace College decided to go with "Shut up or we'll sue you." In a stern letter sent by Catharine Biggs Arrowood, an outside attorney whose firm had been retained by the college, the newly renamed "William Peace University" (part of the intended makeover of the college) demanded that the author of the petition "desist from further distribution of the letter and send letters of retraction to any persons to whom the letter was published, whether they received a letter directly by mail or otherwise."[31] Arrowood also asked that the signees "furnish us with a list utilized to distribute this letter so that we may communicate directly with recipients to correct your misstatements."[32] And this from a school claiming that "the exchange of ideas . . . is essential to the university's intellectual, cultural and social life."[33] Those behind the petition declined to furnish Arrowood with the demanded list of recipients, though they did furnish FIRE with Arrowood's demand letter, which we promptly posted on our website, along with the petition itself.

The cease-and-desist letter roughly hinted that the petition, which contained a combination of opinions and factual assertions, constituted defamation, claiming that the letter's various statements were "not only false but individually and collectively damage[d] the reputation of the University and its President."[34] Of course, any lawyer knows that defamation is very difficult to prove against a public figure (which a university president is); the burden is on the allegedly defamed to show that the alleged defamer either actually knew they were lying or showed "reckless disregard" for the truth.[35] And, as the legal blog known as Popehat pointed out in a post excoriating Peace College's "ham-fisted" attempt to shut down dissent, Arrowood's letter "conspicuously and utterly fail[ed] to specify *exactly what statements in the letter are false*." Popehat aptly commented that "ambiguity in a defamation threat letter is the vanguard of bullshit thuggery."[36]

That astute observation provides the perfect segue to the red herring of swear words.

Swear at Your Own Risk
(a.k.a. Skip This Section If You Can't Abide Cussing)

Warning: This section will involve cussing, swearing, profanity, or whatever you call it. As a First Amendment advocate and a Brooklynite, I have been shocked by how passionately many people who normally agree with me on free speech have a completely different attitude when it comes to "curse words." If you suspect you believe that swearing can never have a meaningful function in debate, dissent, or society, I recommend you skip the following section.

For those of you who are still reading, understand that the fact that a student swore in a case is often little more than an excuse for insulted university administrators to punish someone for criticizing them. In the same way that administrators dupe kindhearted, politically correct students into granting them implicit permission to pass policies that limit their own speech rights, administrators take advantage of society's taboo against "bad" words to justify punishing students selectively based on what they say.

Many universities have speech codes that specifically ban swearing. FIRE has often awarded our Speech Code of the Month (SCOTM) "distinction" to such schools: in June 2006, Coast Community College District, which banned "derogatory posters, cartoons, or drawings" and "habitual profanity or vulgarity"; in October 2006, Ole Miss, which required that "offensive language is not to be used" even in private phone calls; in December 2008,

Lone Star College–Tomball in Texas, which simply banned "vulgar expression"; in November 2010, Moorpark College in California, which prohibited "profanity, vulgarity, or other offensive conduct"; and in October 2011, Sam Houston State University (also in Texas), which banned "using abusive, indecent, profane or vulgar language."[37]

The October 2009 SCOTM was especially striking in its scope: James Madison University's code flatly stated, "No student shall engage in lewd, indecent or obscene conduct or expression, regardless of proximity to campus."[38] To give credit where credit is due, both James Madison University and Ole Miss not only repealed their codes after each was named a Speech Code of the Month (as many colleges do in the face of public embarrassment for receiving this "honor"), but also worked with us so diligently to conform their codes to First Amendment standards that both colleges' policies earned a rare "green light" status from FIRE.

The award for the greatest irony in a code has to go to our April 2006 SCOTM at Barnard College, which printed word for word George Carlin's famous seven dirty words (adding an eighth word, "suck," for good measure) in its prohibition of those words.[39] Did no one at Barnard realize that the code violates itself?

So yes, many public universities have policies against various forms of swearing despite the fact that the Supreme Court, as discussed below, has been exceedingly clear that swearing constitutes protected speech. While I know that some might have sympathy for an attempt to eradicate swears from our institutions of education, when you take a closer look, you realize what is really going on. These codes are incredibly selectively enforced. College students swear an awful lot. Tom Wolfe, himself no stranger to swearing, was taken aback by how much students of both genders swore in everyday life when he went from college to college to investigate campus life for his book *I Am Charlotte Simmons*: "[H]earing women talk like they have acetylene torches inside their mouths still catches my attention."[40] He even came up with a term for how students mix constant swearing into everyday language: "Fuck Patois."[41] I suspect that students will always use these words, if for no other reason than to reject the manners of their parents (perhaps, not realizing that many of their parents spoke the same way in college). Now, consider the fact that hardly any students are disciplined for swearing. These codes come into play only when a student is criticizing the university or the decisions of its staff.

Take the case of Isaac Rosenbloom, a twenty-nine-year-old father of two and a student at Hinds Community College in Mississippi. On March 29, 2010, Rosenbloom stayed after his Oral Communication class with a few other students to talk to the instructor, Barbara Pyle, about their grades on a recent assignment. During the after-class discussion, he said privately to one of his fellow students that his grade was "going to fuck up [his] entire GPA." Professor Pyle overheard him, became angry at his choice of words, and threatened Rosenbloom with "detention"—a sanction available in middle school but not in college. Rosenbloom called her out on this absurdity, telling her he was not in grade school.

Rosenbloom was soon brought up on charges of "flagrant disrespect of any person," an actual offense under the college speech code, and was subject to an official hearing.[42] The professor referred to his comment as a "severe cursing incident" in her complaint against Rosenbloom. Listening to the audio record of the hearing (which Professor Pyle did not bother to attend), you might think that Rosenbloom was facing a court-martial or a congressional investigation rather than an inquiry into a single use of profanity.[43] In his defense, Rosenbloom cited well-established First Amendment law that clearly protects far more offensive speech than simple swearing. The 1973 Supreme Court case *Papish* v. *Board of Curators* could not have been more clear: "the mere dissemination of ideas—no matter how offensive to good taste—on a state university campus may not be shut off in the name alone of 'conventions of decency.'"[44] The Supreme Court has even specified that the much-maligned "F-word" is protected, ruling in its famous 1971 case *Cohen* v. *California* that "while the particular four-letter word being litigated here is perhaps more distasteful than most others of its genre, it is nevertheless often true that one man's vulgarity is another's lyric."[45] Popular music has demonstrated for decades since then that this observation is quite literally true.

Despite his impassioned, reasoned, and 100 percent legally accurate defense, Rosenbloom was found guilty of "flagrant disrespect."[46] He received twelve "demerits," three short of being suspended from the university, and was kicked out of Pyle's course. Worst of all, because of the punishment he lost his Pell grant—a federal scholarship to help lower-income Americans attend college—and all of his other financial aid at Hinds. Without financial aid, Rosenbloom, an EMT, had no hope of completing his paramedic studies, a fact that he told his college hearing board to no avail.

With the help of FIRE, Rosenbloom appealed this finding, but he was twice rejected. Finally, in the face of pressure from FIRE and perhaps realizing it had no chance of winning a lawsuit, the school reversed the decision against Rosenbloom in late July 2010.[47] Nonetheless, I was amazed by how the Rosenbloom case united censors on the conservative right and the speech code left, who came together to blast his use of the F-word. Critics of Rosenbloom insisted that such language would never be tolerated in the professional world. Really? Rosenbloom was an EMT. Do we really expect our paramedics to limit themselves to "Oh, fudge" in the midst of a crisis?

Also, let's be clear on what didn't happen here. A professor retains extensive powers to prevent students from disrupting class. Colleges can certainly intervene when a student is acting in a way that is disruptive or genuinely makes other students or the professor feel threatened. These powers, however, do not create an all-encompassing professorial right to never hear words that offend them when class is over.

Just as the case of Isaac Rosenbloom closed, the case of Jacob Lovell opened. Lovell was a graduate student at the University of Georgia who drove a scooter to get around campus. He was constantly aggravated by the lack of parking for his scooter and what he saw as the rude and dismissive way the Parking Services office conducted itself. So when he saw that Parking Services was requesting both "positive and negative" feedback from students via email, he took the opportunity to vent some frustration:

Why isn't there any scooter parking near Aderhold [a building where he had classes on campus], according to your parking map? There's like a billion places to park on north campus and over by the Georgia center, but nothing anywhere close to Aderhold. What the hell? Did you guys just throw darts at a map to decide where to put scooter corrals? Can I expect you guys to get off your asses and put in a corral near there some point before I fucking graduate and/or the sun runs out of hydrogen?

Thanks for nothing, ever,

–J [48]

In less than four hours, Parking Services responded with a terse email that read only, "Your email was sent to student judiciary." Lovell responded, "So that's a no?" He was quickly contacted by the associate dean of students, who told him he was being charged with "Disruption or obstruction of teaching, research, administration or other University activities" and "Engaging in conduct that causes or provokes a disturbance that disrupts the academic pursuits, or infringes upon the rights, privacy, or privileges of another person. Specifically, it is alleged that Mr. Lovell engaged in disorderly conduct and disrupted parking services when he sent an email to them that was threatening."[49]

I understand that his email is rude, but compared to the kind of complaints I have read while working for both the ACLU and FIRE, Lovell's email was downright affable. Did anyone feel threatened by this email? I doubt it, but institutions, like students themselves, quickly learn what buzz words they have to say in order to punish students who insult them. After a letter from FIRE, UGA dropped the charges against Lovell, though as *Washington Post* columnist Valerie Strauss wrote: "The case was closed. But why was it ever opened?"[50] Many of the writers in the comment section of Strauss's article, however, disagreed. One wrote, "This is no less offensive than spitting on a teacher or administrator. Expel the kid; let him learn manners somewhere else." I have to disagree, as spitting in someone's face constitutes criminal assault. Kvetching about parking, on the other hand, is rightfully protected.

Swearing, profanity, or cussing still retains what is, to First Amendment lawyers like me, a puzzling power to provoke outrage and calls for censorship. When it comes to cussing, some liberals and conservatives start sounding an awful lot like each other in calling for "decency" and "civility." I don't object to certain safeguards, like warning parents if television shows, music, and movies contain "adult situations" or "strong language." But adult life, especially that of a parent, paramedic, or graduate student, is one big "adult situation," and adult situations sometimes include strong language.

And this brings me back to my favorite of the great internal contradictions of speech codes. These codes, much like the one applied at Hinds Community College, are often passed and enforced in the name of tolerance, diversity, and multiculturalism, but as I discussed in Chapter 1, any real commitment to tolerance, diversity, and multiculturalism must recognize that people from different economic classes, different countries, and different backgrounds have different opinions of what is polite and what is inappropriate.

My father was raised in Yugoslavia and often lamented the lack of imagination in English swear words. My mother is Irish but grew up in England, and observed that the working class there used coarse and colorful language to demonstrate their disdain for the soft ways of the upper classes. Before starting college, I spent years working in restaurants as everything from a busboy to a prep chef, in discount retail, and in construction, and each environment had a different appreciation of when and what kind of swears were appropriate (with kitchen staff favoring using them as often as possible). While working with kids from some of DC's toughest high schools before law school, I often thought that my dad might have been wrong about the lack of creativity in American swearing. I now live in an old Italian neighborhood in Brooklyn. If you suddenly started fining people for swearing in my neighborhood, you would soon be rich . . . that is, if you managed not to get your (excuse me) ass kicked. And the kids in my neighborhood would be justified in defending their right to use colorful language as part of tolerance, diversity, and multi-culturalism, pointing out that curse words can be used for everything from expressions of joy to solidarity to simply conveying sincerity.

As some of America's greatest comedians, from Lenny Bruce to George Carlin, have repeatedly stressed in their comedy, we have to "get over it" and recognize that curses are simply words and stop giving them the power to make us behave irrationally. I'm not saying that people shouldn't argue for or urge the use of different or "better" words, but as soon as we start assuming that there is one universal idea of politeness and that certain words must never be spoken, we impose a dreary monoculture on an otherwise vibrant society.

Another interesting aspect of Lovell's and Rosenbloom's cases is that both involved students of "nontraditional age," a little older than their peers. In my experience, older students have a greater tendency to get into trouble in college, in no small part because, having lived in the "real world," they are far less prone to accept the patronizing, infantilizing, and unconstitutional behavior of college administrators. They know their rights and are willing to expose the violations enacted by the campus judiciary, unlike younger students who have never learned these valuable lessons in high school or college.

And now for the story that inspired the intro to this chapter: In late September 2011, Jacob Ramirez was given a $25 parking ticket by Western Washington University (WWU), a public college in Washington State. Irritated, as most students are with university parking departments, he wrote the title of the famous NWA "Fuck tha Police" song on the check he used to pay his fine.[51] Rude? Well, that was the point of that 1988 protest song (which *Rolling Stone* considers one of the top 500 songs of all time and which was co-written by gangsta rapper turned family entertainer Ice Cube).[52] But WWU refused to let this simply slip as an irritated memo note on a student check. On October

19, Ramirez found out he was under investigation for violating the school's "Harassment and/or Threats of Violence" policy. The official notice informed him: "Parking Services and the University Police reported [that he] mailed them payment for a parking violation with the 'F' word written on [his] check and on the parking ticket." So a defiant reference to a song from my youth had become an "unwanted and/or intimidating contact and/or communication of a threatening nature."[53]

The use here of "intimidation" is instructive, as there was approximately a zero percent chance the check placed the campus police in "fear of bodily harm or death" as the legal definition of intimidation requires. Yet again, those who simply didn't like what someone said glommed onto legal tools to persecute him. FIRE quickly became involved, pointing out that the Supreme Court had clearly established that protests like Ramirez's are entirely protected. The college suspended the investigation and actually apologized to the student.[54] The single rarest thing ever received by the students and faculty members that FIRE helps is an apology.

How State Governments (Often) Aren't Helping

As we saw in the previous chapter, the federal government recently made a major move that ignores the problem of censorship on campus and may make due process for accused students much weaker. Are state governments doing any better? The answer depends on what state you're talking about.

Certain states have taken extra steps to safeguard the free speech rights of their students and faculty. California's Leonard Law, for example, extends First Amendment protections, along with similar provisions in the California Constitution, to private colleges and universities.[55] Illinois recently passed the College Campus Press Act, which classifies all student media at public colleges as public forums, strengthening the protection that student journalists at Illinois public colleges and universities have against administrative censorship.[56] And the state of Oregon even extends protection for student journalists to the high school level, bolstering the speech rights of student journalists at both public colleges and public high schools.[57]

Other states, however, ignore the issue of free speech on campus and go right into red-meat culture war issues. Getting back to the hot-button topic of swearing on campus, the Arizona State Legislature proposed a bill in February

2011 that would require all educational institutions in the state—including state universities—to suspend or fire professors who said or did things that are not allowed on network TV.[58] The bill attempted to use "the standards adopted by the Federal Communications Commission" and explicitly targeted "indecency and profanity." The author seemed to be under the impression that FCC standards are clear and orderly, when they are actually a messy hodgepodge of attempts—sometimes constitutional, sometimes unconstitutional—to control the airwaves. Also, the bill was so poorly written that it made no distinction between a classroom setting and the teachers' everyday lives. As Angus Johnson, writing for *The Nation*, wittily observed, "If this law passes, it will be illegal for any 'person who provides classroom instruction' in the state of Arizona to have sex. Or pee. Ever."[59] The proposed law would make it almost impossible to teach serious literature or history or some of the most basic cases in constitutional law, besides being (not incidentally) "hysterically unconstitutional."[60]

In a similar vein, the Maryland Senate took on an issue in April 2009 that I'm sure was the most pressing one facing the state at that moment: the fact that some students at the University of Maryland were hosting an event that showed *Pirates II: Stagnetti's Revenge*, a pornographic tribute to the *Pirates of the Caribbean* films. State senators threatened to cut off funding to the University of Maryland, with Senator Janet Greenip declaring, "Colleges are supposed to be wholesome."[61] The students went ahead and showed the movie anyway, taking precautions to make sure that nobody under eighteen attended it, but this led to a protracted fight between the University of Maryland and the Maryland Senate—which eventually fizzled with no real resolution. (Well, the fight did have one predictable result: *Pirates II: Stagnetti's Revenge* got a lot more press than it otherwise would've received.)[62]

Another embarrassment for state governments came out of the Oklahoma State Legislature in 2009 and involved the famous evolutionary biologist and atheist Richard Dawkins. Dawkins gave a well-attended speech at the University of Oklahoma on March 6, but some state senators objected, attempting to pass two resolutions condemning both Dawkins as a scientist and the theory of evolution as an "unproven and unpopular theory."[63] I learned shortly thereafter that state representative Rebecca Hamilton requested all emails and correspondence relating to the speech; a list of all money paid to Dawkins and the entities, public and private, responsible for this funding; and the total cost to the university, including, among other things, security fees, advertising, and even "faculty time spent promoting this event." I wrote to the Oklahoma State Legislature, pointing out that this constituted a legislative investigation of protected speech, which court cases have clearly demonstrated is a constitutional no-no.[64] I followed up by writing every member of the Oklahoma legislature and heard nothing back, but after the University of Oklahoma stood up for itself, the controversy seems to have quietly faded.

The sad part is that state legislatures could be helping in this fight. FIRE has written numerous state legislatures and even President Barack Obama pointing out how the overwhelming majority of public colleges have speech codes that violate the Constitution; so far, we have seen little in the way of results for our efforts at outreach.[65] This is surprising, as you would think some state legislatures would care either about the issue of free speech on campus or about reforming university codes so they don't find themselves on the losing end of a free speech lawsuit.

Colleges Need to Teach Students to Question Authority, if Only for Their Own Good: The Penn State Child Rape Scandal

The examples we've seen in this section all demonstrate negative lessons that college administrators are teaching a generation of students. Punishing students for questioning authority is probably also the starkest example of how students unlearn liberty. "You'd better watch your mouth if you have anything critical to say about how things are run here, son" is not the lesson you want to give to people who are supposed to be active participants in a gigantic democracy. Colleges need to teach, both in class and by example, the exact opposite of this lesson. They should be asking students for feedback; they should be able to handle harsh criticism; and they should recognize that it is often only through these mechanisms that universities learn the sometimes ugly truths they desperately need to know. Empowering students to question everything, even the administration, may make administrators' lives harder, but it's what you need to do if you want to educate a free people as opposed to an obedient one.

One horrifying example illustrates why universities must create a culture that instills in its members the intellectual and moral habit of questioning authority. On November 4, 2011, former Pennsylvania State University assistant football coach Jerry Sandusky was indicted on forty counts of sex crimes against underage boys—some of which took place on Penn State property.[66] Another assistant coach, Mike McQueary, allegedly witnessed one of the assaults in 2002 and reported it to Joe Paterno, the head coach.[67] After informing the athletic director, Tim Curley, about the allegation, Paterno never mentioned it again.[68] Curley and his supervisor, Gary Schultz, responded by restricting Sandusky's access to campus, but chose not to report the incident to law enforcement—a decision approved by Penn State's president, Graham Spanier.[69] A concerned parent finally brought Sandusky's actions to the police; in the resulting investigation, Curley and Schultz were charged with perjury and failure to notify authorities of the alleged assault.[70]

What kind of campus culture leads five separate individuals to remain silent in the face of such grave accusations? As the details of the incident trickled upward through the Penn State administration, not a single member of the university staff took a potential child rape case to the police. Paterno acknowledged that "[i]t was obvious that [McQueary] was distraught over what he saw," but he justified his own inaction with that age-old defense: "I did what I was supposed to."[71] He and McQueary saw the ineffectual choices of their superiors, yet chose not to question their authority. In doing so, they let a potential child molester remain free for years. Sandusky's indictment lists counts of child molestation dating to 2009—a full seven years after the incident that McQueary allegedly witnessed.

Had Penn State worked to create a different culture on campus, one where people felt comfortable telling hard truths and making their own ethical decisions, these five individuals, and possibly others who may have known, might have chosen to take meaningful action. When a campus values conformity over principled dissent, it has forgotten that the role of the dissenter and the whistle-blower is as good for a college as it can be for the society as a whole.

CHAPTER 8

Student Activities Fair

I**T'S FINALLY FRIDAY AND THE END OF YOUR LAST DAY OF ORIENTATION.** With everything that's happened, with all the new people you've met and new ideas and worries bouncing around in your head, it's hard to believe that classes have not even begun yet. You can't stop wondering about Jason. He is still waiting to hear the charges against him. You apologized to him for telling him about the accountability program, but he kept saying it wasn't your fault. You wish you believed that.

This is on your mind as you step out of the student center onto the quad. Stretching before you are dozens of folding tables with bright banners and signs announcing various causes, organizations, and student groups. Today is the student activities fair, where the different student organizations try to get others interested in joining their groups. There seems to be a student group for every imaginable interest: Students for a Free Tibet, College Democrats, Ultimate Frisbee, the Film Society, several Muslim, Jewish, and Christian groups, and one well-staffed table for a group called Students Against All Hate. Then, right before you, you see a cheery, charming African American student manning the table for the Theater Club. He smiles at you, and you head right towards him. Theater sounds perfect. If it's anything like high school theater, it promises fun, interesting people, probably a ton of laughs, and little chance of serious controversy.

Right?

Stifling Freedom of Association on Campus

This chapter is a broad examination of the shoddy treatment many student groups get on campus these days. These cases—ranging from the silly to the serious—reveal the deep effects of a culture of censorship.

Student groups are part of what makes college life college life. I have spent some of this book talking about the dangers of surrounding yourself with people you already agree with. Having a campus populated by differing groups that are encouraged to interact with each other, however, can actually increase and enliven the flow of ideas. The technical term for the idea that many opposing groups can create better discourse is "second-order diversity," but it might be better known as good old American pluralism. On campuses, student groups can play a particularly important role, as they help to balance out the sometimes heavy-handed attempts by administrators to create a monoculture. But this defining element of campus culture is under threat. Universities have been actively turning the idea of freedom of association on its head, recharacterizing a group's desires to form around shared beliefs as a form of discrimination. The primary motivation for this shortsighted attempt was once to punish evangelical Christian groups for their politically incorrect beliefs, but it has spread far beyond that goal, creating a real threat to the diversity of campus life.

But before getting into this divisive culture war issue, let's start by examining what happened to one student who wanted to bring a little bit of showbiz to his college.

Theater Club

Theater might not seem like a student activity that is likely to generate death threats and mob censorship; indeed, the most serious challenge that most student playwrights face is getting people to show up to performances. In 2005, Chris Lee, a student at Washington State University, inspired by a project in his sociology class, set out to make a comedy musical that, in the tradition of *South Park* and *Howard Stern*, offended as broad a spectrum of people as possible. Unfortunately for him, he succeeded. A mob of forty angry students showed up to disrupt his comedy musical by standing up in the middle of the performance and yelling, "I'm offended," an act that soon escalated to slurs, threats of violence, and even death threats. Chris was afraid for his safety and the safety of his actors. The angry crowd succeeded in stopping the play several times and threatened to turn a theater performance into a full-scale riot. Chris knew that the university promised to protect students, especially African American students like him, from threats of violence, but the campus police did little to stop the mob. After all, why would the university help him when (as he would later learn) his own school had trained, funded, and encouraged the mob to protest his play in the first place?

Chris Lee's comedy musical *The Passion of the Musical* was a loose parody of *The Passion of the Christ*, which had been one of the top grossing movies the previous year. The goal of the play, of which Chris was both author and director, "was to show people we're not that different, we all have issues that can be made fun of" by poking fun at identity politics. (As Harvey Silverglate and I have frequently observed, parody and satire can be risky hobbies on campus.)[1] I have seen the play and have discussed it several times with Chris, a mischievous and likable fellow who used to make a living in part through professional poker. *The Passion of the Musical* is not serious social satire, but an intentionally silly comedy intended to produce belly laughs for being so thoroughly politically incorrect.

Instead, it provoked a wild response from the campus community and beyond. According to media coverage and interviews with Chris, dozens of groups were poised to protest the play, including the Church of Jesus Christ of Latter-day Saints; the Catholic Student Association; the Christian Crusaders; the Gay Straight Alliance; the Women's and Ethnic Studies departments; the Latino and African American centers; the Gay, Lesbian, Bisexual, and Transgender Association; the Department of Psychology; the WSU Office of Campus Involvement; and even the local Pullman Police Department.[2] Most of these protests came in the usual form of angry letters, op-eds, and picketers outside the show, but one of Chris's parody songs pushed the norms of campus political correctness too far, and the protest was racheted up.

That song was Meatloaf's "I'd Do Anything for Love (But I Won't Do That)," which Chris had changed to "I Would Do Anything for Love (But I Won't Act Black)." Keep in mind, the musical was written by an African American student and featured a number of black performers, including Chris himself. And, the entire stated point of the play was to be an equal-opportunity offender and make fun of every identity group in the United States. Chris could not have been clearer about this fact, warning students ahead of time that the play was "offensive or inflammatory to all audiences." These warnings were in ads, on the tickets, and on the doors leading to the theater. Chris even added a warning before the show that students who were easily offended should leave. All this made the mob's cries of "I'm offended" particularly ironic. That was the whole point. For his comedy musical, Chris earned the campus nickname "Black Hitler" from critics with an embarrassingly myopic view of history.

Unfortunately, rather than allowing the play to go on, campus administrators at Washington State University organized students who were angry. The administration held a brief training session showing students how to disrupt the play and even purchased their tickets.[3] If you send angry students to disrupt a play, don't be surprised if they do so with gusto. When the bought-and-paid-for mob got out of hand, the campus police told Chris that they would let the students rush the stage unless he changed the words to the parodied Meatloaf song. The university further dishonored itself the day after the disruption, when the school's president applauded the students for the "very responsible" exercise of *their* free speech rights. Yes, you read that right: WSU's president, V. Lane Rawlins, was quoted in the campus paper as saying that the students in the angry, disruptive, potentially violent, university-organized mob, who shouted physical threats and were poised to rush the stage, "exercised their rights of free speech in a very responsible manner by letting the writer and players know exactly how they felt."[4] In a truly Orwellian turn, university-sponsored mob censorship had become free speech.

For Chris, there was a somewhat happy ending to this story. After taking a bit of a drubbing in the press and from FIRE about its handling of *The Passion of the Musical*, the university changed its tune when Chris put on his next politically incorrect play, *The Mangina Monologues*. Before the play, the school issued a statement to students warning them not to disrupt it.[5] While this warning conveniently glossed over the fact that the administration had helped create the last disruption, the school's position was nonetheless a welcome about-face. WSU seemed to have learned a simple and obvious lesson: If you don't like a play, don't go to it.

America is a very religious country, so it may come as no real surprise that a play that mocked religion and everything else would incite paroxysms of censoring zeal. But Chris's case is not typical, as those who mock religion are not the ones who usually get in trouble on campus. Indeed, look what happened six months earlier when a Christian student group tried to show *The Passion of the Christ* on campus.

Campus Christians

While it sometimes seems like there is no rhyme or reason to what can get a student group in trouble on campus, certain trends emerge over time—in particular, the fundamental misunderstanding of tolerance and freedom of association that is widely applied to evangelical Christian groups. If you told me twelve years ago that I, a liberal atheist, would devote a sizeable portion of my career to defending Christian groups, I might have been surprised. But almost from my first day at FIRE, I was shocked to realize how badly Christian groups are often treated. Whether I personally believe in God or not, I certainly believe in the *right* to follow the faith that you choose.

When I talk about this issue, I often get a lot of pushback: surely the idea that evangelical Christians are disfavored on college campuses is just some kind of right-wing propaganda, and the examples that I cite are just weird flukes, people say. Given my experience, however, I was not at all surprised when a 2007 study of attitudes about religion among faculty performed by the Institute for Jewish and Community Research showed that evangelical Christians were the *only* group that a *majority* of faculty were comfortable to admit evoked strong negative feelings in them.[6] The study also revealed that Jews and Buddhists were the two groups that faculty members felt the most positive about. They also reported positive feelings about Muslims but fairly negative about Mormons.

In the fall of 2004, the members of the Christian Student Fellowship at one of the largest community colleges in Florida were told that they couldn't show *The Passion of the Christ* at their next meeting. An administrator at Indian River State College (IRSC) forbade the viewing because the film was "controversial" and "R-rated." Whatever your feelings may be about the movie, it remains the highest-grossing foreign-language film in U.S. box office history and the highest-grossing religious film of all time worldwide.

When the administration threatened further draconian measures against the Christian group, the students contacted FIRE. When I first saw this case, I found it so ridiculous that I (once again) felt confident that it would only take a letter from us for the university to back down. Instead, IRSC dug in its heels. While the college had the good sense to abandon the "you can't show this because it is controversial" argument (what exactly can you study in college if everything "controversial" is off-limits?), IRSC stood by its purported blanket code against R-rated movies.[7] This argument was outrageous by itself; college students range from teenagers to retirees, from freshmen to professionals, and the lofty mission of higher education would be, to say the least, hampered by a content ceiling of PG-13.

But what made this case so classic was the administration's double standard. Not only had the college *sponsored* the showing of R-rated movies in the previous year, but we also discovered that, at the very same time the school was banning *The Passion of the Christ*, it was hosting a production that included a skit called "Fucking for Jesus"—a piece about masturbating to an image of the Christian messiah.[8]

To be clear, both the skit and *The Passion of the Christ* were protected expression and could not be banned on a public college campus, like them or not. Yet the school's double standard was jaw-dropping. After months of public pressure from FIRE, the college relented, ceased its punitive actions against the Christian Student Fellowship, and allowed them to show the film.[9] Indian River State College was only one of dozens upon dozens of schools that I had already seen demonstrate a fact that I initially found surprising: devoutly Christian groups are often targeted for unfavorable and unequal treatment on campus.

At the University of Wisconsin–Eau Claire, for example, Lance Steiger was a member of Student Impact, UWEC's chapter of Campus Crusade for Christ, along with several other RAs. Its members held Bible study meetings, which took place in various locations on campus, including the dormitories. On July 26, 2005, Deborah Newman, UWEC's associate director of Housing and Residence Life, mailed a letter to several Campus Crusade members who were RAs and were leading Bible study groups.[10] Newman's letter forbade the students from leading any more Bible study groups in their own rooms during their own free time. Reportedly, she had told other RAs previously that Bible studies weren't welcome, but she now claimed that this new, unwritten policy banned the study of the "Koran and Torah" as well. It was a transparent attempt to appear, in some sense, fair. The only RA extracurricular religious activities at issue at UWEC were the Christian Bible study meetings.

Newman gave a strange rationale for her new rule. If residents knew about the private Bible study meetings, she explained, they might not "feel that they [could] turn to [the Bible study-leading RAs] in a crisis, for information, or for support," and she didn't want students to "feel judged or pushed in a direction that does not work for them." According to Newman, the office's decision was intended "to make sure RAs are accessible to all residents." She concluded the letter with a threat: "If this activity were to occur again this year, you would force us to institute disciplinary action."

Steiger was mystified. Was the university really telling him that he couldn't engage in private religious activities in his own room on his own time? His attempts to protest the policy were referred back to Newman, who wrote him in the beginning of the fall semester of 2005 saying, "As an RA you need to be available to your residents both in reality and from their perspective."[11]

Understand what the university was saying here. It was arguing that if students knew Steiger was a Christian who studied the Bible, they might not feel "comfortable" talking to him, so he had to curtail his *private* religious activities. When I spoke at UWEC in 2006, I explained FIRE's concerns with the policy: "Can you imagine a university telling an RA, 'I know you're Jewish and all but we have some terrific anti-Semites on the floor, so while it's totally cool that you're Jewish, could you try to show it only off campus?'" Indeed, if Steiger had been of any religion other than Christianity, I believe that the university would've understood that it is not any state employee's place to tell a person to hide his or her religious identity.

UWEC pulled the trump card of student "comfort" to justify its treatment of Steiger and the other club members, but there is plenty of evidence that Residence Life officials were not overly concerned with student comfort. Just a year earlier, Residence Life had publicly commended another RA who had put on *The Vagina Monologues* as an *official* Residence Life activity.[12] The administration clearly understood that taking students outside of their comfort zone could be a good thing, at least in other circumstances.

To be clear, neither during this time nor when I later gave my speech at UWEC was there any suggestion that the Christian RAs had, in any way, misused their power or position to influence students to join or participate in their Bible study groups. Nevertheless, UWEC doubled down and relied on a strategy I've seen repeated time and time again: claiming against all evidence to the contrary that its sudden decision to come down on campus Christians was part of a heretofore unknown policy that restricted all students regardless of viewpoint and had been in place at the university (unbeknownst to anyone) since time immemorial. Months after Newman first tried to redefine her specific ban on Bible studies as one against all holy books of the Abrahamic lineage, the president of the University of Wisconsin System, Kevin Reilly, wrote to the attorney general of Wisconsin saying that UWEC's "prohibition applies to all activities, regardless of viewpoint, including such activities as partisan politics, religious studies or 'sales party' events," not just Bible studies.[13] But a simple investigation proved that such a policy had never been applied in the past, and the claim was simply another transparent, post-hoc attempt to justify the Bible study ban.

RAs at UWEC were allowed to engage in activities in which they espoused particular viewpoints; in fact, they were *required* to do so publicly and officially as part of their job description. At the time, the university's job description for RAs required them "[t]o help organize and promote educational, recreational, social, and cultural activities that the students want and need," and asked them to "actively assist" in the "political" programs of the dorm.[14] Furthermore, at the very same time the UW System's general counsel Patricia Brady was claiming that "UW–Eau Claire has consistently followed a practice of prohibiting these employees [RAs] from leading, organizing or recruiting students for student organizations or activities within the residence halls in which they work," a starkly contradictory policy was in place at the school, according to one UWEC insider: "The UW–Eau Claire office of Housing and Residence Life is currently sponsoring and funding political/ideological activities on campus and in the community, and University administrators are praising them for it."[15] These included hosting a "Tunnel of Oppression" event; once again putting on *The Vagina Monologues*; sponsoring campus TV programs debating gay marriage and the morning-after pill; and backing productions like "The F-Word," in which—according to the Office of Housing and Residence Life's own materials—participants were "introduced to feminism as a non-threatening, productive, socially necessary way of thought. The objectives for this lesson are to have participants share their views on feminism, examine their beliefs about feminist thought, and learn the importance of the feminist movement."[16] These events also included organizing an activity called a "Privilege Walk," which the Office of Housing and Residence Life described as an "intense and sometimes emotional program [that] helps people realize just how privileged members of our society are and what they can do to minimize these disparities between people in our society."[17] Whatever you may think of these programs, it is impossible to argue that they were without an officially endorsed viewpoint.

The University of Wisconsin case seemed to grind on and on. Making matters worse, in early 2006 a working group recommended that *any* school in the whole UW System could have such an unequal policy because they had "the right to establish reasonable restrictions on RA activities."[18] The recommendation did not define "reasonable," and it left "the determination of where the meetings may be held . . . to the discretion of the individual institutions." In other words, UWEC was free to continue banning the Bible studies.

It took a long publicity campaign, an Alliance Defense Fund lawsuit, and negative attention from across the country just to get the UW System to adopt the reasonable standard we had suggested from the very beginning. Finally, on March 14, 2006, nine months after the public controversy began, the University of Wisconsin System Board of Regents approved a policy that gave RAs the right to "participate in, organize, and lead any meetings or other activities, within their rooms, floors or residence halls, or anywhere else on campus, to the same extent as other students."[19] This commonsense rule protected both the right to put on *The Vagina Monologues* and the right to participate in Bible study meetings. But the tooth-and-nail fight to restore common sense to the university's policy speaks volumes about the disparate treatment that Christian groups receive on too many campuses. One wonders how UWEC hoped to produce students who could interact with those of the Christian faith—the majority of the American population—after graduating and entering a world where administrators could not protect them from the "horrors" of the private practice of Christianity.

Contrast: The Muslim Students Association at Louisiana State University

In contrast to how the University of Wisconsin–Eau Claire dealt with Bible study groups, Louisiana State University showed that college administrators are able to understand freedom of religion, for non-Christians.

The Louisiana State MSA chapter had existed for thirty years before it was derecognized in 2003 because it refused to add language to its constitution that indicated it would not "discriminate" on the basis of "religion" or "sexual orientation." Derecognition means that an organization becomes a nonentity on campus. At LSU, it meant that the MSA could not use on-campus facilities, sponsor speakers and public performances, raise funds, distribute literature, or enjoy the many other benefits of being a student organization.

Usually when we talk about discrimination in the contemporary United States, we mean invidious or illegitimate discrimination on the basis of unchangeable characteristics such as the color of your skin or your gender. There is a strong distinction, however, between excluding someone on the basis of "status"—that is, the immutable state of being of a particular race or ethnicity or gender—and on the basis of belief. The Supreme Court has long recognized that the ability to exclude people on the basis of shared *beliefs* is part and parcel of what it means to be able to form organizations around shared beliefs. In other words, LSU may require a religious organization like the MSA not to exclude Muslims who, for example, are not Arab, but the MSA has every right to "discriminate" against people who do not share its beliefs. Without the freedom to exclude those who do not share your faith, the freedom to form religious organizations means next to nothing. Forming a group around shared beliefs is the very meaning of freedom of association, a cherished principle of democratic society that the First Amendment protects.

Therefore, the issue of whether the MSA should be allowed to exclude people on the basis of religion was a fairly easy legal question, at least at the time. The Supreme Court understood that the right to freedom of association includes the right to exclude those who disagree with your entire purpose for having the association in the first place. As the Court observed in a decision in 1984, "There can be no clearer example of an intrusion into the internal structure or affairs of an association than a regulation that forces the group to accept members it does not desire."[20] The Court concluded, "Freedom of association therefore plainly presupposes a freedom not to associate."[21]

The issue of whether the MSA could exclude people on the basis of "sexual orientation" was a somewhat more complicated matter, as the phrasing "sexual orientation" placed the prohibition somewhere between the status of being gay and the belief in the propriety of homosexual conduct. The MSA is a Muslim group that believes that homosexuality is sinful. Yet it is certainly the case that some people are gay and also devout Muslims.

These complexities aside, when FIRE became involved in reinstating LSU's recognition of the MSA, all it took was an exchange of letters between FIRE and various LSU administrators to win the case.[22] Throughout the thoughtful exchange, it became clear that LSU was struggling to reconcile tolerance for the faith and culture of the MSA with protection for the rights of gay students. At the conclusion of this dialogue, FIRE asked LSU to recognize the MSA, and a week later, the group was restored to the community of student organizations.

LSU is the only case I've seen in my career in which an antidiscrimination rationale was used to derecognize a Muslim group. When we brought it to the university's attention, LSU decided to engage in constructive dialogue, and ultimately decided that it couldn't, in good conscience, tell another faith and culture what it had to believe and how it had to honor those beliefs. This is a night-and-day difference from what I've seen with regard to evangelical

Christian groups. The fans of religious liberty for Muslims are often vehemently on the other side when the group in question is Christian.

Between 2002 and 2009, dozens of colleges across the country threatened or derecognized Christian groups because of their refusal to say they would not "discriminate" on the basis of belief. These colleges included, to name a few, Arizona State University, Brown University, California State University, Cornell University, Harvard University, Ohio State University, Pennsylvania State University, Princeton University, Purdue University, Rutgers University, Texas A&M University, Tufts University, the University of Arizona, the University of Florida, the University of Georgia, the University of Mary Washington, the University of New Mexico, the University of North Carolina at Chapel Hill, and Washington University.[23] The MSA case at LSU and these dozens of cases rest on the exact same concept of religious tolerance, but the polarized sides of the culture war see these issues as totally different for groups with whom they sympathize and those with whom they do not.

This lack of objectivity is a threat to every student who wishes to engage in controversial speech, and is the kind of hazard that the First Amendment was designed to eliminate. The necessity of protecting expression extends to a wide range of student groups, from Chris Lee's theater company to Campus Crusade for Christ and the Muslim Students Association. A controversy at Central Michigan University in 2007 involving the Young Americans for Freedom helps to illustrate the consequences of misunderstanding freedom of association and its significance as a constitutionally protected right.

Young Americans for Freedom at Central Michigan University and Hostile Takeovers

Young Americans for Freedom (YAF) is a national organization of conservative students that has been around since 1960. Its founding document, the Sharon Statement, lays out the group's belief system, including a commitment to liberty, economic freedom, the Constitution, and the following principle: "Foremost among the transcendent values is the individual's use of his God-given free will, whence derives his right to be free from the restrictions of arbitrary force."[24]

FIRE first defended YAF in 2000 at Penn State University. The Penn State Young Americans for Freedom, an independent student group sharing its name and mission statement with the national organization, was told by the student government that its mention of "God-given" rights constituted religious discrimination. This action took place a full eight years after the organization had been founded, during which time it had been continuously operating with this statement in its constitution. After YAF appealed the finding, the appellate board ruled that YAF had to strike the mention of God from its mission statement.[25] Thankfully, after FIRE wrote to Penn State's president, he intervened. Within days of receiving a letter from FIRE, the appellate board reversed its decision.[26]

Unfortunately, this was not the first or the last time a YAF chapter would find itself in trouble on campus. By 2007, the Central Michigan University chapter of YAF had earned itself a reputation for controversy far beyond mentioning God in its mission statement. This chapter had enraged students because some of its members had attended politically incorrect events (such as "Catch an Illegal Immigrant Day") organized by the far more controversial Michigan State University YAF chapter, and because one Central Michigan YAF student had allegedly chalked anti-gay language at CMU. ("Chalking" is a fairly standard practice at many colleges, where students write messages to each other and to the community in chalk on designated parts of the university sidewalks.) The student accused of the chalking was later kicked out of the group.

As a result, many students at CMU were fed up with YAF, so the student government tried but failed to get the group derecognized in 2006. At that point, students from several progressive and liberal groups began attending, and allegedly disrupting, YAF meetings. Opponents also established a group on Facebook for "People who believe the Young Americans for Freedom is a Hate Group." While they had every right to set up a critical web page, they took their plan of attack a step too far. On February 13, 2007, two members of the Facebook group publicly discussed strategies to eliminate YAF from within. One student wrote the following:

> The best way to get rid of them, is for everyone in this group to go to their meetings and we all vote eachother [*sic*] on to the eboard [executive board] and dissolve the group. Another thing we can do is make it public that we intend to bring in a ton of people and watch them change their membership requirements which might make them slip up and break a cmu [*sic*] discrimination policy.[27]

After reading this, CMU's YAF president, Dennis Lennox, emailed Thomas H. Idema, the assistant director of student life, asking if the group could lawfully deny membership to "someone who disagrees with us or our stated purpose."[28]

In response, Idema quoted from the CMU nondiscrimination policy in the student group handbook, which stated that a registered student organization "may not discriminate in its membership criteria or leadership criteria on the basis of age, color, disability, gender, familial status, height, marital status, national origin, political persuasion, race, religion, sexual orientation, veteran status, or weight."[29] Just to be clear, Idema wrote, "you may not require members to be 'like-minded' as that opens yourself up to [a charge of] discrimination based on political persuasion."

Idema was interpreting the campus nondiscrimination policy as an "end run" around the freedom of association that any group might employ in the face of sufficiently determined opponents. According to this administrator, nothing could be done to keep students from destroying an organization from within, even if those students were willing to put in writing that they intended to do so.

After FIRE contacted Michael Rao, the president of Central Michigan University, he quickly grasped the situation and spared YAF from destruction at the hands of its enemies. In a mass email to every single registered student organization at CMU, he clarified the student organization policy, saying "A belief-based registered student organization may use its belief system as a criterion for selection of membership or leadership."[30]

Seems obvious, doesn't it? A belief-based organization should, of course, be allowed to choose members on the basis of whether or not they share the core beliefs of the group. As we shall see, however, this principle is currently under attack from the highest legal authority in the nation.

Christian Legal Society v. *Martinez*

In 2005, the University of California Hastings College of the Law in San Francisco injected itself into the ongoing fight over freedom of association and religious liberty on campus. There, a chapter of the Christian Legal Society (CLS)—which had been active for several years at the law school—was derecognized because it insisted that members sign a statement of faith affirming the organization's evangelical Christian beliefs. These beliefs included what CLS deemed "biblical principles of sexual morality," and a statement of faith that stipulated:

> A person who advocates or unrepentantly engages in sexual conduct out-
> side of marriage between a man and a woman is not considered to be living
> consistently with the Statement of Faith and, therefore, is not eligible for
> leadership or voting membership. A person's mere experience of same-sex
> or opposite-sex sexual attraction does not determine his or her eligibility
> for leadership or voting membership. CLS individually addresses each
> situation that arises in a sensitive Biblical fashion.[31]

The national CLS responded to the derecognition by filing a lawsuit claim-ing that it was a violation of the group's First Amendment rights. As in the University of Wisconsin case, Hastings soon changed its story about why the Christian Legal Society was the only group it had ever derecognized for this reason.

During discovery (the process in a lawsuit when all parties have to share their relevant documents), the law school settled upon the argument that it was not actually singling out CLS for "discriminating" on the basis of belief. Rather, the law school's dean, Mary Kay Kane, testified that the school had *always* had a policy requiring that all students be able to join all organizations, regardless of what they believed. This was a far cry from Hastings' description of the nondiscrimination policy in the earlier stages of the case. Previously, the school had stated that its policy "permits political, social, and cultural student organizations to select officers and members who are dedicated to a particular set of ideals or beliefs."[32] What's more, at the time CLS filed suit, Hastings recognized student groups such as La Raza (a Latino student group), Outlaw (a gay student group), and other groups that conditioned membership on sharing the group's beliefs (and, in the case of La Raza, their ethnicity). But Hastings had decided that *only* CLS's decision to do the very same thing warranted derecognition.

When I first heard about Dean Kane's attempt to claim that the "all comers" policy had been Hastings' true policy since the 1990s, I was sure it would be seen by the courts as an obvious dodge. The facts of the case made it clear that the law school was employing a transparent, post-hoc rationale for punishing a Christian group—just like the University of Wisconsin,

Indian River State College, and countless other schools. That is why I was stunned when, in June 2010, the Supreme Court handed down its decision in *CLS* v. *Martinez*.[33] In a 5-4 ruling that bitterly divided the Court, Justice Ruth Bader Ginsburg's majority opinion took the law school at its word despite the plain evidence to the contrary. The majority held that any public university could pass a rule that required all student organizations to accept any students, regardless of whether or not they believed in the tenets of the organization. While the Court did send part of the case back to the U.S. Court of Appeals for the Ninth Circuit to decide if Hastings had in fact singled out CLS, the opinion displayed a remarkable amount of unwarranted trust in Hastings' administration to do right by conservative Christians. Justice Samuel Alito's dissent railed against the majority's decision, arguing that freedom of expressive association meant nothing if student organizations had to admit any student regardless of beliefs.

In the majority opinion, Justice Ginsburg treated recognition of a student group as if it were some sort of special gift the law school bestowed on organizations, which goes against decades of Supreme Court precedent supporting the rights of students and student organizations. Indeed, in the landmark case of *Healy* v. *James* in 1972, the Supreme Court found that Central Connecticut State University (CCSU) could not derecognize a chapter of Students for a Democratic Society because other chapters of SDS had been engaged in violence on other campuses and because the CCSU chapter would not specifically renounce violence as a tactic.[34] The Court's powerful interpretation of the right of student groups to be recognized as official student organizations in *Healy* cannot be squared with *CLS* v. *Martinez*.

Nor can *Martinez* be reconciled with two more recent Supreme Court decisions: *Rosenberger* v. *Rector and Visitors of the University of Virginia* (1995) and *Board of Regents of the University of Wisconsin System* v. *Southworth* (2000).[35] *Rosenberger* established the principle that religious groups cannot be excluded merely because they have a religious point of view. *Southworth* held that student fee funding must be distributed to student organizations without any reference whatsoever to the beliefs they hold. These decisions demonstrated the Supreme Court's understanding (at the time) that diverse opinions are especially crucial on college campuses, given the importance of robust and creative debate, and that any barriers to excluding groups from campus should be high. *CLS* v. *Martinez* makes a hash of this tradition, and in doing so—as Justice Alito wrote in his dissent—"the Court arms public educational institutions with a handy weapon for suppressing the speech of unpopular groups."[36] And as we have seen, Christian organizations make up a surprising number of these "unpopular groups."

Without the ability to exclude students who are hostile to their mission, student groups are in danger of being taken over by their opponents in a cynical ploy to get rid of them. This concern was dismissed as "more hypothetical than real" by Justice Ginsburg and the majority, despite the fact that ideologically motivated takeovers are demonstrably a real threat. We saw at Central Michigan University the planning of the exact kind of deliberate takeover that Justice Alito warned against in his dissent. Ginsburg's own musing on hypotheticals is both confusing and contradictory. She apparently had a change of heart on this issue midway through the opinion, positing a hypothetical and nonexistent "Male Superiority Club" to make the point that distinguishing between status and belief (which the Court has done on numerous occasions) was too difficult for a campus to manage.

The distinction between status and belief was readily apparent at Hastings; in 2003, one of the handful of members of the club (then called the Hastings Christian Fellowship) was openly lesbian. I have seen this pattern repeated at Harvard University, Tufts University, and Cornell; in each case, evangelical Christian groups have been happy to have members who acknowledge they may be gay but still subscribe to all the principles of evangelical Christianity. Whatever we may think of religious ideas about sexual orientation, the fact that many devoutly religious citizens are also gay demonstrates that the status of being gay and the belief in orthodox religion are not incompatible. Similarly, a Zionist organization would probably be happy to have a Palestinian member if he agreed with the Zionist movement, just like a gay group would likely welcome an evangelical Christian who disagreed with the Bible's condemnation of homosexuality. But as the Supreme Court has it, the Zionist group would have to admit not just a pro-Zionist Palestinian but also an anti-Zionist Palestinian who might be joining solely to find out what his enemies are strategizing about.

Perhaps most troubling of all, the majority opinion argued that the impact of Hastings' refusal to recognize CLS was moderated by the fact that CLS could still exist like other "secret societies" and unofficial student groups on campus. This is a stunning argument. Justice Ginsburg seemed to be telling CLS, "It's okay—I hear the catacombs are nice this time of year." Previously, the Supreme Court has understood that withholding campus recognition means that, for all intents and purposes, a group is a nonentity on campus.[37] The Court had concluded in earlier cases that to subject a student group to second-class status because of what they believe was an unacceptable violation of First Amendment rights.[38]

Forcing a student group to have a secret existence is not an acceptable alternative to official recognition. That should be obvious, but apparently it wasn't to the Supreme Court. The following example from Hampton University in Virginia should help explain the dangers of this approach.

The Campus Lesbian and Gay Association, and Tolerance for All

Hampton University, a historically black college in Virginia, was founded in 1870. But the story of Hampton goes back even further, to the first year of the Civil War, when a professor willingly violated Virginia's law against teaching slaves by holding class underneath what is now known on campus as "Emancipation Oak." Hampton boasts, among other illustrious alumni, Booker T. Washington, and is a symbol of the power of minorities to overcome adversity, no matter how great. That is, sadly, unless you want to start a gay student group at Hampton.

In 2007, FIRE launched a publicity campaign against Hampton University because it refused to recognize what would have been the only gay and lesbian organization on campus. The group, known as Students Promoting Equality, Action and Knowledge (SPEAK), had twice tried and failed to receive recognition at Hampton. SPEAK's proposed mission was to "serve as a bridge between the Gay, Lesbian, Bisexual, Transgender and Straight communities of Hampton University," with the purpose of "providing a safe place for students to meet, support each other, talk about issues related to sexual orientation, and work to end homophobia."

I love the mission of SPEAK. I believe that not just tolerance but acceptance of different sexual orientations is a necessary step towards a more enlightened society. FIRE argued that, consistent with its contractual promises of free speech, the school had an obligation to allow SPEAK on campus. Unfortunately, Hampton officials refused to address our concerns, and the fifty-four students who expressed interest in joining SPEAK graduated from Hampton without there ever having been a gay or lesbian group on campus.[39]

One Hampton University official did respond to a query on this issue from the *Richmond Times-Dispatch*, claiming that the school had a moratorium on new student groups.[40] Despite this assertion, no fewer than eleven new groups were approved at Hampton that year, while SPEAK was denied approval two years in a row, even with a relatively large number of students expressing interest. Hampton currently boasts 110 student organizations, but there is not a gay and lesbian organization among them.

In the comments section of an article by *Inside Higher Ed* concerning the denial of recognition to SPEAK, a Hampton student wrote the following:

I understand you think homophobia on the campus isn't as bad as it is. But as a gay student here at [Hampton], all I can say is you are wrong. You are dead, dead wrong. It hurts being on campus most days. It hurts like hell. And I hope you and the other students in power will really help to change that one day. In the meantime, many of us are suffering. *We are regretting we came here under false pretenses of equality.* [Emphasis added.][41]

Again, just as in the case at Hastings with CLS, forcing students away from campus life and making them second-class citizens who do not enjoy the rights of every other student group on campus is not an acceptable alternative to recognition.

The Hampton University case is also a lesson in why the tension between evangelical Christians and gay students is so profound. Not so long ago, gay student groups were the disfavored ones on campus. Gay students across the country felt—and feel to this day—condemned and shunned by conservative Christians. Indeed, in the 1986 Supreme Court case *Bowers* v. *Hardwick*, the Court made a strange leap from the legal into the religious by appealing to "Judeo-Christian moral and ethical" standards to justify a Georgia law that effectively criminalized homosexual sex.[42] *Bowers* was a powerful statement that gay Americans were not yet full citizens possessing the rights granted to all others.

But things change. When it comes to gay rights, we have all seen things improve dramatically within our own lifetimes. While the Supreme Court will go to great lengths to avoid overruling itself in a previous decision, in the landmark 2003 case *Lawrence* v. *Texas* the Court recognized its error in 1986 and overturned a Texas law that criminalized homosexual sex.[43] The *Lawrence* decision demonstrated how far our court and our society had progressed in just seventeen years, and it opened the door to equal rights for gay Americans. Meanwhile, most college campuses today run programs designed to increase tolerance towards gay students. In a sign of solidarity with gay Americans, many colleges across the country opposed allowing military recruiters on campus because they believed the military's former "don't ask, don't tell" policy discriminated against gays.[44]

I believe that it is this positive shift—a far more supportive, even activist attitude about gay rights—that accounts for the dozens of instances in which universities have derecognized evangelical Christian groups across the country. In order to make campuses friendlier to gays, universities are attempting to eliminate any groups that believe homosexuality is sinful. However, a university should not take turns deciding which moral majority it gets to ban, disband, or chase off campus; instead, its goal should be to end this process altogether. Universities need to understand that they are promoting *intolerance*, not tolerance, by trying to derecognize Christian groups for what they believe. We should also remember that most common religions in the United States, in one form or another, have in the past or do currently believe strongly that homosexual behavior is sinful, wrong, and even punishable. Muslims, Mormons, Orthodox Jews, and even Baha'is believe this to be the case, but any backlash against these groups on campus has not been nearly as widespread as that against Christian groups, in part because they are not seen as part of the "oppressive" structure of the United States. When attention is focused on these other groups, administrators suddenly remember the importance of respect for different cultures and different value systems.

Admittedly, it took me a long time to take religious objections to homosexuality seriously, but I think those of us who would like to see acceptance of homosexuality become the norm can sometimes be blind to an important aspect of tolerance. Many religious people genuinely believe that homosexual acts are wrong, and this has been the case for hundreds if not thousands of years. My dislike of this fact doesn't make it any less true. In trying to punish Christian evangelical groups for believing that homosexuality is sinful, campuses are fundamentally misunderstanding why the First Amendment protects freedom of assembly and free speech in virtually the same breath as it prevents interference with the free exercise of religion and establishes freedom from state-imposed religious norms.

Those who, like me, would like to see major religions shift from condemning homosexuality to accepting it can argue, advocate, and bear moral witness for this change. But it is *not* a change we can, or should even wish to, achieve through coercive tactics like banning Christian groups from campus. That is not the way you create cultural transformation in a free society. It is, in fact, almost guaranteed to stiffen resistance to that change.

I ask people who support kicking CLS chapters off campus to think about the kind of society we would live in if the government could force masses of citizens to the periphery if they refused to abandon their deepest beliefs. I believe that is not a society most Americans would want to live in, even if it produced some temporary "victories" for causes we care about. And do not underestimate the backlash that a gradual move to push evangelical Christian groups from campus will cause. Most Americans consider themselves Christian, and evangelicals already feel insulted, marginalized, and dismissed in higher education these days. In the wake of *CLS v. Martinez*, they are right to feel this way. They must ask: How can our universities reject the faith of most Americans while protecting the rights of other religious groups that believe the same thing?

As we have seen, and will see further in the next chapter, attitudes in higher education towards everyday Americans can often be grotesque caricatures. The fallout of the *CLS* v. *Martinez* decision will be felt for years to come and will result in a worsening of our larger societal culture wars by deepening the divide not only between the religious and the nonreligious, but also between higher education and everyone else. And it will teach college graduates that selective application of religious intolerance to disfavored religious groups is a legitimate weapon to fight disfavored beliefs.

The Fallout from *Martinez*: San Diego State and Vanderbilt

The *CLS* v. *Martinez* holding is rippling through the American justice system, and the resulting rulings reveal the deep flaws in the Court's reasoning. Take the August 2011 case of *Alpha Delta* v. *Reed*. In its holding, the Ninth Circuit Court of Appeals dealt a serious blow to freedom of association on college campuses by permitting San Diego State University (SDSU) to deny official recognition to two student groups, a Christian fraternity and a Christian sorority, based on their requirements that members share the groups' religious convictions.

Alpha Delta Chi, the sorority in question, required members to attend church regularly and demonstrate "personal acceptance of Jesus Christ as Savior and Lord," while the fraternity, Alpha Gamma Omega, required members to "sincerely want to know Jesus Christ as their Lord and Savior." Alpha Gamma Omega also asked its leadership to sign a "Statement of Faith" attesting to similar religious commitments. SDSU denied official recognition to these groups several times, claiming that their requirements violated SDSU's nondiscrimination policy. The groups filed suit against the university, and the resulting court case found its way to the Ninth Circuit. The appeals court justified its opinion in favor of SDSU through a reading of *Martinez* that was even more troubling for religious groups than the Supreme Court opinion.

Although *Alpha Delta* v. *Reed* did not involve an "all comers" policy but one that was applied only to religious groups, the Ninth Circuit upheld it.[45] In doing so, the court ignored the only nod the Supreme Court had made towards the rights of free association on campus in *Martinez*—that is, if a college is going to ban groups from selecting members on the basis of belief, it must apply the rule to *all* groups. The burden and impracticability of making sure that all belief-based groups admit hostile members is probably what made some university counsels think twice about adopting an "all comers" policy.

To determine whether SDSU's nondiscrimination policy was "reasonable," the Ninth Circuit borrowed another troubling concept from *Martinez*. It found that because student groups like the fraternity and sorority have access to other means of communication with members—most notably, online speech—the school's exclusion of these groups was reasonable.[46] The Ninth Circuit's casual assumption on this point—lifted straight from *Martinez*—signals that courts increasingly believe that because student groups denied official recognition still have access to social media outlets like Facebook and Twitter, courts need not intervene, leaving virtually all student groups with minority viewpoints at the mercy of universities that want to exclude them from campus.

What about the discriminatory effect that such a policy has against belief-based groups? The Ninth Circuit actually admitted that "under this more limited policy, a student Republican organization could permissibly exclude Democrats because the policy does not forbid discrimination on the basis of political belief, but a Christian group could not exclude a Muslim student because that would discriminate on the basis of religious belief."[47] Despite its full understanding that the policy targets religious groups, the court decided that this "incidental" burden did not constitute viewpoint discrimination because the policy had not been enacted with the *intent* or *purpose* of suppressing the groups' viewpoints. But as we saw in *Martinez* and the University of Wisconsin case—and, as I've seen in countless other cases—a school can easily hide or misrepresent the intentions behind its discriminatory policy, and even the highest court in the land can decide to defer to the school's false claims.

So, even though the Ninth Circuit relied on *Martinez* in considering SDSU's application of its nondiscrimination policy, its decision in *Alpha Delta v. Reed* contradicted *Martinez*'s narrow focus on the "all comers" policy at issue in that case. Yet the Supreme Court declined to reconsider *Alpha Delta v. Reed* in March 2012.

Vanderbilt University decided to enter the fray in April 2011, when it deferred approving the constitution of its chapter of the Christian Legal Society, claiming that the constitution violated the school's nondiscrimination policy. The document required the group's officers to subscribe to its "Statement of Faith" and to lead Bible studies and prayer at chapter meetings. The school announced that "Vanderbilt's policies do not allow any student organization to preclude someone from a leadership position based on religious belief."[48]

The resulting firestorm of national criticism included condemnation from FIRE, the National Association of Evangelicals, and the U.S. Conference of Catholic Bishops, and even a letter of protest signed by twenty-three members of the United States Congress. But Vanderbilt refused to back down, and instead held a three-hour town hall meeting to defend its position. At the meeting, Provost Richard McCarty faced intense opposition from the Vanderbilt student body, but insisted that the school did not "want to have personal religious views on good decision making on this campus."[49] When a student challenged McCarty's assertion that faith should not guide one's daily decisions, he stressed, "No, they shouldn't. No, they shouldn't. No, they shouldn't."[50]

Provost McCarty has every right to make decisions based on criteria other than religion, but does his personal refusal to do so give him the right to prevent a religious group from choosing officers based on religious criteria? Unfortunately, *Martinez* leaves the door wide open for such a blatant attack on freedom of association to take place. As I write this book, eleven Christian groups on Vanderbilt's campus have formed a coalition called Vanderbilt

Solidarity to challenge the school's policy, refusing to remove faith-based requirements for leadership positions from their constitutions, and another student group, Vanderbilt Catholic, has decided not to register as an official student organization.[51] The story will continue to unfold over the coming months and years, and seems likely to further deepen an already immense cultural divide.

From PETA to Guns: More Causes That Can Land You in Trouble on Campus

Lest I give you the impression that the punishment of student groups relates only to those with religious views, gay student groups, young conservatives, or politically incorrect theater, here are two more examples of the veritable rainbow of causes that can get you censored (or worse) on campus.

PETA: Providing a classic example of why administrators should not be allowed the power to censor, an administrator at Seminole Community College in 2005 forbade a student, Eliana Campos, from distributing literature about People for the Ethical Treatment of Animals on campus, despite the fact that numerous other groups were allowed to hand out their own materials. When asked to justify the exclusion of PETA, the administrator wrote, "PETA instills a feeling in me that I can't, and won't, take a chance on campus [*sic*]."[52] In other words, "I personally don't really like PETA, so no free speech for you." As a consolation prize, the administrator offered Eliana the use of a tiny "free speech zone," but no one seemed clear about where the zone actually was.

The Gun Club: Given how many innocuous ideas can get you in trouble, it is probably no surprise that organizations that advocate for students to be allowed to carry concealed weapons on campus face censorship. The intensity of this censorship heated up after the shootings at Virginia Tech and Northern Illinois University. While many of us felt these incidents provided an argument against guns on campus, several organizations pointed out that if students had been armed at either school they might've been able to limit the extent of the massacres. It's a provocative and controversial point, but in a country that does have a strong right to bear arms and in which several states ban officials from *interfering* with a concealed carry permit, it is an opportunity for rich debate and discussion.

In 2009, Christine Brashier, a student at the Community College of Allegheny County in Pittsburgh, was prohibited from handing out pamphlets encouraging students to join a proposed new campus chapter of Students for Concealed Carry on Campus, a national organization. She was accused of punishable "solicitation" for trying to "sell" students on her *ideas* (yes, that is actually what they said) and even ordered to destroy her pamphlets.[53] Meanwhile, in both 2008 and 2009, students at Tarrant County College in Texas were told that they had to go to the school's tiny "free speech zone" if they wanted to protest for concealed carry, and that they could not conduct a symbolic "empty holster protest" even within the confines of the zone.[54] Fortunately, in 2010, a district judge agreed with a FIRE/ACLU lawsuit, finding that it was unconstitutional to limit the students to symbolic protest in such a heavy-handed manner.[55]

Even just discussing or joking about Second Amendment rights can get you in trouble. In the fall of 2008, a professor at Central Connecticut State University *called the police* after a student gave a presentation in his speech class arguing for the safety value of concealed carry.[56] Meanwhile, at Lone Star College near Houston, a student group was threatened with dissolution for distributing a tongue-in-cheek flyer listing "Top Ten Gun Safety Tips."[57] The banned flyer listed such "tips" as "No matter how excited you are about buying your first gun, do not run around yelling 'I have a gun! I have a gun!'" In the spring of 2008, students at Colorado College were found guilty of "violence" for making a clear parody of a feminist flyer by focusing on macho topics like "chainsaw etiquette," "tough guy wisdom," and the range of a sniper rifle.[58] The college stands by this finding to this day.

During the same semester, a college in Arkansas banned Stephen Sondheim's fanciful musical *Assassins* "out of respect for the families of those victims of the tragedies at Northern Illinois University and Virginia Tech, and from an abundance of caution."[59] The previous year, a student in Minnesota was suspended after he sent an email suggesting that the Virginia Tech massacre might have been stopped if students had been armed, a professor in Boston was fired after leading a classroom discussion about the Virginia Tech massacre in which he and a student exchanged pretend gunshots, and Yale briefly banned the use of any realistic-looking weapons in theatrical productions, be they switchblades, rapiers, or six-guns.[60] (Yale now allows such prop weapons, provided that the audience is warned about them in advance.) Whatever your position on the Second Amendment or gun control, I hope we can all agree that censoring toy guns from stage productions achieves little more than making the administrator who came up with that idea look tragically silly.

Unlearning How to Live with Each Other

The ongoing war between college administrators and student groups that stray from campus talking points is one of the most dramatic manifestations of the lack of tolerance for meaningful dissent that our universities are instilling in their students. Universities seem to have forgotten that a healthy, diverse environment includes providing a forum for groups that might be diametrically opposed to each other. A university that recognizes devout Mormon, Christian, and Muslim associations as well as pro-choice, gay, liberal, and atheist groups is showing how healthy its culture is, not revealing a shameful failure to reach consensus.

A recent public controversy demonstrates how entrenched an uncritical ideological certainty has become in our society. During the 2010 debate over the so-called "Ground Zero mosque," advocacy groups (in my mind, rightfully) argued that the planners had an unquestionable right to build a mosque in downtown Manhattan under their constitutional right to freedom of religious expression. These groups correctly saw the significance of protecting freedom of association and religious expression when it came to the mosque. I was deeply disappointed, however, by the hypocrisy I saw illustrated by several groups and acquaintances during this debate. Some of the same people who were all for kicking evangelicals off campus were now singing the praises of religious freedom and tolerance in this case. The same principle of religious tolerance should protect all sides.

If colleges followed through on their rhetoric that people with radically different points of view should get to know each other, they might create greater awareness that ideological, philosophical, or religious opponents can often find common ground. This could help foster critical thinking, debate, and discussion, while signaling to members of disfavored groups that they have a right to be there and to talk in class. Instead, today's universities are trying to impose a preconceived notion of what good, moral people should believe. They are purposefully building a culture of conformity—an echo chamber in which students learn that there is only one "right way" of thinking, and that expression that deviates from it should be kept between you and your clique. This not only alienates a substantial portion of their students, but also denies other students the practice and understanding of what it means to live in a truly diverse and pluralistic society. We are not training students to be equal members of a multicultural society; we are training them to be soldiers in an endless culture war.

CHAPTER 9

Finally, the Classroom!

I's Monday, the first day of classes. The weekend was extraordinary, in an odd way; so many new people, so many interesting backgrounds, so many dating possibilities. But whenever anybody asked you what your week was like, you had to leave out the most important things that happened to you. Jason is still waiting to hear what he was charged with, and he made you promise not to talk about what happened.

Today is a momentous day, but it has already been soured by your session at the Student Accountability Training seminar. This morning, your "counselor" showed you the "Power and Control Wheel," and you are still wracking your brain to figure out if what you said to your RA represented "intimidation," "emotional abuse," or the still not entirely understood offense of "using privilege." You know this is an answer you have to get right.

As you sit down in your very first college class and open your textbook for Sociology 101, the smell of binding glue is strangely soothing. The moment is short-lived, however, as your mind at once turns to the absurd cost of your textbook and the fact that it seems like everyone else in the classroom has an iPad or, at the very least, a laptop. Your professor hands out the rules of the class. You assume they are standard and obvious rules like "No texting during class." But as you read them, you see that the rules list a number of required "assumptions" for class discussion. One rule says that overall and for all discussion purposes, "Let's assume that people are always doing the best they can."

Something about that strikes you as a little strange. But what's the harm? At least it seems nice.

Mandatory Assumptions and Pleasant Little Lies

Asking students to repeat by rote what their teachers think they should believe is antithetical to the development of critical minds. It also arrogantly places professors in the position of all-knowing arbiters of truth as opposed to their role as mentors helping students figure out the world for themselves. The mandatory "assumptions," political litmus tests, and ideological criteria discussed in this chapter are at odds with what a liberal education is supposed to be. They are also intellectually lazy, and therefore they foster uncritical thinking in the next generation.

Take, for example, the mandatory ideological ground rules for discussion developed by Lynn Weber, a professor of women's studies at the University of South Carolina.[1] In a 2010 Internet search I found versions of Weber's "rules" in courses including Sociology at Southern Illinois University at Carbondale and Kansas State University, Southern History at the University of Texas at Dallas, Social Work Practice and Policy Advocacy at the University of Minnesota, and even World Politics at my own undergraduate alma mater, American University. A 2004 version of the guidelines included that students must, among other more detailed positions, "Acknowledge that racism, classism, sexism, heterosexism, and other institutionalized forms of oppression exist," and "Assume that people—both the people we study and the members of the class—always do the best they can."[2]

As Alan Charles Kors pointed out to me, it is not the role of professors to tell students what assumptions they *must* have in order to take a class. Just like the pledge to civility, kindness, and inclusivity that Harvard tried to coerce students into signing in 2011, it is as if the professor had said: "Yeah, these are debated, and many disagree, but I don't, and I don't really want to explain why. So just believe them, okay?"

Take, for example, the statement, "Acknowledge that racism, classism, sexism, heterosexism, and other *institutionalized* forms of oppression exist" (emphasis added). While the syllabus defends this assumption by saying,

"We are not going to spend time debating whether the world is flat, whether sexism, et al., exists," this position misses a major point.[3] While I may agree with this statement, I am not so arrogant as to assume that this should be unquestionable dogma. I would feel differently if it weren't for the word "institutionalized," which implies that racism, sexism, and classism are currently and intentionally maintained and propagated throughout the American government and other institutions. Conservatives I have spoken with about this cultural critique respond that the Fourteenth Amendment, the Thirteenth Amendment, the Voting Rights Act, affirmative action, the Civil Rights Act, numerous Supreme Court decisions overturning racial discrimination, Title IX, Title VII, the Office for Civil Rights, hate crimes legislation, public service announcement campaigns, and numerous other legislative, judicial, and private actions indicate that our country has gone to great lengths to institutionalize *anti*-racism. Barely anyone would argue that racism is not a problem, but it isn't crazy to point out that there are institutional and systematic attempts to combat it. Placing such a fundamental argument outside the realm of discussion is also incompatible with any meaningful definition of academic freedom.

What struck me most about Weber's guidelines and their popularity is the seemingly innocuous requirement to "[a]ssume that people—both the people we study and the members of the class—always do the best they can." While that sounds nice, it's demonstrably untrue. People absolutely *do not* always do the best they can. People can be lazy, self-interested, dishonest, conniving, deluded, and even sociopathic. Weber's rule is not even a useful assumption in the classroom setting, where cheating and plagiarism are all too common and where your fellow students can be apathetic, manipulative, dishonest, or doing just enough to get the best grade possible with as little work as possible. Professor Weber herself admitted that "a handful of students" had dropped her classes "because they felt uncomfortable with the guidelines, primarily because the students were unable to commit to working under the assumption that 'people are always doing the best that they can.'"[4]

This false assumption also is a way of circumventing what are probably the most important, divisive, far-reaching, and sometimes bloody debates in history. As Steven Pinker elegantly summarized a key argument of Thomas Sowell, a senior fellow of the Hoover Institution at Stanford University, many of the culture wars we currently face and have faced throughout history fall along the fault lines of whether you take a "tragic" or a "utopian" view of humanity.[5] In the tragic view, mankind is fallen, corrupt, selfish, and flawed, and there's no way around that. In the utopian vision, mankind is basically good, almost infinitely malleable under the right social conditions, naturally inclined to cooperation, and, ultimately, perfectible. There very well may be *no* greater question in philosophy, politics, social policy, history, psychology, and government than whether man is essentially good or essentially corrupt. I am not saying that a class needs to take the position that human beings *are not* perfectible, but to actively discourage students even to *discuss in class* the idea that people are not always "doing their best" denies one of the most important arguments in human history a place at the academic table. I don't think even the sunniest utopian would go so far as to say that people are always doing "the best they can."

You cannot ask your students to think hard and come to their own conclusions while at the same time demanding that they unconditionally agree to uncritically parrot untruths. When you ask people to adopt certain assumptions with deep philosophical implications, you undermine critical thinking by denying them the opportunity to argue out these issues on their own and thereby come to understand why they believe what they believe. Furthermore, you chip away at the ever-crucial skepticism that helps protect both our individual and our collective rights. A free people should not be trained to accept comforting falsehoods just because someone in power told them to.

While the problem with such ideological classroom guidelines may be philosophical in nature, many of the abuses that take place in classrooms are perfectly concrete. Before I start discussing the abuses of student rights in the classroom, it is important to establish what I am *not* saying.

Academic Freedom, Free Speech, and Ward Churchill

It is perfectly legitimate for critics both within and outside the academy to criticize what they see as political bias on the part of professors. However, attacks on "liberal bias" sometimes jeopardize the academic freedom that makes higher education possible. In defending professors' rights, I have been involved with protecting some famously unpopular speech. Perhaps the most notorious case was the uproar over Professor Ward Churchill from the University of Colorado at Boulder. In 2005, Churchill was investigated by the university after the public became aware of an article he had written in 2001 arguing that the people killed in the World Trade Center on 9/11 had it coming. Churchill contended that the people who worked there were part of America's capitalist infrastructure and that because that system has so much blood on its hands, these individuals were comparable to Nazi administrators who ran the death camps in the Holocaust. Churchill's argument felt like a slap in the face to most Americans—and to me, as I was born in and now live in New York City, and my sister (who bears no resemblance to Adolf Eichmann) worked in the World Trade Center up until a few months before the terrorists steered the planes into it. Briefly taking off my First Amendment advocate hat, I will say that Churchill's unhinged arguments typify much of what is wrong with the state of American discourse.

Nonetheless, we must learn to take a deep breath when we hear speech that deeply offends us and remember the principles at stake. Both the law and the theory of academic freedom accept that oftentimes a speaker's entire objective is to be provocative. We must not punish such speech because it is successful in its goal of provoking. Whatever I felt or thought about his remarks was irrelevant, and FIRE and I went to bat for the free speech rights of Ward Churchill.[6] I even devoted my column in the *Daily Journal* of San Francisco and Los Angeles to the Churchill case.[7] We received a good deal of hate mail for our defense of Churchill, but that is nothing new; to paraphrase a friend who also works in civil liberties (the same one who reminded me not to think like a "Generalissimo"), you are not really a First Amendment advocate until you get hate mail.

While Churchill's case is sometimes labeled as an incident concerning "liberal" speech, I suspect only a tiny minority of people agree with his view. And that is precisely why it needs to be protected. A definition of free speech that excludes offensive speech provides no real protection at all. A university investigatory committee agreed with this analysis, as did a district court judge. Churchill was, in the end, fired for plagiarizing and other academic misconduct accusations that had been around for years prior to his becoming a nationally hated figure. While the First Amendment does protect your right to be provocative, it does not include a right to plagiarize.

Plagiarism is, of course, not the only professional responsibility binding what professors say. You can fire a professor for being a poor instructor, engaging in shoddy research, or just failing to live up to the expectations of quality teaching. Even tenure does not provide complete protection for actual incompetence. But if you allow professors to be fired for being strongly opinionated, you open the door to eliminating those professors whose politics do not align with those of the university.

Ironically, it is often conservatives who argue for the tightening of pedagogical and other professional standards using a limited interpretation of academic freedom that would allow them to root out professors who infuse their classes with their politics. This is shortsighted, however. Given that most universities tilt decidedly left, it is far more likely that such policies would end up being used against conservative professors than those to the left of the spectrum. For example, how many conservative professors would like to defend themselves against a committee of Lynn Webers after making the mistake of declaring that some students can be lazy, dishonest, and deceitful? The primary result of the attempts of conservative professors to push for a more limited view of academic freedom would almost certainly be even fewer conservative professors on campus.

As for concerns about professors indoctrinating their students, if you believe in student rights, you are arguing for what I call a "strong student model." That is, if you believe students can take part in a robust exchange of ideas, tolerate slights and insults, and even deal with offensive ideas or words, you are assuming that students, for the most part, are strong enough to live with freedom—and this includes the discomfort of hearing professorial opinions that they consider dead wrong. It's a "model" because I recognize that some students may not be up to this task, but it is best to design a system that assumes that most students would rather not sacrifice everyone's education for the comfort of the thinnest-skinned student on campus.

The primary source of abuses on college campuses, however, is not the faculty. While many professors have played an unforgivable role in propagating speech codes and seriously undermining the philosophy of free speech, and of course some professors engage in questionable pedagogy, the actual regimes of censorship on campus are put in place primarily by the ever-growing army of administrators you have met so often throughout this book.

This does not mean that professors are entirely blameless. Sometimes professors and entire departments do cross the line into serious abuses of their students' right to freedom of speech and even the right to private conscience.

Mandatory Lobbying for Progressive Causes

My first experience with a professor abusing his or her power to coerce students into specific political speech took place at Citrus College in California. In 2003, an adjunct professor named Rosalyn Kahn offered an extra-credit assignment in her Speech 106 class: students had to write letters "demanding" that President Bush not go to war in Iraq.[8] This was not a creative writing assignment; the letters were actually to be sent to the White House. Some students asked if they could write letters in support of the war instead and were flatly told they couldn't. FIRE brought the case to the attention of Citrus College's president, Louis E. Zellers, who responded confirming that Kahn "did abuse her authority" over her students on this and at least one other occasion.[9] Zellers understood that the assignment was both an abuse of power and an embarrassment to the college. He suspended Kahn, apologized to the students, and even sent a letter of apology to President Bush.[10]

The case at Citrus College had an almost comic air. How could a professor think she had the right to use her power over grades to influence her students to take particular, public political action? Unfortunately, I've seen many more serious cases of professors requiring students to lobby the government—even for causes the students did not support.

The still-unfinished odyssey of Bill Felkner, a student at the Rhode Island College School of Social Work, is a case in point. Bill is somewhat of a rare breed: a conservative who was trying to get a degree in social work. While he likely had tension with his chosen department from the start, I first became aware of his case after he emailed a professor in the School of Social Work (SSW) to object to the fact that professors were showing Michael Moore's anti-Bush, anti-Iraq-war documentary *Fahrenheit 9/11* in their classes shortly before the 2004 election. To Felkner, this seemed like a transparent attempt to influence how the SSW students voted. Professor Jim Ryczek responded to his email by explaining, "In the words of a colleague, I revel in my biases. So, I think anyone who consistently holds antithetical views to those that are espoused by the profession might ask themselves whether social work is the profession for them."[11]

The full email assumed that the only values a social worker could have would be the same as Ryczek's. It wasn't even up for argument that libertarians, conservatives, and, for that matter, nonconformists might have values that could be conducive to helping people.

Still, Ryczek did not violate Felkner's rights by offering this opinion. Ryczek and the Rhode Island College School of Social Work, however, crossed a bright line when they required students in the school, including Felkner, to lobby the state government for "progressive" (a word that was repeated over and over again in department materials) change in order to complete their major. Causes he was allowed to lobby for, but which he did not believe in, included gay marriage and various social policy initiatives such as government-provided "income supports." Felkner objected but was told that he could not complete his degree in social work if he did not lobby for a cause against his conscience.[12] Felkner sued in 2007 but, as of this writing, the case has not come to a resolution.

For all its heavy-handed ideology, the School of Social Work at Rhode Island College was a portrait of tolerance in comparison with the one at Missouri State University. Emily Brooker, a petite, Missouri-bred redhead, wanted to go to Missouri State University so she could stay in the community she wished to serve when she graduated. In her freshman year, she was given an assignment for a class about diversity that required her to go out and display homosexual behavior in public and write a paper about the experience. This is an odd request and must have seemed particularly strange for Emily, who was an evangelical Christian and believed homosexual behavior was a sin. She did not go out and behave as if she were gay in public, but wrote the assignment as if she had. She decided after that experience that she was not going to compromise her beliefs again.

In her senior year, Brooker took an advanced class in social work in which the professor assigned a group project that involved lobbying the state government for the rights of gays to adopt or foster children. While many, including myself, might agree with this goal, lobbying for it would have gone directly against Emily's religious beliefs. As part of the project, Emily's professor required her and other students to sign a letter, on university letterhead, to the state legislature advocating for gay foster parenting and adoption. Emily completed the assignment as if it were a position paper, but would not take the final step of signing the formal letter to the state legislature.

That is when Emily got in real trouble. Her attempts to explain her faith to her professor failed. Instead, she was told to show up to a meeting with seven professors who proceeded to interrogate her. She was not allowed to bring a witness or her parents or even to record the meeting.[13] Over the course of two and a half hours, she was asked questions like, "Can you not do this assignment because you are a Christian?" "Are you a sinner?" and "Do you think I'm a sinner?" To stay in the program, Missouri State forced Emily to sign a contract pledging that she would "close the gap" between her beliefs and those of the social work department, and that she would attend weekly reviews with faculty members.

Brooker decided to sue in part because she "witnessed other students who also agreed with [her] but said nothing out of fear." She waited until after she graduated to file the lawsuit, which she brought in 2006 with the help of the Alliance Defense Fund. MSU quickly settled the case in Brooker's favor.[14]

Then something surprising happened: the president of MSU came out and admitted that there was something wrong at the MSU School of Social Work and brought in the deans of the social work departments of two other universities to evaluate the department. In my experience, such "reviews" are usually whitewashes—attempts to get someone to say that the university was, is, and has always been right. Instead, the two evaluating deans issued a scathing indictment of MSU's behavior, not just in the Emily Brooker case, but overall. The report stated: "Both external reviewers have extensive experience in several institutions of higher learning and both have conducted numerous site visits for reaccreditation. Neither of the reviewers ha[s] ever witnessed such a negative, hostile and mean work environment."[15] It also confirmed that "'bullying' was used by both students and faculty to characterize specific faculty." The report stated: "It appears that faculty have no history of intellectual discussion/debate. Rather, differing opinions are taken personally and often result in inappropriate discourse." One of the report's suggestions for handling the problem was to "[c]lose down the School; disband the faculty and restart the School after a short period (start from scratch)."[16] After the review, four faculty members were dismissed and four others were transferred to other departments.

While the story of what happened at Missouri State University's School of Social Work made the news, other social work departments learned nothing about the importance of tolerating dissenters.

The Limits of "Social Justice" Advocacy

Andre Massena, a black immigrant from Haiti, is an avid proponent of "social justice." You might have expected him to fit right in, ideologically speaking, at Missouri State or Rhode Island College—or at Binghamton University's (formerly SUNY–Binghamton) Department of Social Work, where he was studying. The problem, however, was that in 2008 he publicly criticized his own department. The Binghamton Housing Authority, whose executive director was a prominent Binghamton alumnus, had evicted a family from public housing in a manner that Massena found "inhumane," and his department had recently hired the BHA executive director to the faculty. Massena put up posters criticizing his department for having hired a person whose actions seemed to go against the department's "social justice" mission.[17]

Within a week, Massena's department suspended him for a year and would not let him return unless he completed a draconian remediation plan.[18] The plan included a formal retraction and multiple formal apologies to be sent to a preapproved list of university and government officials, plus a paper of ten to twelve pages on the ethics of social work. He appealed twice, whereupon his department chair, Laura Bronstein, submitted approximately fifty pages of materials including details on entirely new allegations, with a recommendation that Massena be expelled.[19]

FIRE took the case public the day before the hearing on his second appeal. The next day, Massena received a one-sentence letter from Bronstein: "Due to procedural misunderstandings, the case pertaining to you is no longer being pursued."[20] Protected by the public's eyes on his case, Massena went on to graduate with his master's degree. But Binghamton University's president, Lois DeFleur, did not have the foresight to follow MSU's example and seek an independent review of the social work department.

The Andre Massena case is yet another example of the lack of tolerance for dissent on campus. It also shows how any institution that believes it has figured out what something as hotly debated as social justice means is at risk of treating its critics like heretics who deserve ostracism, if not outright expulsion from the community. A higher education environment that invited debate, welcomed dissent as an opportunity to inch closer to the truth, and understood the discipline required in critical thinking would not have overreacted so badly. But how could it be possible that entire departments are so unfamiliar with debate that they treat criticism as blasphemy and teach students to do the same? Maybe it's because some departments are trying to discourage potential scholars and professionals with divergent points of view from entering their chosen professions in the first place.

"Dispositions" and Political Litmus Tests

In 2005, Professor KC Johnson of Brooklyn College brought the higher education community's attention to a new kind of political litmus test. In his *Inside
Higher Ed* article "Disposition for Bias," Johnson focused on how education
schools had institutionalized the process of evaluating their students according to their "dispositions," including their commitment to "social justice."[21]
As Johnson pointed out, "There would seem little or no reason why academic
departments would seek to promote social justice, which is essentially a political goal."

Yes, "social justice" sounds lovely. We all agree that the world should be
socially just. But the problem is, we do not agree on what on earth "social
justice" means. (Just ask Andre Massena, Laura Bronstein, Bill Felkner, or
Emily Brooker.) I challenge you to think of how you could evaluate someone's
"commitment to social justice" *without* reference to your own opinions about
their politics. As Johnson pointed out, "Though the concept derives from
religious thought, 'social justice' in contemporary society is guided primarily
by a person's political beliefs: on abortion, or the Middle East, or affirmative
action, partisans on both sides deem their position socially just."

Vague, subjective, and politicized evaluation standards are dangerous.
They invite administrators and faculty members to substitute their own
opinions and political beliefs for fair, professional criteria to evaluate students'
demonstrated skills as members of a profession—as teachers, social workers,
counselors, or psychologists. Many of us can think of teachers and professors whose politics we may not have agreed with but who were nonetheless
exceptional educators. Having the "correct" political beliefs no more makes
someone a good teacher than having "incorrect" beliefs necessarily makes
someone a bad teacher.

In the article, Johnson also brought up his own college's response to
several students who complained of a teacher in the school of education
showing *Fahrenheit 9/11* in class shortly before the 2004 election. In response,
according to Johnson, "One senior was told to leave Brooklyn and take an
equivalent course at a community college. Two other students were accused
of violating the college's 'academic integrity' policy and refused permission
to bring a witness, a tape recorder, or an attorney to a meeting with the dean
of undergraduate studies to discuss the allegation." He also said the same

professor "demanded that [her students] recognize 'white English' as the 'oppressors' language.'"

In the wake of the article, administrators and professors held an "emergency academic freedom" meeting where they discussed having Johnson investigated by a disciplinary board. On June 20, he received a scathing letter on the school's letterhead signed by dozens of professors in the School of Education, expressing their "contempt" for the claims in his article.[22] They demanded he stop his "attacks" on the professor he mentioned in the article, on the School of Education, and on the use of "dispositions." The letter was also sent to the Brooklyn College president, Christoph M. Kimmich, to the CUNY chancellor, Matthew Goldstein, to every Brooklyn College department chair, and to every member of the CUNY Board of Trustees. While the department was within its rights to criticize Johnson for challenging it, the looming possibility of a secret investigation by the "integrity committee" for public criticism was unacceptable. Thankfully, after receiving a letter from FIRE, the school disavowed the investigation.[23]

In a nod to the problems posed by these standards, in 2006, the National Council for Accreditation of Teacher Education (NCATE), one of two major accrediting bodies for schools of education, dropped its recommendation that teachers' colleges evaluate students on the basis of their commitment to social justice.[24] The decision came in the face of criticism from a number of groups, including FIRE.

Meanwhile, even after NCATE's reversal, many top professional schools of education have maintained such policies. Take, for example, perhaps the most famous education school in the country, Columbia University's Teachers College. The college's "Conceptual Framework" states that education is a "political act" and that teachers—and hence teachers in training, or students—are expected to be "participants in a larger struggle for social justice."[25] At times, the standards are remarkably specific: "To change the system and make schools and societies more equitable, educators must recognize ways in which taken-for-granted notions regarding the legitimacy of the social order are flawed." The policy adds that students are expected to recognize that "social inequalities are often produced and perpetuated through systematic discrimination and justified by societal ideology of merit, social mobility, and individual responsibility."

I asked in an article in the *Chronicle of Higher Education* about such policies, "Does Teachers College really believe that a student who thinks 'social responsibility' and 'merit' are positive societal values would not make a good teacher?"[26] Both FIRE and the New York Civil Rights Coalition wrote to Teachers College and pointed out how such standards involve tests of opinions and political beliefs rather than professional assessments of teaching skills.[27] Only after FIRE took its objections public in October did Teachers College respond, stating that it did not "assess or grade [its] students on their attitudes or beliefs."[28] FIRE replied, "If Teachers College is arguing that while it maintains these 'dispositions' on paper, it will not actually utilize them in practice, then the college should rewrite them to reflect this reality." We also pointed out: "While the problems posed by officially sanctioned and politically charged evaluation criteria are very serious, the solution to this problem is rather simple. FIRE asks only that a personal 'commitment to social justice' or any other vague or politically loaded term no longer be *required* of Teachers College students."[29] We received no response to that letter, so we wrote again six months later, in May 2007.[30] We finally received a reply asserting that while Teachers College does not in practice coerce its students to adopt certain beliefs, they would be clarifying the language of their policies to reflect that.[31] Years later, however, Teachers College still has not reformed its policy.

One would hope that we were long past the time when higher education was viewed as an opportunity to inculcate "correct" and unchallengeable answers to philosophical, moral, and societal questions. Attempts to impose mandatory orthodoxies are as old as society, whether those beliefs concern "social justice," "individualism," or "patriotism," but standing up to such attempts is the sign of a free society. For example, in 1943, the Supreme Court invalidated a mandatory requirement that children pledge allegiance to the U.S. flag. As Justice Robert H. Jackson wrote then, efforts "to coerce uniformity of sentiment in support of some end thought essential" have proven destructive throughout history, raising the bitter question of "whose unity it shall be." He concluded: "Compulsory unification of opinion achieves only the unanimity of the graveyard."[32]

College administrators and professors who believe they need to do nothing more than impart correct beliefs to students—without training them to think critically, question authority and dogma, and have meaty and thoughtful debates—cannot hope to produce serious thinkers. Instead, they produce students who know what they're supposed to believe but have very little inclination or even ability to explain why.

Another case, this time at Syracuse University, demonstrated again that something has gone wrong in campus schools of education. In 2011, the Syracuse University School of Education effectively expelled a graduate student over a comment he made on Facebook in response to a remark that he considered an insult to himself.[33] While tutoring at one of the most troubled middle schools in Syracuse, New York, Matthew Werenczak overheard a representative of the city's Concerned Citizens Action Program complain that the city schools should be hiring tutors from historically black colleges instead. Werenczak, who was white, took offense and vented about the incident on Facebook: "Just making sure we're okay with racism. . . . I suppose I oughta be black or stay in my own side of town."[34] The comment eventually reached the School of Education's administrators, who suspended Werenczak from school and required him to complete psychological counseling for anger management issues, take a course on cultural diversity, and write a reflection paper demonstrating "progress and growth . . . in relation to issues regarding cultural diversity"—just to earn the mere chance of readmission.[35] His other option was to leave the program and not come back.[36]

In *Academically Adrift* (see the introduction), Richard Arum and Josipa Roksa found that students in schools of education and social work showed the lowest improvement in critical-thinking skills during their time in college.[37] The only other students who did as poorly were business students (while those in math and the sciences showed the greatest improvement). That departments of social work and education are the most likely to try to impose mandatory ideological conformity on their students is, I believe, related to why students in those departments are not developing the ability to think critically. And if that is the case for those we are training to teach the next generation, the prospects for future generations appreciating the rigorous philosophy of free speech and free minds are bleak indeed.

"So, Are You SURE I Can Write Whatever I Want in This Assignment?"

Stepping away from the heavy and politically charged world of social work and education schools, a bizarre case at Oakland University in Michigan highlights the dangers of being a bit too freewheeling with your creativity on campus. In the fall of 2011, Joseph Corlett was taking an Advanced Critical Writing class that included a "daybook" assignment in which students were encouraged to engage in "free writing/brainstorming" and to write "creative entries" in this "place for a writer to try out ideas and record impressions and observations."[38] Corlett, at fifty-six, had returned to college after dropping out more than thirty-five years earlier. Thus, he was another nontraditional student; having spent the last three-plus decades working for a living, he was also not steeped in the cautious culture of the contemporary campus.

Corlett had gotten high marks after writing on sexual themes in previous assignments for his critical writing course and had even won an honorable mention in a student essay contest a couple of years earlier.[39] According to Corlett, after asking his professor three times if it was really okay to write anything he wanted, he penned an entry called "Hot for Teacher." For those of us who were kids during the golden age of Van Halen, it is almost impossible to hear those words together and not get the song or images of its wonderfully bizarre video stuck in your head. (If you do, by the way, I find that "The Girl from Ipanema" is good at pushing any other song out.)

In the daybook, he riffed on the theme of "Hot for Teacher" and talked about being distracted by his attractive professors.[40] The course's instructor, Pamela Mitzelfield, played a role in some of the entries. In one, he wrote, "Kee-rist, I'll never learn a thing. Tall, blond, stacked, skirt, heels, fingernails, smart, articulate, smile." In a separate September 23 entry he described her as being like Ginger from the television series *Gilligan's Island*, while comparing another professor to Mary Ann.

As someone who has taken literally dozens of writing classes (both creative and otherwise), I can attest that students love to write about racy topics—drugs, violence, but most of all, sex—and are often rewarded with high grades for doing so. I don't dispute that Corlett's entries could "creep out" the professor and cause her to regret emphasizing that it was really okay for him to write anything he wanted. It would've been perfectly appropriate for her to explain that she thought his take on the assignment was unacceptable. But that's not what happened.

Instead, the professor complained to the administration, stating in an email that "either Mr[.] Corlett leaves or I do."[41] The university, apparently unable to convince itself that Corlett's behavior was harassment, charged him with "unlawful individual activities" on the basis of the journal alone. On January 20, 2012, he was found guilty of this vaguely defined offense, barred from campus under penalty of criminal trespassing charges, suspended for three semesters, and made to undergo counseling for his "sensitivity issues" before ever taking a class at Oakland University again.[42] FIRE intervened, bringing substantial media attention to his treatment. (Word of the case even made it to Portuguese, Croatian, and Indonesian Van Halen–related websites.)[43] Corlett appealed with FIRE's help, but on March 5, Oakland denied his appeal, stating that the public university was not bound by "technical legal definitions and standards."[44] Oakland will likely get to see how their arguments stand up in court.

Teaching Censorship by Example

This chapter has largely focused on attempts by professors and departments to impose ideological conformity on their students, abandoning the principle that free and open thought is needed in a complex and dynamic world. While many of the pressures placed on students to ideologically conform are subtle, most of the examples in this chapter have been anything but. Perhaps the most direct illustration of unlearning liberty I've ever seen, however, is the case of a university professor at Northern Kentucky University teaching censorship as a noble, romantic, and heroic calling. In 2006, Professor Sally Jacobsen urged students in one of her classes "to express their freedom-of-speech rights to destroy [an anti-abortion] display if they wished to."[45] The display—which was a field of approximately four hundred tiny crosses—had been erected by a student pro-life group with permission from the university. Jacobsen was later photographed with several other students destroying the display and tearing down the crosses in broad daylight. When asked about her decision to both encourage and engage in mob censorship and self-righteous vandalism, Jacobsen said, "Any violence perpetrated against that silly display was minor compared to how I felt when I saw it. Some of my students felt the same way, just outraged."[46]

Professor Jacobsen turned individual freedom on its head and transmogrified it into a mandate for enforced conformity. Thankfully, the president of Northern Kentucky University, James Votruba, had no patience for this, stating: "Freedom-of-speech rights end where you infringe on someone else's freedom of speech."[47] Jacobsen was suspended for her actions, and she retired at the end of the semester.

Sally Jacobsen's example may seem extreme, but as we will see in Chapter 11, students are learning the lessons of censorship all too well. Meanwhile, the off-campus world has many Sally Jacobsens of its own. Bill Bishop cites some particularly telling examples in *The Big Sort*, but the award for the perfect real-world version of Sally Jacobsen would have to go to the youth minister at the Owens Crossroads Methodist Church in Alabama. In the last days of the 2004 Kerry v. Bush campaign, he organized a "scavenger hunt" to steal pro-Kerry signs from people's lawns to be brought to the minister and then burned.[48] As a testament, though, to our physical isolation from people we disagree with, Bishop explains that the "scavengers did the best they could, but in Republican Huntsville they found only eight signs, barely enough for kindling."[49]

Some might see Sally Jacobsen's censorship as a justified "tit for tat" in light of this example—they censor us, so we censor them. But that is a sad view of the world and denies the very reasonable hope that one could learn to handle the existence of opinions one dislikes and even welcome them as a chance to learn something new. Campuses are one of the only settings that can teach this disciplined, thoughtful disposition on a mass scale, but if they are doing the opposite, the vicious cycle of "who gets to censor whom next" will continue as if humans have never learned a thing.

CHAPTER 10

If Even Your Professor Can Be Punished for Saying the Wrong Thing...

IT'S MID-OCTOBER OF YOUR FRESHMAN YEAR and you enter your Introduction to Latin American Studies class looking for someone. Weeks have passed since your accountability training ended and you are relieved that your probation will be lifted if you stay out of trouble until the end of semester. You don't talk much to Jason anymore, as he seems to have developed the habit of getting in trouble, but you do sometimes still check out what he has to say on Facebook.

He claims that your Latin American Studies professor, Dr. Roth, has been found guilty of racial harassment for explaining where the racial epithet "wetback" came from. This is not shocking to you, as you were startled to hear the word being discussed in class, even though the professor condemned its use while explaining that it arose from stories about immigrants literally swimming across the Rio Grande. Dr. Roth seemed weirdly incautious about how he spoke; adding that to the fact he was probably in his seventies, you figured it was just a matter of time before he got in trouble. But still, you're not sure Jason was telling the truth. He wrote that the Big State U administration had placed an official monitor in his class to make sure he didn't use such language again.

But there he is. The assistant provost sitting in the back row with his pen in hand, listening intently to everything your professor says. Dr. Roth does not quite seem himself today, as he tries to talk about the role of race and class in colonial Peru. You think to yourself that it is right for Dr. Roth to feel chided—he should have known better.

Learning on Eggshells: The Hindley Case at Brandeis

Recall that in the *Engaging Diverse Viewpoints* survey published by the Association of American Colleges and Universities in 2010, faculty members scored the absolute lowest of any group on the question of whether they "feel safe to hold unpopular views on campus," with a dismal 16.7 percent answering that they strongly agree with that statement.[1] That finding is no coincidence, and it forces an important question: If the people who know campuses the best and the longest are this pessimistic about the safety of merely holding unpopular views on campus, what does that say about the overall environment for ideas? The punishment of even tenured professors for their speech teaches students unforgettable lessons about both the danger of verbal missteps and the power of claims of outrage and offense to silence just about anyone.

The opening scenario of this chapter comes directly from the case of Donald Hindley, a professor of politics at Brandeis University. In 2007, Hindley, who had been a professor for nearly half a century, was found guilty of racial harassment for discussing the word "wetbacks" in his Latin American Politics course. He explained the origin of the word—it derives from immigrants crossing the Rio Grande—to *criticize* its use. For that, he was found guilty without a hearing and without even knowing the specific allegations against him. Professor Hindley was informed by Provost Marty Krauss in a caustic follow-up letter that "The University will not tolerate inappropriate, racial and discriminatory conduct by members of the faculty," and that Krauss was placing the assistant provost, Richard Silberman, as a monitor in Hindley's classes for however long Krauss thought it would take "to ensure that you do not engage in further violations of the nondiscrimination and harassment policy."[2] Finally, Krauss required Hindley to attend "anti-discrimination training" where the trainer would "assess your ability to conduct classes without engaging in inappropriate, racial and discriminatory conduct." This exemplifies the arrogance of college administrators who think they know the fine points of scholarship and moral philosophy better than their most seasoned professors.

This incident is especially galling at a university that uses the glowing pro-free-speech language of Justice Louis Brandeis throughout its promotional materials and on the actual campus. After all, Louis Brandeis is arguably the most important justice in the history of the First Amendment, since it was in part through his efforts and wisdom that the Supreme Court came to understand the importance of robust protections of speech.

The one bright side of the case, however, is that it was a notable exception to the rule of student and faculty acceptance of censorship. The Faculty Senate unanimously adopted a resolution condemning the university's failure to consult with them on its decision (as was required by the school's own policies), and the faculty's Committee on Faculty Rights and Responsibilities later granted Hindley's appeal—a decision that was rejected by the provost.[3] Furthermore, Brandeis students at the time and in the years since the Hindley incident have risen to the professor's defense.[4]

The heavy-handed tenacity with which the administration fought off all criticism from faculty, students, FIRE, the ACLU of Massachusetts, and the local and student media has seldom been equaled and is worth examining in detail in our document archive on the case.[5] The university eventually removed the monitor and issued a letter essentially saying that Hindley had learned his lesson. But the harassment finding remains to this day despite years of attempts to get the university to officially overturn it.

It is fairly easy to find parallels to this case in education over the past decades; however, they normally occur in K–12. Writing for *The Atlantic* in February 2012, Wendy Kaminer lamented one case of a Chicago sixth-grade teacher being suspended in a similar incident:

> Someday, perhaps, the idiocies of equating critical references to epithets with malicious uses of them will be self-evident. Someday we may conquer our phobias and stop compiling a lexicon of words that may be known only by their initials, if at all, like the sacred Name of God, or Voldemort. In the meantime, we have to persist in arguing the obvious: Words are not incantations; they do not cast spells. Instead, they take their meaning and power from the contexts in which they appear.[6]

Beyond the knee-jerk response to epithets, there is another dimension to the Hindley case. Some have speculated that Hindley's harassment charge was a smoke screen to hide the university's real reason for wanting to punish him: Hindley's pro-Palestinian stances at a largely Jewish college.[7] Whether or not this is true may never be known, but it does highlight the special role of the culture wars in the classroom setting. When administrators have unfettered power to punish students or teachers for protected speech, you can practically guarantee some of them will use that power to persecute those who merely disagree with them.

Culture Wars, Censorship, and the Professoriate

One of the many disappointing things about the state of American discourse that I encounter when I give speeches, either on college campuses or in front of more ideological groups, is how often people want me to give a simple, pat answer to why there is so much censorship on campus. If it's a more conservative group, people sometimes want me to tell them that "it's all political correctness run amok"; more liberal groups are particularly focused on how people with opinions like theirs are persecuted. Unsurprisingly, neither simple narrative is entirely true. For example, Professor Hindley is a political liberal but the justification for punishing him—preventing hostile-environment harassment—is also considered a liberal cause. In fact, many of these cases that might be considered examples of "PC run amok" involve people who consider themselves liberal being punished by the administration. As I have already argued, however, I believe students and faculty are often duped by appeals to tolerance and diversity to justify the punishment of professors or students who are simply disliked by the administration or by a particular administrator.

Sometimes, college administrators feel no need to even try to hide the ball, as in the case of Gale Isaacs at Shaw University in Raleigh, North Carolina. In the fall of 2002, an anonymous petition was circulated on campus that criticized "the present atmosphere of contention and distrust of the Faculty and Staff . . . with regard to The Shaw University Board of Trustees, the Academic Administration and the sitting President."[8] On November 12, 2002, Gale Isaacs, a professor at the university since 1986 and chair of the Department of Allied Health, admitted to being one of the authors of the resolution; she was immediately stripped of her appointments and on November 16 received a letter signed by the president of the university, Talbert O. Shaw, firing her explicitly for the resolution.[9] Notwithstanding the university's clear promises of free speech ("Faculty and staff, as citizens, are entitled to the fullest freedom of political thought and activity"), the letter stated that the resolution "demonstrated faithlessness in and disloyalty to the University and exhibited an unwillingness to work for the common good of the University."[10] Professor Isaacs was escorted from her office by campus security that same day.

The case proved impossible to win, despite the efforts of the AAUP and FIRE, because ultimately Isaacs decided, understandably, that she did not want her job back.[11] What has always struck me about the case is that a university president would proudly sign his name to a letter firing a professor for nothing more than her speech. This clueless pride in being a censor was reflected years later in a 2006 case at the State University of New York at Fredonia involving Steven Kershnar, a professor of philosophy.

The SUNY Fredonia case, however, was anything but apolitical. Kershnar wrote a biweekly column in the local *Dunkirk-Fredonia Observer* newspaper. In February 2006, he wrote two pieces: one titled "Are Conservatives Being Shut Out of the Academy?" (he concluded it wasn't totally clear that they were but thought it was a valuable question); and the other, perhaps more dangerously for a professor, "Against Affirmative Action at Fredonia."[12] When he applied for promotion to full professor two months later, the response from the university president, Dennis L. Hefner, was remarkably blunt. He denied the promotion, citing Kershnar's "deliberate and repeated public misrepresentation of campus policies and procedures (e.g. student conduct code, affirmative action, admissions) to the media," which he claimed "has impugned the reputation of SUNY Fredonia."[13] Notably, Hefner offered no support for his claim that Kershnar's opinion pieces contained errors.

We don't often get university presidents signing letters saying "In the name of your publicly expressed opinion, I, as a president of a public university, despite the First Amendment, hereby punish you," but it actually got worse. After FIRE wrote on Kershnar's behalf, President Hefner proposed a settlement that would allow Kershnar's promotion to full professor if he agreed to be bound by a committee that would review all of his writing about SUNY Fredonia and would have to "give unanimous consent prior to publication based on their determination that there is no misrepresentation."[14]

This is what is known as a "prior restraint." Even before the First Amendment was strongly interpreted in the United States, there was near-complete agreement that it meant the government could not punish members of the press before they spoke or require authors to submit their writing for official approval before publication. Even John Milton knew this in 1644, when he argued in his *Areopagitica* against the print licensing system in Britain. But apparently, President Hefner did not.

Kershnar refused to agree to these laughably unconstitutional conditions and was once again denied promotion. Finally, FIRE took the case public and wrote an article about it in the *New York Post*.[15] After a hearty round of bad press, Hefner reversed course and granted Kershnar's promotion on August 11, 2006.[16]

That same year, Walter Kehowski, a professor of mathematics at Glendale Community College in Arizona, was placed on forced administrative leave after emailing George Washington's Thanksgiving address to the college district's listserv.[17] Kehowski had always been an outspoken conservative and controversial figure, and he linked the Thanksgiving address to Pat Buchanan's website. Reportedly, several district employees were offended by the anti-immigration opinions expressed on Buchanan's site. The case led to a lawsuit and Kehowski reached a settlement that allowed him to return to class.[18] (An earlier lawsuit involving Kehowski's un-PC emails resulted in a strongly free speech protective decision by the Ninth Circuit in 2010.)[19]

Meanwhile, Mike Adams, a conservative columnist and professor in the Department of Sociology and Criminology at the University of North Carolina Wilmington, has been through more than his fair share of battles in the culture war. My first involvement defending Professor Adams' rights came from an incident four days after the September 11 attacks, when a UNC Wilmington student sent an email to students and faculty at the university blaming the United States for the attacks. The student quoted the World Socialist Web Site and argued, "The American ruling elite, in its insolence and cynicism, acts as if it can carry out its violent enterprises around the world without creating the political conditions for violent acts of retribution."[20] She invited readers to forward the email in the interest of "open, unbiased, democratic discussion." Adams wrote back:

> I will certainly forward this to others and I hope they will respond. My response will be brief as your "statement" is undeserving of serious consideration. Your claimed interest in promoting rational discussion is dishonest. It is an intentionally divisive diatribe. The Constitution protects your speech just as it has protected bigoted, unintelligent, and immature speech

for many years. But, remember, when you exercise your rights you open yourself up to criticism that is protected by the same principles. I sincerely hope that your bad speech serves as a catalyst for better speech by others.[21]

The student then alleged that she had been defamed, and additionally accused Adams of intimidation and false representation. Amazingly, even though the university counsel acknowledged that her claims were without merit, UNC Wilmington's administration capitulated and ordered the opening of Adams' email account for investigation.[22] Because the case involved only speech that was clearly protected on both sides, there was nothing to investigate. But the university, bowing to the student's repeated demands and escalating threats, proceeded with the investigation despite Adams' objections.

Years later, in 2007, Adams filed suit against the university with the help of the Alliance Defense Fund, after his application for promotion was denied, in part due to his work as a conservative columnist. UNC Wilmington argued that because Adams had included samples from his years of published work in his application, the writing was not protected speech. The university based this claim on the Supreme Court's 2006 decision in *Garcetti* v. *Ceballos*, which held that public employees' speech made "pursuant to their official duties" is not insulated from employer discipline.[23] While I view *Garcetti* as a very flawed ruling, the Supreme Court explicitly noted that the decision's application to university professors (specifically, to "expression related to academic scholarship or classroom instruction") raised additional questions that would not be decided in that decision.

A federal district court ruled against Adams, but in April 2011, the U.S. Court of Appeals for the Fourth Circuit (which is not known for its high regard for academic freedom) reversed that decision and held that UNC Wilmington had unconstitutionally stretched the *Garcetti* opinion in a way that could devastate academic freedom.[24] Critically, the Fourth Circuit found that simply because Adams had included his columns in his application for promotion, that act alone did not transform them into speech made pursuant to his duties as a government employee. The court also held that the columns implicated Adams' right to academic freedom, because it is understood that faculty provide such commentary as a function of their role as academics. Overall, Professor Adams' case was not just a win for him personally, it also provided a landmark ruling from a federal appellate court protecting academic freedom for professors.

Despite the labels above, in my daily life, I try not to label professors "liberal" or "conservative" too often, because the meanings of those terms change tremendously both over time and depending on whom you talk to, and also because I think overreliance on these loaded terms is part of the problem for the state of American debate. However, there is one fairly clear trend in my work defending free speech on campus: if the professor or student is being punished because of speech that is considered "too liberal," the impetus usually comes from off campus. As you've seen, being a political liberal is no protection from politically correct censorship on campus, but the public is also often on the lookout for offensive comments and ideas being generated by their campuses. Universities have done an awful lot to earn public suspicion, but when they heed the public's calls to censor unpopular speech on campus, they only make things worse.

Take the 2011 case at Gainesville State College (GSC) in Georgia involving a Confederate flag. Of course, a Confederate flag is certainly a divisive and controversial symbol both on and off the modern campus, but in this case a professor drew public ire for making artwork that was *critical* of the Confederate flag. A January 2011 exhibit at the college featured a painting by Stanley Bermudez, a GSC art professor, called "Heritage?"

The painting features a Confederate flag superimposed over images of, among other things, a torch-wielding Ku Klux Klan member and a lynching. The Venezuelan-born professor explained his thoughts about the painting:

Source: *Stanley Bermudez*

[On] the KKK web site the rebel flag is used often. [This and other] things strengthen my negative view of the Dixie flag and the reason for this painting. This painting represents what I feel and think of when I see the flag. However, after living in Georgia for the last 4 years and talking to several people from Georgia, I have also learned that there is a strong heritage and pride associated with the flag that has nothing to do with the KKK or racism. As is the case in many of the paintings, I do like to show two sides of the coin. I am in the process of creating an accompanying painting of a Rebel flag that shows the image in a more positive manner.[25]

After the Southern Heritage Alerts blog publicly criticized the painting as "despicable" and encouraged people to contact the president of GSC, Martha T. Nesbitt, the school buckled under pressure and removed the painting.[26] According to Bermudez, Nesbitt herself, along with one other GSC administrator, went into the gallery where Bermudez's piece hung and removed it—without notifying Bermudez or anyone else.[27] Nesbitt defended her choice of censorship over discussion, stating that she had to consider the "health and reputation of the institution" and that the painting had "been perceived as aggressively hostile in other areas of the country."[28] Multiple entreaties by FIRE and bad press couldn't change GSC's mind.

Gainesville State College's response is a lesson on where the logic of campus censorship leads; after all, if you are going to justify speech codes and speech zones by the sensitivities of those on campus, it looks hypocritical not to consider those off campus as well. The problem with this, of course, is that by following a "sensitivity for everyone" as opposed to a "free speech for everyone" model, you create the risk that nobody will be allowed to say anything interesting at all. As for Bermudez, discouraged by the college's spinelessness, he never made that companion piece. He told FIRE, "I do not want the people that did not like the image to think that I am doing it to just make amends or to appease them."[29] At the opening reception for the faculty exhibition, the spot where "Heritage?" was to have hung sat empty, save for the explanatory statement quoted above.[30]

At virtually the same time as GSC's controversy, in my very own borough, Brooklyn College fired Kristofer Petersen-Overton, an adjunct instructor who was to have taught a course on Politics of the Middle East, before he was able to lead a single class session. Just days earlier, Dov Hikind, a New

York assemblyman, had complained about Petersen-Overton's pro-Palestinian views, stating that his course's syllabus "reads like a Who's Who of Palestinian sympathizers and historical revisionists," and calling Petersen-Overton "an overt supporter of terrorism."[31] Brooklyn College initially claimed it fired Petersen-Overton, a Ph.D. student at the CUNY Graduate Center, because he lacked the credentials to teach the masters-level course. Reporters including *Salon*'s Justin Elliott were easily able to find student instructors at Brooklyn College whose similar credentials apparently presented no such problems.[32] FIRE got involved in the case and the public backlash quickly led to Petersen-Overton's reinstatement.[33]

In a similar vein, consider the case of William Robinson, a professor at the University of California, Santa Barbara. In a January 2009 email he sent to students in his Sociology of Globalization course, Robinson drew parallels between the Warsaw ghetto and the blockade of the Gaza Strip. It is worth noting that Professor Robinson is Jewish, and that this comparison was also drawn by the UN investigator Richard Falk and covered by the Israeli news service *Haaretz*.[34] UCSB undertook an investigation of Robinson after the Anti-Defamation League wrote to Professor Robinson and other UCSB officials, asking him and UCSB to repudiate the emails, and after two students dropped the course and filed complaints against the professor.[35] Both FIRE and the AAUP argued that Professor Robinson's speech was clearly protected by academic freedom because it was related to the topic of the class, and that any investigation or threat of punishment should be ended.[36] The administration took several months to reach the same conclusion, finally deciding to end the investigation after a faculty committee found that Professor Robinson's speech was protected by academic freedom.[37] The case was predictably polarizing. Outside critics saw it as a prime example of a growing anti-Israel sentiment on campus and called for action to be taken. But as I have attempted to explain many times, attitudes about Israel on campus would only worsen if students and faculty suddenly found themselves punished for criticizing Israel.

The chilling power of investigations is conveyed in a FIRE case that took place before I joined the team in 2001. Once again, it involves a professor who considered herself liberal running afoul of the shifting norms of cultural sensitivity. Linda McCarriston, a creative writing professor at the University of Alaska, published a poem in 2000 called "Indian Girls." It is a powerful and complex short poem, and it incorporates haunting images of child sexual molestation within an Alaskan Native tribe.[38] But Diane Benson, a student in her class who would later run for governor and lieutenant governor of Alaska and for the House of Representatives, was offended and led a protest of the professor and the poem.[39] McCarriston was accused of hate speech, and an investigation was launched. On March 13, 2001—after months of debate, controversy, and the looming possibility of punishment for art—the university's president, Mark R. Hamilton, issued what remains the best statement I have seen of the proper official response to calls to "investigate" clearly protected speech:

> What I want to make clear and unambiguous is that responses to complaints or demands for action regarding constitutionally guaranteed freedoms of speech CANNOT BE QUALIFIED. Attempts to assuage anger or to demonstrate concern by qualifying our support for free speech serve to cloud what must be a clear message. Noting that, for example, "The University supports the right to free speech, but we intend to check into this matter," or "The University supports the right of free speech, but I have asked Dean X or Provost Y to investigate the circumstances," is unacceptable. *There is nothing to "check into," nothing "to investigate."* [Emphasis added.] Opinions expressed by our employees, students, faculty or administrators don't have to be politic or polite. However personally offended we might be, however unfair the association of the University to the opinion might be, I insist that we remain a certain trumpet on this most precious of Constitutional rights.[40]

If every university president took such a brave and principled yet commonsense stance on the importance of free speech and academic freedom on campus, I could happily retire. Sadly, it does not seem likely that this will happen anytime soon.

Not Letting the Cases Blur Together:
The Very Real Consequences of Censorship on Campus

It is impossible to do justice to all the cases involving the punishment of professors I have seen over the years. Even though we are hardly a name known to most students, FIRE receives hundreds of direct requests for help from students and faculty each year and hundreds of additional reports of censorship on campus through the student media and from friends and allies across the country. We've always been a much smaller organization than people assume (sometimes with as few as six employees, and for many years I was the only lawyer on staff), and the crush of cases can sometimes make our office feel like an emergency room. Given these circumstances, it can be all too easy to lose sight of the fact that each case involves real individuals and affects their families, friends, wives, husbands, and children, as well.

Professor Lisa Church at Rhode Island College helped remind me of how terrifying a campus prosecution can be. In 2004, Dr. Church was an associate professor and was volunteering her time as a coordinator at the cooperative preschool program at the college, which was open to the family of staff, faculty, and students. On February 19, 2004, three mothers of children who were part of the co-op got into a heated argument about welfare and race. One of the mothers, who was an administrator at the college, complained to Dr. Church and demanded that the college take action including disciplinary proceedings against the other two mothers. Church responded that mediation would be preferable to disciplinary action. She was also aware that disciplinary actions would involve First Amendment concerns for a public college like Rhode Island College, a situation made even trickier because this was a she said, she said situation.

The mother filed charges with the college's Affirmative Action Office alleging discrimination and intimidation—by Lisa Church. Dr. Church was mystified as to how she could be charged when she had tried to be helpful, but she also knew that a public college could not constitutionally punish the parents. When she tried to find out why she was being charged, all she received were bizarre and legally dead-wrong responses that even cited the university's wildly unconstitutional speech code. (The student guide at the time prohibited "jokes or demeaning statements about a person's gender, race/ethnicity, disabling condition, etc.")[41] Keep in mind that there was no allegation whatsoever that Church herself had said anything that was unprotected, but because she had correctly interpreted her duties as a public employee, she was now facing charges that could end her career. The charge against her was "hostile environment racism."

When FIRE and the ACLU of Rhode Island became involved, the faculty union also joined in challenging Rhode Island College's speech code.[42] After Church's case made it into the Associated Press and after the *Providence Journal* condemned the college, it handed down a decision that, after months of process and a closed-door hearing, Church's case did not require "further formal action."[43] President John Nazarian, who had publicly defended the campus prosecution and the university speech code, never conceded that the issue had anything to do with free speech and never apologized to Church.

This case might have faded from my memory in the blur of cases I saw that year, if not for a visit to Providence where I got to sit down with Lisa Church and her husband. I got to see for myself the panic in their eyes as they talked about the months-long investigation and how afraid they both were that this would spell the end of Lisa's career. Even that early in my work at FIRE, I had gotten too used to such abuses, and this was a much-needed reminder to always think of the real people at the core of these stories.

Of course, feelings cut both ways, and the reason why we see so many cases at FIRE is often because the college is bending over backwards to accommodate the feelings of others, in this case one staff member. But the difference is that while the complaining mother had every right to decry what she had heard, she did not have the right to have someone punished for it, let alone for refusing to punish the alleged speakers. Lisa Church's ordeal is all the more powerful because she was resisting a punishment that was unlawful from the very start, but in the parallel universe of university justice, this did not seem to matter.

Adam Kissel, FIRE's vice president of programs, had a similar personal experience with a professor of English at East Georgia College whose case was finally resolved in 2011. Professor Thomas Thibeault attended a mandatory faculty training in 2009 in which he complained that the campus sexual harassment policy was flawed because it did not offer sufficient protection for false or malicious accusations. In his real-life example of a case that he thought would be "ridiculous" if it counted as harassment, a student had decorated her cleavage with "some sort of sparkly material" and then had complained about another professor looking at it.[44] Thibeault recalled that another "female student then said, and I hope you're not offended by her actual words, 'if you don't want anyone looking at your titties, I'll lend you a T-shirt. I have one in the truck.' The first student then said, 'No. I'm proud of the way I look.'" Thibeault explained drolly that he "left the conversation at that point."

Thibeault was right to be concerned about procedural protections, as professors have been fired or punished for attempting to navigate the eroticism- and taboo-filled world of literature along with the schizophrenic nature (one minute sex-positive, the next quasi-Victorian) of some campuses, especially when the students refuse to play by such rules. And his concerns proved prophetic. Just two days later, he was contacted by the college's president, John B. Black, who ordered him to resign or else be fired and have his "long history of sexual harassment . . . made public."[45] This came as a shock to Professor Thibeault, as he had never before been charged with any sort of harassment. As a popular English professor with an irreverent, wry wit and excellent student reviews, he enjoyed reading and talking about a wide range of literature including texts with the frank and colorful style of contemporary writers, but had never before run into trouble for doing so. Thibeault refused to resign, and like Professor Isaacs, was escorted from the college by campus police.

East Georgia College had provided Thibeault with no hearing and no support for the allegation that he had a pattern of sexual harassment. Black couldn't even get his story straight about whether he had fired or suspended Thibeault. When the Office of the Attorney General of Georgia started investigating the case, Thibeault was reinstated—but only temporarily.[46] President Black censured him for his "offensive" speech and told him that he would not be rehired in 2010. Seeing no other option, Thibeault filed suit in 2010, and the suit eventually settled for $50,000.[47]

Adam Kissel met Thomas Thibeault and his wife in 2010 when he gave a speech in the local community center in their small town of Swainsboro. He stayed in their house, later edited Thibeault's first novel, *Balto's Nose* (which is about, among other things, administrative overreach), and now attends his wife's annual music retreat in the Blue Ridge Mountains of North Carolina. Thibeault eventually landed on his feet—no longer a professor, now a novelist—but Black's violation of his rights made havoc of his life for two years.

The Outrage Culture, from the Campus to the Real World

Reading the story of Dr. Hindley at Brandeis and many of the other examples in this book may remind some people of Philip Roth's 2000 novel *The Human Stain*. In this national bestseller, an elderly professor sees his career collapse after he is unjustifiably accused of racism for asking of two students who had never shown up for class, "Does anyone know these people? Do they exist or are they spooks?"[48] Professor Coleman Silk had no idea the two students in question were black, but when it turned out they were, the university outrage machine turned on, claiming that Professor Silk had meant the term "spooks" as an epithet instead of how he actually meant it: as ghosts.

I'm sure the scenario may seem far-fetched to some readers, but it sounds like a day at the office to me. The novel also offers a great deal of insight about the strange links between political correctness, Puritanism, and the danger of crusaders wanting to have a "hero narrative" about themselves. One thing it does especially brilliantly is convey how the sudden turn against Professor Silk was motivated not only by political correctness, but also by decades of bad feelings relating back to when the professor had been a demanding dean, and other personal and private resentments that found focus in opportunistic outrage. The outrage became hopelessly entwined with a mix of self-serving interests.

Abraham Lincoln once observed, "The philosophy of the school room in one generation will be the philosophy of government in the next," and I believe some of the bad habits of campus are increasingly bleeding their way into the larger society. A striking example of this happened in March 2012, when the conservative radio host Rush Limbaugh mocked Georgetown law student Sandra Fluke, calling her a slut (among other things) after her Senate testimony about contraception. Rush Limbaugh, who rarely apologizes for anything, publicly apologized as the uproar increased.[49] In an attempt to find a liberal double standard, some commentators turned their attention to the comedian Bill Maher, who had never minced words about or hesitated to insult Sarah Palin, among others.[50] The spiral of blame reached its crescendo, however, when Newt Gingrich demanded an apology from President Obama after Robert De Niro made a joke that included a reference to Gingrich's wife, Calista.[51] The joke was: "Calista Gingrich. Karen Santorum. Ann Romney. Now do you really think our country is ready for a white first lady?"

In response to all these controversies, Bill Maher wrote a March 21 op-ed in the *New York Times* titled "Please Stop Apologizing."[52] Maher poked fun at the culture of outrage in our society and proposed, "Let's have an amnesty—from the left and the right—on every made-up, fake, totally insincere, playacted hurt, insult, slight and affront. Let's make this Sunday the National Day of No Outrage. One day a year when you will not find some tiny thing someone did or said and pretend you can barely continue functioning until they apologize."

Maher was saying something that our society and especially our campuses need to hear. Outrage can, of course, be real, but it also can be insincere, tactical, and self-serving, and once people start to understand the power of outrage, they can easily use it to manipulate others against their own pet targets. While many were outraged at Limbaugh and Maher, and maybe some were even angered by De Niro, others simply saw it as an opportunity to go after someone whose politics they did not like. This phenomenon is not new, but I believe it has become so much more common in our larger society because outrage is a weapon of choice that is widely used and legitimized on college campuses. Students are learning that a claim of outrage can get whichever professor you dislike punished (including entirely innocent people like Lisa Church), whichever cause you dislike silenced, or just let you take the moral high ground in an argument you were losing. We should not be surprised that students bring this useful tool with them into the real world or that our national discussion suffers for it. Yes, there are many things in the world to be outraged about, but if campuses want to produce a generation that knows how to solve problems rather than resort to cheap tactics to shut down debate, it needs to teach the habit of hearing the other side without throwing a fit.

Chapter 11

Student Draftees
for the Culture War

Y<small>OU'RE WALKING HOME FROM THE LIBRARY AT MIDNIGHT</small> on the day before first-semester finals. All week long, you've been walking around in a daze, caught somewhere between nervousness, giddiness, and melancholy, trying to comprehend how much has changed in your life in less than four months. College has been somehow both more and less exciting than you expected, both more and less different from high school than you had guessed, and both more and less challenging than you thought it would be. But for all these paradoxes, you know you'll be going home for winter break a very different person.

As you meander across the quad, you see the first few flakes of snow float by a solitary lamp. Then you notice something strange. Three students are running from the student center with gigantic piles of newspapers in their hands. They are theatrically dressed in black with their heads covered by hooded sweatshirts, but it doesn't do a great job of concealing their identities. You recognize the president of Students Against All Hate, and realize what is happening. Throughout the semester, the official student newspaper, the conservative journal, and the supposed "humor" magazine (which you only occasionally find funny) have each provoked fits of outrage for investigatory pieces, editorials, op-eds, or satirical articles they have published. On several of those occasions, the publications wrote stories about how some of your fellow students had stolen and destroyed thousands of copies of the issue that angered them. You weren't sure if this had been true, but even if it had been, many of your friends on campus thought these so-called student journalists had it coming.

You try to remember what the controversy was about this week and which publication had started it. Was it that conservative columnist who is always on about affirmative action or illegal immigration? Was it that fundamentalist columnist who argues against *Roe* v. *Wade*? Was it another tasteless parody gone wrong? Was it an article about allegations of date rape by a member of the football team or a fraternity? Was it that sex columnist who always seems to be in trouble? Or was it members of the student government angry about allegations of misspending student money again? No, if Students Against All Hate is involved, it's probably something highly offensive, hurtful, or insensitive. It might even be hate speech, which you know has no place on campus.

So you stand and watch as one of the three students in black sweatshirts throws bales of newspapers into a dumpster, while another, hands still full of newspapers, runs over to try to get yet another stack out of one of the distribution bins. You know they don't see you. You ask yourself if you should report them, but you quickly dismiss that idea. Yes, if you make it through to the end of the semester, your probation will finally be lifted, but from what you've read the administration seems dismissive and even vaguely supportive of the alleged thefts. Besides, the social consequences alone would be bad enough, and who knows, these students might even be striking a blow against hate. So you're torn between two options: do you just walk away and say nothing, or should you do your part for progress and lend a hand?

Students Destroying Student Newspapers

It surprises me how few people know how often newspaper theft occurs on campus. These thefts involve students, alone or in groups, stealing large numbers of student newspapers, journals, magazines, or other publications, with the goal of preventing an unwanted opinion or story from getting out, or punishing a publication for running an article. This is, sadly, a fairly regular part of the collegiate landscape. Newspaper theft is a sign of just how harmful the culture of censorship has become, revealing how the lessons of speech codes, overzealous prosecutions, and restrictions on unpopular expression have turned everyday students into active censors.

FIRE, the First Amendment Center, and, most thoroughly, the excellent Student Press Law Center have documented hundreds of cases of newspaper theft since 2000. This is a marked increase over the number reported in the previous decade, and we are confident that only a small percentage of such incidents get reported.

Since 2005, several large-scale incidents of newspaper theft have occurred at schools across the country: at the University of Arizona, where 10,000 copies of the *Daily Wildcat* were stolen; at Catholic University, where 3,000 copies of the student newspaper were trashed; at Ball State University, where 7,000 copies of the *Ball State University Daily News* were taken; at the University of Southern Indiana, where 2,300 copies of the student newspaper were stolen; at Kansas State University, where 8,000 copies out of a run of 11,000 copies of the *Kansas State Collegian* disappeared; at the University of Rhode Island, where almost the entire 5,000-copy press run of the student paper was stolen; at the University of Utah, where 8,500 copies went missing; and at Loyola Marymount University, where 4,000 copies of the *Los Angeles Loyolan* were taken.[1]

Sometimes the numbers don't do justice to the thefts. For example, the loss of 2,000 copies of the student newspaper at Nicholls State University in Louisiana in 2007 constituted the elimination of 90 percent of the print run, and the 2009 theft of approximately 1,900 copies of the Vincennes University student paper meant that it lost 95 percent of its press run.[2] Such large-scale mob censorship results in the loss of tens of thousands of dollars for college newspapers and, potentially, the loss of important advertising for future editions.

The motivations for individual acts of newspaper theft and destruction vary widely. Student newspapers often run into trouble for reporting on abuses in the student government. For example, at the University of California, Riverside, up to 1,500 copies of the main student newspaper disappeared in 2009 when it featured a front-page article reporting on a student government president who allegedly spent almost $5,000 to fly herself and another student to a conference without approval.[3] In 2007 at UNC Charlotte, thousands of newspapers were stolen after the paper neglected to mention a candidate for student government.[4] Even stories involving homecoming queens have prompted thefts: at the University of Texas at El Paso in 2008, 3,500 copies of the paper were stolen because an article revealed that a homecoming queen used to be a stripper; and in 2004 at the University of Central Florida, a homecoming queen was sentenced to sixteen hours of community service for throwing away 1,000 copies of the student newspaper because it reported that she had a criminal record.[5] Covering campus crime can also be risky. Take, for example, the 2007 case at Rowan University, where two students admitted to stealing hundreds of copies of the student newspaper after it reported about a friend's arrest on drug charges.[6]

Criticizing fraternities can often result in mob censorship. At the University of North Carolina at Chapel Hill in 2007, a fraternity admitted responsibility for the theft of 10,000 issues of the main student paper, the *Daily Tar Heel*.[7] The paper had run a front-page story on the fraternity's three-year suspension for hazing. Sororities occasionally engage in mob censorship of their own, such as in 2006 when a sorority at Stetson University in Florida admitted to stealing hundreds of copies of the student newspaper after it printed an article that claimed their sorority house was plagued with mold.[8] To their discredit, Greek organizations can be tied to the theft of no fewer than 58,000 copies of student publications in the previous decade.

Of course, the drama of the culture wars often rears its head in cases of newspaper theft. A conservative magazine at Bucknell University called *The Counterweight* reports that its issues are regularly stolen. This includes a 2008 incident in which virtually *all* copies of the magazine disappeared after it ran an article that questioned the scientific certainty around global warming and mocked universities' attempts to be "green."[9] More recently, students at my undergrad alma mater American University invoked "hate speech" to justify trashing copies of the student paper when Alex Knepper, a gay columnist, wrote a column saying that girls who drink too much and go home with anonymous strangers should not "cry date rape" if they later regret having sex.[10] I understand why students were offended, but that does not excuse brazen censorship. One student even publicly admitted to having been involved in the theft and destruction of the papers, but the university chose not to sanction her.[11] Not to be left out, conservatives sometimes get in on the act of newspaper theft, too. At the University of Southern Indiana, nearly the entire press run of the student newspaper disappeared after being condemned as showing "softcore porn" for running a picture of two women in bed.[12]

The scariest cases are those where newspapers are burned. One spectacular example occurred at Louisiana State University in 1998, when a student burned 1,000 copies of the student newspaper because an article allegedly "took him out of context."[13] College students have maintained this shameful tradition with newspaper burnings at Boston College in 2005, Dartmouth in 2006, and the University of Wisconsin in 2007.[14] At Boston College, members of a minority student group set fire to copies of the student newspaper *The Heights* after it ran the headline "RDs [Resident Directors] Resign Following Drug Bust." The students who burned the newspapers claimed that because the three RDs in question were African American, the use of the term "drug bust" was racist.

In 2006, Dartmouth students burned copies of *The Dartmouth* after a campus-wide outcry relating to an editorial cartoon. Why? The cartoon had four panels featuring a male student holding a beer, arm in arm with a visibly drunk girl, while talking to Friedrich Nietzsche. Here is the entire content of the cartoon:

NIETZSCHE: Yeah dude.

MALE STUDENT: This girl's acting all into me but she's really wasted. I don't want to do the wrong thing.

NIETZSCHE: Dude, assert your will to power. Take advantage of her.

MALE STUDENT: For real? My prof said you are against that stuff.

NIETZSCHE: No way bro, that's just liberal academic revisionism. Do it!

MALE STUDENT: Man, I am so beyond good and evil right now.[15]

The "will to power" refers to one of Nietzsche's famous concepts, and "beyond good and evil" to one of his most famous works. Nietzschean philosophy is often criticized for dismissing conventional morality and even encouraging human evil.[16] The cartoon is another argument in that long history. Personally, I think its jibe at the bizarre affection some liberal professors show for Nietzsche is spot on.

The student reaction to a cartoon spoofing the "will to power" was a great demonstration of the "will to be offended." Whether they were engaging in melodramatic grandstanding or genuinely misunderstanding the point of the cartoon, critics accused the cartoonist and the paper of advocating date rape. One student wrote a column comparing the cartoon to showing "a black student being lynched" or "a group of students from Hillel being marched off to a gas chamber under a giant swastika."[17] The overheated rhetoric didn't end there, of course, as students gathered outside the office of *The Dartmouth* to burn copies of the paper.

These newspaper burnings bring up some interesting free speech questions. Citizens have—and should have—a right to burn symbols, even the American flag (the Supreme Court ruled that flag burning was protected in *Texas* v. *Johnson* in 1989), as a form of protest.[18] While burning a small number of newspapers could count as protected symbolic expression, the rights at stake change when the goal is to destroy so many papers that the publication's message does not get out. There was no ambiguity between symbolic expression and grassroots censorship at the University of Wisconsin–River Falls when a student admitted in 2007 to stealing and then burning hundreds of copies of the student newspaper that reported he had received a citation for underage drinking.[19] The fact that so few students are repulsed by actions like this—despite the pernicious examples of the book burners of the twentieth century—is chilling, to say the least.

While students receive grim lessons about living with free speech at every stage of their college experience, some lessons are more direct than others. The bad examples start at the top, as in 2002, when the mayor of Berkeley, California, pleaded guilty to stealing 1,000 copies of UC Berkeley's student newspaper for endorsing his opponent.[20] Mayor Tom Bates was charged and fined, he apologized, and as penance he enacted a tougher law against the theft of student newspapers. Or consider a 2008 case at the University of Tampa, where a professor admitted to stealing copies of the student newspaper because he didn't want incoming students to be frightened by a story about crime on campus.[21] Or the April 2012 case at Christopher Newport University in Virginia, in which administrators were caught hiding stacks of the student newspaper because it featured a story about a suspected meth lab on campus.[22] Or, worst of all, the 2010 example of Coach Guy Morriss at Texas A&M–Commerce, who praised his football team for going out and stealing the entire press run of the school's student newspaper for publishing a story about a team member arrested in a "drug bust."[23] After finding out about what the team had done, the coach was quoted saying, "I'm proud of my players for doing that. This was the best team building exercise we have ever done." As Adam Goldstein of the Student Press Law Center put it so well in the *Huffington Post*, "If these are actually Guy Morriss' words, he shouldn't be coaching students. He shouldn't be coaching a foosball table."[24] Morriss later offered a somewhat testy apology, which to my mind only served to demonstrate that he didn't really think he or his team had done anything wrong.

Some critics of higher education may be surprised to see how broad the range of motivations that lead to newspaper theft and obstruction are. It is true that if an article is going to be targeted for its political point of view, it is likely a socially conservative one, but newspaper theft is frequently not "political correctness run amok." Often, it is as simple as students wishing to silence criticism of their organizations or themselves.

Why? After decades of speech codes, bad examples from administrators, and omnipresent threats of censorship, students increasingly accept that eliminating the opinions they dislike is a legitimate option. If you have not been taught to debate but instead have learned that painful interaction with your fellow students is a sign of something gone wrong, it makes a primitive kind of sense to shut down and destroy opinions that you disagree with or view as offensive. Students haven't learned how to deal with opponents like adults; they have been taught that their fellow classmates are children who cannot handle having their feelings hurt or their beliefs challenged, and who therefore need to be protected. In other words, today's students have been taught to think like censors.

So, which is more worrisome: crusaders who believe censorship is a romantic, noble, and moral pursuit; or students who think they should not be inconvenienced by speech? I tend to think that the romantics are more dangerous, as an anti-free-speech morality is a formidable force. Yet there is something insidious about speech being blotted out for reasons of cold self-interest, compounded by ignorance of what that action really means. Besides, it is often hard to tell where one motivation ends and the other begins. What isn't hard to discern is that both ideological and self-serving censorship are alive and well on campus, and they affect more than student newspapers.

Student Government Gone Wild

Something that should probably keep you up at night is the fact that student governments, which are often seen as training grounds for future politicians and lawmakers, harbor attitudes towards basic free speech and due process rights that are more akin to petty dictatorships than to the American Founding Fathers. In fact, early on at FIRE, we decided that we could not intervene every time a student government tried to do something that was an insane violation of student rights unless the college declined to take action to prevent the student government from following through. The first reason for this is that colleges have a nondelegable duty to protect the constitutional rights of their students and their contractual promises of student rights. Second, if we did try to take on student governments every time they attempted to violate student rights, we would need a staff many times our current size.

A case that is almost beyond parody occurred in 2008 at the University of Wisconsin–Milwaukee (UWM), where the student government passed legislation that the sponsors named the "Sedition Act." That's right, the Sedition Act. The legislation promised action and "civil relief" in the case of any students who "disseminate[d] untrue or otherwise misleading statements about the Student Association."[25] Apparently, the student government at UWM was not aware that America's own 1798 "Alien and Sedition Acts" are now considered to virtually define unconstitutionality and are invoked as a shameful moment in American history, not one to be emulated. The fact that an attempt to force this rule would've put the University of Wisconsin System yet again at the losing end of a free speech lawsuit also didn't seem to concern these young politicians.[26] Thankfully, after the Student Press Law Center, the local ACLU, and the UWM students and faculty heartily condemned the act and pointed out that it would be laughed out of court, the student government vetoed it two days after passing it.[27]

Another college whose student government had an impressively short memory was the College at Brockport (State University of New York), which had repealed its unconstitutional speech code in 2005 in the face of a FIRE-coordinated lawsuit.[28] But in 2011, the SUNY Brockport student government threatened the student newspaper, *The Stylus*, for publishing a negative story about it.[29] Besides demanding the author's resignation from the newspaper, the student government also claimed that *The Stylus* should understand it was only an arm of the student government. This self-serving claim of authorial control over student publications should come as no surprise, since many college administrations, including Harvard, have taken authorial control of once independently run alumni magazines.[30]

At the University of Massachusetts Amherst in 2009, students organized to get rid of copies of a conservative newspaper that mocked student government officials.[31] A UMass police officer stood by as angry students tore copies of the newspaper out of the hands of another student. Rather than distance itself from this effort at censorship, the student government later passed a resolution in support of shutting down the newspaper if it did not apologize for mocking them. The university eventually rejected the resolution to punish the paper, but only after FIRE stepped in.[32]

A banana republic–worthy incident took place at the Community College of Rhode Island in 2010, when the chief executor of the paper reported that the president of the student government had locked the paper out of its office and would only grant access back to the paper in exchange for positive coverage.[33] A year earlier, at West Georgia College, the student government eliminated all funding of the student paper the *West Georgian* after it published articles critical of the student government.[34] It is well-settled constitutional law, by the way, that student governments cannot use student fees to punish student newspapers or student groups on the basis of their viewpoint.

Many student governments are oblivious not only to laws that make it unconstitutional for them to act like tyrants, but also to the philosophical and moral reasons why they shouldn't. Take, for example, East Carolina University, which in 2011 prevented any funding of a Young Americans for Liberty (not to be confused with Young Americans for Freedom) "Hemp Fest" event.[35] Despite the fact that hemp is perfectly legal, the student government justified its action with little more than its discomfort with the event. A similar case took place at Northern Illinois University, where the student government refused to recognize a chapter of Students for Sensible Drug Policy, attempting to justify this by passing a rule that prevented both political and religious groups from receiving funding.[36] The supposedly broad-based rule could be enforced only with double standards; the school was funding a model UN and an environmentalist group, and granting full recognition to a victims' rights group that was engaged in lobbying. I have run into the same kind of excuse to ban groups many times. In 2005, to give a notable case, the University of Wisconsin–Eau Claire refused to fund *The Flip Side*, a politically liberal student newspaper, because it did not have a "neutral viewpoint."[37] This is a remarkable inversion of the law, which requires the student government to be "viewpoint-neutral" in how they hand out student fees and explicitly prevents them from discriminating against groups on the basis of their viewpoint. The paper would continue battle with the student government for years.

The follies of student government are vast and would make for a great satirical novel. However, we should not be lighthearted about the fact that so many of these burgeoning young politicians think even the most clearly self-

serving act of censorship is acceptable. Of course, there are student governments out there that excel in protecting freedom of speech; unfortunately, I
have found them to be overwhelmingly in the minority.

The "Irvine 11": Misunderstanding Free Speech

Some campus controversies gain national attention for campus speech rights
even though they involve a profound misunderstanding of freedom of speech.
On February 8, 2010, students who were affiliated with the Muslim Student
Union at the University of California, Irvine orchestrated prolonged and
repeated disruptions of a speech by the Israeli ambassador Michael Oren.[38]
During the speech, no fewer than ten students stood up and screamed at the
ambassador. Having watched the video repeatedly, I can tell that their remarks
were prepared, but it is very difficult to make out what many of them were
saying because the rest of the organized students screamed so loudly in support of the disruption that even the disruptors could not be heard.[39]

UC Irvine officials repeatedly came up and explained that this behavior
was against the university's policies, that it was an attempt to disrupt a speech,
and that students who continued would be punished. The students did continue, however, culminating in the ambassador having to stop the speech
and return later, once again to be met with repeated attempts to shout him
down. The group, somewhat ironically, finally staged a mass exit before the
question-and-answer period—the time when students could have challenged
Oren directly.

It's hard for me to imagine that anyone watching the video of Oren's
disrupted speech could come to any other conclusion than that this was an
orchestrated act of civil disobedience that was hostile to the value of free and
open discourse, not supportive of it. Nonetheless, many students have angrily
asked me why FIRE has never come out in support of the "Irvine 11" after the
university chose to prosecute them under criminal law. The latest discussion I
had about this was in late 2011 at UCLA, where a student told me that people
suspected FIRE had decided not to defend the students due to what, frankly,
sounded to me like a Jewish conspiracy theory. As a Catholic-raised atheist, I
found this insinuation bizarre on many levels. It is true that the university's
decision to subject the students to criminal prosecution was a step beyond
what I would've done had I been the local prosecutor, but the students at UC

Irvine were on the wrong side of free speech, and we would no more defend them than we would the students who tried to shut down Chris Lee's play. Too many students seem to believe they have a free speech right to take over or in some cases completely shut down speech they dislike. This is a perversion of what free speech means, but should we really be surprised given the terrible example that administrators have been setting for decades?

Student Censorship of the Right

In 2006, an incident at Columbia University took me by surprise. During a speech by Jim Gilchrist, the founder of the anti-illegal-immigration group the Minutemen, students rushed the stage to chase him off, while their classmates in the audience howled in approval. The video circulated the world, eliciting condemnation by everyone from Fox News to Jon Stewart.[40] But the students' behavior was not what shocked me; I see incidents like this on a fairly regular basis on campuses across the country. What took me by surprise was that, after years of student censorship being ignored, this was the case that got worldwide attention. The crucial factor was the then relatively new phenomenon of YouTube. Watching students at an elite college chase off an unpopular speaker was a novelty—for the moment.

Unfortunately, future incidents would not catch the public's attention in quite the same way. In April 2009, when Congressman Tom Tancredo—who is known for being a vociferous opponent of illegal immigration—attempted to speak at the University of North Carolina at Chapel Hill, some students went to battle, interrupting the speech several times and shattering a window during the protest.[41] This out-of-control behavior caused the event to be shut down. When the university allowed the student group to invite another opponent of illegal immigration to campus, students tried again (this time unsuccessfully) to halt the event, going so far as to pull fire alarms. In the same month, students at the University of Massachusetts Amherst shouted down a speech by Don Feder, a conservative columnist.[42]

Unsurprisingly, pro-lifers often face student-led censorship on campuses. For example, in 2008, students at Missouri State University (the same university that had recently interrogated Emily Brooker) stepped on, crushed, and rode their bikes over an administration-permitted pro-life display of tiny wooden crosses.[43] Much of this vandalism was filmed and posted online.

When the pro-life group confronted one of the vandals and asked her why she did it, the student proudly replied on camera, "I feel like I have the right to walk across campus without seeing that."[44]

Online, you can also see a video of another 2008 case in which Roderick King, a student at the University of Wisconsin–Stevens Point and member of the student government, tore up crosses that were part of a pro-life display while shouting, "Since [abortion] is a right, you don't have the right to challenge it."[45] It is hard to overstate what a fundamental misunderstanding of basic rights this statement represents. And even without Professor Sally Jacobsen (see Chapter 9) to lead them, students once again tore down the crosses of a pro-life display at Northern Kentucky University in 2010.[46] The university made the news again in April 2012, when three students were arrested for tearing down yet another pro-life display, this time of baby clothes with a red "X" (to indicate an aborted baby) marked through every fourth garment. This vandalism took place three times before the students were caught. When questioned about his motives, one of the vandals attempted to twist the First Amendment to justify his actions: "Tearing it down was expressing our right to free speech."[47]

The quotes from the censoring students in these cases demonstrate a strange inversion of the idea of rights. Students have internalized the idea that it's a violation of their own rights to be presented with arguments, protests, or displays that disturb or offend them—and that they have the *right* to silence those arguments or destroy the displays. Some antics by students are surreal, including Ann Coulter being hit by a pie at the University of Arizona or Pat Buchanan being doused with salad dressing during his speech at Western Michigan University.[48] But few campus speakers have as many stories to tell as David Horowitz, a former leftist who is now a conservative writer and the founder of Students for Academic Freedom.

Horowitz has been the target of pie hurling himself. During a speech at Butler University on April 6, 2005, he was struck by a pie—just eight days after the conservative pundit Bill Kristol was "pied" at Earlham College.[49] In November 2006, a student at Ball State University threw a pie at Horowitz during a speech about the political agendas of university professors.[50] When Horowitz attempted to give a speech on "Islamo-Fascism" at Emory University in October 2007, calling attention to the horrific practice of female genital mutilation, he was forced to leave the stage after a protestor shouted, "'Everyone stand up! They can't take all of us!'"[51] Some universities have even refused to allow him to give a speech or engage in a debate. Saint Louis University banned Horowitz from speaking on campus twice in less than six months. In September 2009, administrators would not permit Horowitz to speak on "Islamo-Fascism"; the university claimed that the issue was too divisive and that Horowitz was required to have a speaker with an opposing viewpoint on stage.[52] He attempted to address those concerns in February 2010, changing the topic of his speech to academic freedom and inviting a strong critic of his (Cary Nelson, president of the American Association of University Professors) to appear with him on stage for a debate.[53] This time, the administration decided that Horowitz needed to invite a *third* speaker who represented a Catholic perspective.[54] Nelson also criticized the university for its position. "I think what the university is now trying to do is not so much offensive as completely ludicrous," he was quoted as saying; it was "as if the keystone cops" had responsibility for academic freedom at Saint Louis University.[55]

The sad truth is that university administrators often play a role in the censorship of speakers, and sometimes even encourage students to disrupt them, just like in the Chris Lee case at Washington State University. One administrator certainly crossed that line when Roger Clegg, president of the Center for Equal Opportunity, gave a press conference near the University of Wisconsin–Madison on September 13, 2011. Clegg was giving a speech critical of affirmative action in college admissions at the Madison Doubletree Hotel and was scheduled to participate in a debate at the university later in the day. On September 12, Damon Williams, UW–Madison's vice provost for diversity and climate, posted an "Important Invitation to Students" on the university's website, calling Clegg's press conference "a threat to our diversity efforts" and urging students "to participate so we can be in community regarding our response."[56] More than 150 students showed up to the meeting, where Williams "stressed the need for students to mobilize," and told them, "'Don't wait for us to show the way.'"[57]

The students took Williams at his word and began to plan an attack. The following day, they left campus and reached the Doubletree Hotel as Clegg was finishing his press conference. Pushing past the hotel staff and even throwing some of them to the ground, they poured into the room.[58] According to Peter Wood of the National Association of Scholars, Clegg fought his way through the mob towards an exit and entered an elevator, but the protestors continued to pursue him. They held the elevator doors open until hotel staff members managed to push them back. Vice Provost Williams actually attended the press conference (although he left before the violence broke out) and later had the audacity to praise the mob's actions from his official university Twitter account: "*Back in Bascom. Students were awesome.*"[59] No students were arrested for their actions, and Williams remains vice provost for diversity and climate.

"I Believe in Free Speech ... Except When I Don't Like It": Students Come to Expect Protection from Free Speech

Not so long ago, I was contacted by Nadine Strossen, former president of the ACLU and a member of the editorial board for our Student Guide series. She wanted to know if there were some legal development she was unaware of to explain why she was suddenly getting calls to speak on campus about "hate speech." Nadine was perplexed because she believed that this was an old fight that had been fought and won in the 1990s, and that there was no new argument to be made. I told her that while no courts have ever recognized anything like a "hate speech" exception to the First Amendment, for some reason the concept that "hate speech" is a form of unprotected speech remains tremendously popular on campus. This is problematic for a number of reasons, not the least of which is that nobody really seems to know what "hate speech" means. Wikipedia defines it as, "outside the law, any communication that disparages a person or a group on the basis of some characteristic such as race or sexual orientation," but even this expansive definition does not contain the extent to which allegations of hate speech are tossed around on campus.

One of my favorite examples comes out of Gonzaga University in Washington, where conservative students had posted flyers for a speech by the author Dan Flynn back in 2003.[60] The flyers prominently featured the title of Flynn's book *Why the Left Hates America*. They were taken down by administrators who argued that they constituted hate speech because they included the word "hate." This standard would, of course, make hate speech a very hard thing to fight, as battling hate speech without using the word "hate" would be quite a challenge. Perhaps the administrators could rename it h-speech to avoid this problem? The university backed away from the decision after FIRE became involved.[61]

Identifying something as "hate speech" has become an irresistible rhetorical tool precisely because evoking "hate" is so effective at shutting down painful or difficult campus debates. It plays on the guilt and compassion of those who hear the accusation and casts suspicion on anyone who should question it. Once you dub something hate speech, defending it implies that you, well, love hate. The fact that students still use the term "hate speech" is a public relations victory for the advocates of collegiate censorship.

A quick review of student editorials demonstrates that many students believe hate speech is not protected speech. Perhaps it is the vagueness of the concept that explains its popularity as an emotional cudgel to delegitimize ideas that someone dislikes. It probably wouldn't surprise anyone that the term is invoked to argue for punishing, banning, or suppressing everything from the image of Santa Claus in a bear suit on a 2010 episode of *South Park* (because he was pretending to be the prophet Mohammed in a bear suit), to Ann Coulter, to the speech by Don Feder at the University of Massachusetts Amherst, to Kanye West for his mean interruption of Taylor Swift's acceptance speech at the MTV Video Music Awards in 2009.[62]

A perfect example of the campus outrage machine came out of Cornell in March 2012. Students defaced dozens of posters for a show by the Asian American comedian Margaret Cho, whose performance sponsors included Cornell's African, Latino, Asian, Native American (ALANA) Programming Board.[63] The objection? The poster, which had been approved by Cho's management, used the font called Chop Suey, which resembles the one used on Chinese restaurant menus. Following the vandalism, the community was assailed by angry missives from a shadowy "antiracist" group calling itself Scorpions X, condemning the university as if it had committed an atrocity. The university and ALANA, of course, apologized to the vandals and sought to make amends, but the righteous outrage of Scorpions X could not be assuaged.[64] The group rejected ALANA's apology and, perhaps fearing they hadn't caricatured themselves enough, claimed they had been unfairly painted as "militant, confrontational, and angry." Even though Margaret Cho's shtick often relies on an ironic twist on racist stereotypes, and the Chop Suey font seemed to be in that spirit of playful irony, Cho herself joined the hand wringing. She claimed that she was "numb" to the hurtfulness of the typography and was used to "swallowing racism down without argument or splatter."[65] Worse, Cho endorsed the methods of Scorpions X, saying she "appreciate[d] the effort that someone has gone to on my behalf." Here we see the will to be offended, the desire to grandstand, and, for Cho, one of the most remarkable applications of selective uptightness I've ever seen, all working together to turn an Ivy League college into a frenzy over a font.

A video filmed at California State University, Fresno in 2011 further reveals that students who profess to believe in freedom of speech are willing to advocate for remarkably broad measures to suppress speech.[66] In the video, several members of the campus community, both young and old, were approached with a petition to remove talk show hosts including Rush Limbaugh and Glenn Beck from the radio and to "limit the speech of conservatives and Republicans" on air. Many of the students who signed the petition explained that they did so because figures like Beck were "not nice" or engaged in hateful speech: "What bothers me [is] the spewing of hatred." Oddly, several of the signees specifically asserted their belief in freedom of speech while signing the petition. One man stated, "Come on, man, this is America! Really? You know, these guys should have an opportunity to be able to express their opinions." Yet he went on to sign the petition, declaring, "I hate them bastards." It would be difficult to better encapsulate the hypocrisy in how "hate speech" is often invoked: it doesn't mean targeting hate itself (hating conservatives was clearly fine), it means targeting opinions you dislike.

Infecting the Law Schools and Infecting the Law

While I was in law school in the late '90s, free speech was already getting a pretty bum rap among many students. I was surprised by how hostile some of my fellow students and instructors were to my internship at the ACLU of Northern California—not because they were right-wingers who hated the ACLU, but rather because they thought of free speech as that pesky principle that got in the way of admirable hate speech prohibitions and campus speech codes.

Law school should be expected to cultivate some greater respect for free speech by its very nature. When you argue all day long, you get used to hearing arguments that offend you, fact patterns that shock you, and ideas that do not comport with your own beliefs. For this reason, law schools *should* be unusually resistant to the idea of limiting free speech. But this resistance has failed over the past decades, with schools like my alma mater Stanford leading the way: in the early '90s, the law school helped Stanford University pass its own speech code. (It was later ruled a violation of the state's "Leonard Law.") I fear that the belief in free speech and even the understanding of the principle are being eroded over time by the implicit acceptance of "benign" censorship on campus and in society as a whole.

A scant regard for free speech was on display among students and faculty at Syracuse University College of Law (SUCOL) in 2010, when some students complained about crude comments on a satirical blog about life in law school, called SUCOLitis. In response, Professor Gregory Germain acted as a self-styled "independent prosecutor" and launched a months-long investigation of Len Audaer, a student at the law school, for his alleged involvement with the blog. The professor threatened to have Audaer expelled, even though the material on the SUCOLitis blog would plainly have been protected as satire and parody under the First Amendment—and under Syracuse's own free speech promises.[67] The school backed down only after I named it one of the worst schools for freedom of speech in my first-ever list of such offenders in the *Huffington Post*.[68]

In the summer of 2010, I was a guest on the Fox Business Network show *Stossel* discussing free speech on campus. During the program, the host John Stossel showed a video of his interview with students at Seton Hall Law School. He was pretty shocked to discover that even law students had adopted the "I believe in free speech, but ..." attitude. Stossel said that most students did offer some defense of free speech, but many suggested that the following categories should not be protected: hate speech, flag burning, blasphemy, corporate speech, and—going a large step beyond normal cruelty rationales—videos of people hunting. Taken together, these exceptions could ban everything from the ACLU or FIRE defending the rights of students (both groups are corporations) to Martin Luther's 95 Theses (considered blasphemy by many in Luther's day), and could be used to punish every incidence of protected expression cited in this book.

A favorable view of "well-meaning" censorship is not limited to Seton Hall. In April 2009, the *Harvard Law Review* published an unsigned student comment (the law student equivalent of a law review article) that vehemently disagreed with the decision by the Third Circuit Court of Appeals in 2008 to overturn Temple University's speech code.[69] The comment was a sweeping defense of harassment-based campus speech codes, arguing that they were constitutional on a wide variety of grounds.

As my former colleague Kelly Sarabyn pointed out on FIRE's blog, the comment *failed to cite a single case in the twenty-year history of speech code litigation* (over a dozen decisions overturning campus speech codes, as of this writing), misrepresented and ignored relevant Supreme Court holdings, and matter-of-factly asserted that college students should have even fewer rights to speak freely than grade school students or private employees in professional offices.[70]

It is more than disturbing that students who work for what is almost certainly the most influential law journal in American history would ignore the law and aggressively come to the defense of campus speech codes.[71] As a result, the hundreds if not thousands of scofflaw institutions that maintain speech codes were handed ammunition with which to defend their codes. And yes, even a sloppy, unsigned student comment in the *Harvard Law Review* helps their case. In fact, almost as soon as the comment was published, it was cited in a motion defending a campus speech code in a case in Los Angeles.

Most troubling is that this comment demonstrates that after decades of university attempts to dupe the public into believing that speech codes are okay by recharacterizing them as harassment policies, people in influential positions are starting to believe it. If you repeat a lie long enough, people forget what the truth is. If lawyers come to agree that free speech should be curtailed for the greater good, their views will eventually be reflected in the law itself.

As Learned Hand observed, a popular belief in the importance of the values inherent in the U.S. Constitution may be more important than the Constitution itself. If citizens are promised certain rights by law but nobody knows they have them—or enough people believe they shouldn't have them—the law ends up mattering little.

We should not take our current strong interpretation of the First Amendment for granted. It was only in the 1920s that the Supreme Court recognized that the First Amendment protected American citizens from infringements on their free speech rights by state governments, not just the federal government, and it was not until the second half of the twentieth century that these protections were found to be as powerful and expansive as those we take for granted today. Prior to that, as argued by Michael Kent Curtis in *Free Speech, "The People's Darling Privilege,"* the strongest protections of freedom of speech came not from the courts but from a shared popular belief that minority views must be protected for the sake of a healthy democracy.[72] The Founding Fathers understood that the rights enshrined in the Bill of Rights would be best protected when individual citizens internalized these principles as personal values.

In the very same way, however, the ideology behind censorship can also become an internalized value, and colleges, through example and miseducation, are teaching students the wrong lessons about freedom of speech. Public opinion plays a significant role in influencing how laws and even constitutional amendments are interpreted. If a generation of students is consistently shown and taught that censorship is not only acceptable but may even be a noble or romantic pursuit, one would expect to see the robust protections that we currently enjoy under the First Amendment erode, not only in the court of public opinion but eventually in the courts of law.

"Bullying," the "Blame Free Speech First" Attitude, and What It Means for All of Our Liberties

The fact that negative attitudes about the right to free speech are penetrating beyond the walls of campus and into our society becomes clearer by the day. These attitudes are increasingly focused on blaming free speech itself when bad things happen, as was the case in the immediate reactions to the mass shootings in Tucson, Arizona, in early 2011. It was also apparent in the wake of Tyler Clementi's tragic suicide in the fall of 2010.

Clementi, a freshman at Rutgers University, killed himself after discovering that two students, one of whom was his roommate, had used a webcam to spy on him during a same-sex encounter in his dorm room and had broadcast the video through social media. Clementi complained to his resident assistant about his roommate's shocking behavior, and shortly thereafter jumped to his death from the George Washington Bridge.

This is a heartbreaking story, and few would deny that what Clementi's roommate did to him was unconscionable. However, this invasion of privacy was already a crime under New Jersey state law and a violation of Rutgers' existing policies.[73] Free speech does not mean that you have a right to spy on people when they're engaged in intimate behavior in the presumed privacy of their own rooms. No new laws needed to be passed in order to prevent a tragedy like this; rather, the ones already in existence simply needed to be enforced. What lay at the heart of the Clementi case had nothing to do with free speech; it was a criminal invasion of privacy.

Nonetheless, legislators and commentators across the country invoked the now well-known yet loosely defined offense of "bullying" and proceeded to call for an expansion of the law to increase the scope of regulations of hurtful speech on campus. The problem is that advocates of these antibullying laws seem confused about the crucial differences between adults and children (and thus between the college and grade school settings), and also confused about the difference between what can and should be banned—like stalking, vandalism, actual harassment, or true threats—and what cannot and should not be banned—like coarse, sharp, or merely hurtful speech. That this new national campaign against bullying is a threat to free speech may not be immediately obvious; but it is dangerous because it takes our deep and righteous anger over the cruelty of children to other children, and harnesses it to efforts at policing the everyday interactions of adults. By dubbing words as "bullying," you gain the same uncritically emotional reaction that any allegation of harassment once held, whether reasonable or not. When that is accomplished, the allegation of "bullying" speech becomes yet another trump card that chills free speech and closes down open discussion and candor.

The idea that we should campaign against hurtful speech among adults arises from a failure to understand that free speech is our chosen method of resolving disagreements, using words rather than weapons. Open debate is our enlightened means of determining nothing less than how we order our society, what is true and what is false, what wars we should fight, what policies we should pass, whom we should put behind bars for the rest of their lives, and who gets to control our government. This is a deadly serious business. While protecting *children* from abuse is a noble goal, an overly expansive definition of bullying cannot be allowed to hobble the gravely important exchange of ideas among *adults* upon which our nation depends. The new emphasis on collegiate "bullying" treats adults like kindergarteners and forgets entirely the gravity of the issues we face in our democracy every single day and the rightful passions they ignite.

But legislators, often with the encouragement of students and activists, have moved ahead to pass vague and broad laws designed to stamp out the social evil of adult-on-adult "bullying." In the fall of 2010, Senator Frank Lautenberg and Representative Rush Holt, both of New Jersey, sponsored a bill in Congress called the Tyler Clementi Higher Education Anti-Harassment Act.[74] If passed into law, the Tyler Clementi Act would dramatically contradict the controlling standard for student-on-student (or peer) harassment in the educational setting, as laid out by the Supreme Court in its 1999 decision *Davis* v. *Monroe County Board of Education*.[75] Specifically, the law would eliminate the objective, "reasonable person" component from the Supreme Court's definition of peer harassment, meaning that harassment could be deemed to have taken place even when a reasonable person would not have found the behavior harassing. This omission means that the most sensitive students—or those most aggressive in their drive to silence "offensive" opinions—could be granted the power to decide what can and cannot be said on campus. Unfortunately, Lautenberg and Holt missed the more than two decades' worth of legal precedent that has defined peer harassment as speech that is not merely subjectively offensive to any particular person, but part of a serious pattern of behavior directed at someone on the basis of gender, race, or similar immutable characteristics that effectively denies that person equal access to an education.

Lautenberg and Holt were also either unaware or unconcerned that the bill promises to condemn colleges to decades more of losing litigation, as attempts to impose the new definition of peer harassment run into the reality of administrators' often overzealous desire to punish speech they dislike.

The same impulses led the New Jersey legislature to pass an even more expansive antibullying bill in the wake of the Clementi tragedy. The new bill—signed into law by Governor Chris Christie in early 2011—is a disaster for student speech. In defining "harassment, intimidation and bullying," it reproduces the worst flaws of the Tyler Clementi Higher Education Anti-Harassment Act and then makes things worse still. For one thing, the law requires every college in New Jersey to enforce a policy outlawing speech that "has the effect of insulting or demeaning any student or group of students," places a student in "reasonable fear" of "emotional harm," or "severely or pervasively" causes "emotional harm."[76] Of course, without an objective, reasonable person standard, the most hypersensitive and easily offended students will be able to decide what speech is and is not "insulting," "demeaning," or "emotionally harmful."[77] The new law also ignores the fact that colleges and universities are *already* required by federal law to prohibit harassment—so, as a result of this new state law, the federal definition of peer harassment supplied by the Supreme Court and the state definition of harassment provided by New Jersey's legislation are now at odds.

A number of states are following New Jersey's lead, drafting laws that would impose new restrictions and regulations as part of an effort to eliminate "bullying" and offensive speech on campus. For example, in March 2012, the Arizona State Legislature passed a law declaring that it is unlawful "for any person, with intent to terrify, intimidate, threaten, harass, annoy or offend, to use any electronic or digital device and use any obscene, lewd or profane language or suggest any lewd or lascivious act."[78] Despite the law's clear unconstitutionality—does Arizona really wish to punish any online speech that is merely intended to "annoy" someone, or that includes "lewd" or "profane" language?—the law passed both legislative houses.[79] Thankfully, citing the First Amendment concerns expressed by many commentators, Arizona lawmakers then decided to review the bill again.[80] Among those who had voiced their free speech concerns were Eugene Volokh, a law professor and noted First Amendment scholar, and Harvey Silverglate.[81] As of this writing, the bill remains under review by members of the Arizona legislature.

Similarly, a bill introduced in Connecticut's legislature in March 2012 defines "Electronic Harassment" as any electronic transmission of information that (a) is based on a person's "actual or perceived traits or characteristics," (b) causes that person "substantial embarrassment or humiliation within an academic or professional community," and (c) is done with the intent to "annoy" or "alarm" the person.[82] In 2011, Tennessee enacted a law that made it illegal to "transmit or display an image" electronically without a "legitimate purpose" if (a) one does so with "the malicious intent to frighten, intimidate or cause emotional distress" or "[i]n a manner the defendant knows, or reasonably should know, would frighten, intimidate or cause emotional distress to a similarly situated person of reasonable sensibilities," and (b) "[a]s the result of the communication, the person is frightened, intimidated or emotionally distressed."[83] Finally, in February 2012, Alabama's legislature introduced a bill that defines "cyberbullying," in relevant part, as (a) transmitting, posting, displaying or disseminating, through electronic communications "with the intent to harass, annoy, or alarm," (b) any communication, image, or information that is (c) based on the actual or perceived traits of the recipient and that (d) "has the effect of causing substantial embarrassment or humiliation within an academic or professional community."[84] Each of these laws or proposed laws is pretty clearly unconstitutional on its face, yet that hasn't deterred public servants sworn to uphold the Constitution from drafting or enacting them.

The solution to bullying is ultimately a cultural one. That is, our culture should not tolerate seriously abusive acts of children against children. But that cultural transformation is well underway, with multimillion-dollar media campaigns letting students know that bullying is not okay and that "it gets better." Free speech isn't the problem; it is, once again, the solution, especially as it also allows important critical voices to push back when crusades to address moral panics go too far.

Unfortunately, there are many forces at work that will co-opt any cause they can find to treat free speech like a hostile, stubborn legalism standing in the way of progress. The ongoing deterioration of First Amendment rights at our universities in particular has wreaked havoc on our national discourse and threatens to undo the right of free speech itself. Unless colleges do a better job of teaching students that free speech is the solution far more often than the problem, the days of free speech being strongly protected may be behind us and the marketplace of ideas will be forever distorted.

Unlearning Liberty
and the Knee-Jerk Society

Throughout this book, I have shown examples of both policies and practices that are teaching students the wrong lessons about what it means to live in a free society. These stories represent only a tiny percentage of the outrageous cases I have seen over the last decade, and there are assuredly many more violations of free speech rights on campus that never reach our attention at FIRE. It takes a rare student (and an even rarer faculty member) to stand up to infringements on their rights. Most students will choose to go along to get along rather than take on the administration; and given the poor state of education about basic constitutional rights, many of these students probably don't even know that their rights are being violated in the first place.

Taken together, the threat of punishment for expressing the wrong thoughts, the omnipresence of codes warning students to be careful about what they say, and the politicized, self-serving redefinition of tolerance and civility all reinforce the social pressure to either half-mindedly agree or avoid vigorous debate altogether. Analysts of higher education have noted this reticence in the "millennial generation," but they often characterize it as a historical peculiarity, sometimes attributing it to a more "collectivist" ethic that somehow materialized among today's younger people. Few have considered that this hesitance to debate has been habituated in part through coercion by those in charge—through a perfect storm of feeble free speech rights in K–12 schooling, a lack of meaningful civics education, and a collegiate environment that makes dissent too risky.

The modern academy has the power to move our nation closer to or further from liberty. By threatening or punishing mainstream (and yes, often socially conservative) opinions on campus, academic authorities are dismissing the views of many Americans and silencing important public discussions. They are also marginalizing higher education itself. In this time of hyperpartisanship, universities could help bridge that political gulf by fostering discussions across political and personal divides. If they continue selectively silencing voices they disagree with, however, they will never be trusted to take on that role. Unless speech codes, campus censorship, and the heavy-handed techniques that stifle debate come to an end, the academy cannot expect to be treated as the honest broker we so desperately need in the arena of political and cultural controversy. In fact, until then, the academy won't deserve that role.

When you remove the process of open debate and discussion from colleges, you take away higher education's reason for existence. An educational system in which the authorities believe they should decide what is right without being questioned is more like a seminary or madrassa, not anything deserving of the name *university*. Without an open process of debate and discussion, we can expect the ideas produced by academics to grow increasingly incoherent and useless to our society.

Ending illiberal lessons and censorship on campus will not, by itself, end the culture wars. But if higher education would live up to its highest function by teaching students that it's okay to disagree, that thought experiments— even those that offend us—are crucial parts of intellectual development, that ideals we disdain may hold some element of truth we had not previously considered, and that concepts that at first seem outlandish might, in fact, be paths to greater insight, it could revitalize itself and, in turn, renew the national discourse. In order to impart these values, it is not sufficient that censorship merely stop; students need to be taught to actively seek out opinions and information that contradict what they believe, and to take the risk of being wrong in the process of hypothesizing solutions. Colleges are uniquely situated to counter the bad intellectual habits our country has developed— and even to spread strong intellectual habits throughout the world with the help of their international students. We could break from our information cocoons and become more nimble and agile thinkers if we were trained to approach ideas and arguments, satire and parody with enthusiasm as opposed to reluctance, fear, and caution.

I can say one thing about the future with great confidence: change is coming to higher education. In retrospect, the '90s and the '00s seem like a fantasy world where the price of college could keep on expanding into infinity, much like the prices of American real estate. This bubble, too, was bound to burst. Multiple studies now show that college students are paying more than ever and going into a lifetime of debt to learn less than they ever have before—and people on the right, left, and center are demanding change, calling for higher education that is leaner and cheaper, as well as more rigorous. My great hope is that the essentiality of free and open give-and-take will be rediscovered in this coming transformation. The encouragement of free thought and open discussion is key to developing a better class of students, a new generation of creative thinkers, a more interesting curriculum, and a more productive national dialogue.

Unfortunately, too many of our educators today are ambivalent about free speech, imagining that if they really did allow all opinions to be expressed, the result would be a nightmarish landscape of nonstop bigotry and ignorance. I think this apocalyptic point of view, which masquerades as sophistication, is a childish oversimplification of the actual interaction of people in everyday life and especially in an academic setting. But perhaps more importantly, the advocates of benign censorship fundamentally miss a simple truth that Buddhists have known for millennia: life is pain. Most Americans find this statement jarring at first, but when you think about it for even a moment and accept that there is nothing strange or odd about the challenges inherent in being alive, life becomes less painful. As philosophers and popular writers have argued, much of our unnecessary emotional pain comes from our obsession with avoiding pain. The sometimes painful process of intellectual growth and living in the world needs to be accepted, not fled from, and that acceptance needs to be taught. If you warn students that an unnatural, unforgivable crime has taken place anytime they are offended or challenged, you are dooming them to a life of feeling like they are constantly under attack. After all, there is no perfect escape from pain, ignorance, human failings, or challenging ideas. And even if there were, I don't believe anyone would really want to live in that cave.

Committing yourself to practicing the intellectual habits of a free people, on the other hand, can lead to a sense of liberation. It means that you can learn to handle arguments that go against everything you wish to be true, and in the end be wiser; it empowers you to sort through those challenges with humility and reason. While free speech certainly does not mean the end of ignorance, biases, or prejudices, it does mean that *you* are empowered—not controlled by paternalistic authority figures with biases, ignorance, and prejudices of their own—to navigate your own way through life, understanding that even an ignorant argument is an opportunity to increase your knowledge of the world, your fellow human beings, and yourself. We must stop apologizing for believing in free speech and embrace it as the best tool we have yet devised for the growth of knowledge and understanding.

It may surprise you to hear at this point that I deeply loved my academic experiences in college and law school. I value those moments when I had to bend my mind to understand why I was wrong on a particular issue I'd always thought was clear-cut. I love the chaotic paradise that universities can be. The promise of a population educated in the best traditions of higher education is nothing less than thrilling. Imagine a national dialogue where most of our citizenry critically examine the debates of the day instead of falling back on sound bites or the beliefs of their parents or peer groups. Imagine a country where disagreement is welcome, where thought experimentation and playful candor are encouraged, where people are at peace with the knowledge that they might be proven wrong. To me, at least, that place sounds like heaven compared to the bipolar mindlessness of today's public square.

Things are going to change for higher education; there can be no doubt about it. But maybe in this coming transformation, we will remember that the best hope for the advancement and improvement of our society is to educate the next generation in the exciting and liberating intellectual habits of free human beings.

Acknowledgments

In late fall 2001, I found myself in a windowless office in Philadelphia sifting through piles of case submissions from students and faculty members across the country who needed help protecting their basic freedom of speech and due process rights. The piles had been building since the Foundation for Individual Rights in Education's founding in 1999 and it seemed as though I would never reach the bottom. Though I studied First Amendment law and had been an avid student of the history of free speech for some time, I was not prepared for the brazenly unconstitutional and hypocritical behavior that I would discover in those files. I had seen free speech controversies during my time at Stanford and American University and read of them in Alan Charles Kors and Harvey Silverglate's *The Shadow University: The Betrayal of Liberty on America's Campuses,* but it was quite another thing to talk to frightened students and realize that academic careers were being ruined despite the clarity of the law and the basic values of higher education. We were a very small organization and there was no way we could assist all those pleading for help, but it was not long before I started thinking that someone had to write a book that picked up where *The Shadow University* left off and tried to explain the seriousness of the situation on campus. *Unlearning Liberty* is my attempt to do justice to the plight of these students and faculty, both those we could help and those we couldn't.

As with any large-scale undertaking, the number of people who need to be thanked are far too numerous; countless friends, colleagues, and generous FIRE supporters made this possible. I'd also like to note that while most abuses of student rights have been committed by campus administrators, there are many good administrators across the country who have directly worked with FIRE or referred wronged students to us. We wish every campus administrator shared such a commitment to free speech, due process, and the values of a liberal education.

I would first like to thank the people who helped day after day to get this book ready. Chief among them is my dedicated, brilliant, no-nonsense assistant, Bridget Sweeney. The advice, dedication, and remarkable skill of Araz Shibley were also invaluable. The entire FIRE staff was exceedingly thoughtful and helpful during this process, especially Adam Kissel, Robert Shibley, Will Creeley, Alisha Glennon, Peter Bonilla, Azhar Majeed, Daniel Schwartz, Jaclyn Hall, and Samantha Harris. FIRE interns also proved very helpful, especially Rachel Cheeseman, who contributed her experiences to the book, and Nico Perrino, who offered advice on its later drafts.

I am especially thankful for the outstanding advice of Catherine Sevcenko and to Jonathan Rauch for introducing me to her. Similarly, Leslie Watkins was incredibly generous with her time and excellent advice, and I'd like to thank Virginia Postrel for connecting us. Of course, I want to thank my exceptional editor at Encounter Books, Carol Staswick, and the entire team there, especially their commander-in-chief, Roger Kimball.

This book would not have been possible without the support of FIRE's Board of Directors and staff, both of which gave me the time and encouragement necessary to write it. I would also like to thank four people who have been special inspirations to me: Alan Charles Kors, cofounder and chairman emeritus of FIRE and a professor at the University of Pennsylvania; Professor Kathleen Sullivan, former dean of Stanford Law School; David Rubenstein, my former boss at the EnvironMentors Project and head of the Best Shot Foundation; and Harvey Silverglate, FIRE cofounder and tireless civil liberties champion, who managed to find me in San Francisco and bring me to Philadelphia to work at FIRE.

I also want to thank my family and friends who put up with me during the antisocial depths of my "book hole."

Finally I would like to thank my fiancée, Michelle LaBlanc. I met her back in January 2010 when I first began *Unlearning Liberty*, and the week before this book is slated for release she will become my wife. She's been with me through this strangely intense, joyous, obsessive, and emotional roller coaster, and I simply cannot thank her enough.

NOTES

Since FIRE's founding in 1999, we have collected and posted online tens of thousands of documents relating to censorship on campus. Many of these are primary documents—including disciplinary letters, memos, emails—that arise directly from the cases discussed. We archive these on the FIRE website, along with media coverage of the cases, so that free speech advocates and skeptics alike can see the facts for themselves. Much of the documentation in the following notes can be found on the FIRE website.

Some material in this book has been replicated and/or updated from the author's previous columns and blog posts.

INTRODUCTION: THE DANGEROUS COLLAGE

1. T. Hayden Barnes' Letter to the Editor of VSU "Spectator," http://thefire.org/article/8525.html.

2. Photo Collage on T. Hayden Barnes' Facebook.com Page, http://thefire.org/article/8530.html.

3. Notice of Administrative Withdrawal from Valdosta State University President Ronald Zaccari to T. Hayden Barnes, http://thefire.org/article/8521.html.

4. Statement of Appeal from the Board of Regents of the University System of Georgia in T. Hayden Barnes' Case, http://thefire.org/article/8529.html.

5. FIRE's Letter to Chancellor of the University System of Georgia, Erroll B. Davis, October 23, 2007, http://thefire.org/article/8523.html.

6. Letter from Associate Vice Chancellor of the University System of Georgia, J. Burns Newsome, to FIRE, October 24, 2007, http://thefire.org/article/8583.html.

7. Malynda Fulton, "Expulsion reversed," *Valdosta Daily Times*, January 17, 2008, http://thefire.org/article/8830.html.

8. Opinion in *Barnes* v. *Zaccari*, Case No. 1:08-cv-00077-CAP (N.D. Ga. Sep. 3, 2010) (Pannell, J.), http://thefire.org/article/12223.html.

9. Ibid.

10. *Barnes* v. *Zaccari*, 669 F.3d 1295 (11th Cir. 2012), http://thefire.org/article/14137.html.

11. For a parody of some of the co-op's politics, see *The Daily Show*, March 27, 2012.

12. Derek Quizon, "Increasing Share of Adults Have College Degrees, Census Bureau Finds," *Chronicle of Higher Education*, April 26, 2011.

13. Among Brooks' many works, see his coverage of the Tucson tragedy for a sense of his views on the current state of the national dialogue: David Brooks, "The Politicized Mind," *New York Times*, January 10, 2011. Also, Paul Krugman, "Climate of Hate," *New York Times*, January 9, 2011. Jon Stewart famously mocked

the state of discourse with his "Rally to Restore Sanity" in 2010: Brian Montopoli, "Jon Stewart Rally Attracts Estimated 215,000," CBS News, October 30, 2010. Also, Kathleen Parker, "American Id-eology," *Washington Post,* March 23, 2012; Kathleen Parker, "The Omen in My Mail," *Washington Post,* October 1, 2008; Tom Brokaw, "Are We Becoming an Uncivil Society," *Time* Specials, January 19, 2011. In the wake of the Tucson tragedy, President Obama gave a speech in support of reforming American discourse. Former presidents George H.W. Bush and Bill Clinton have also commented on the issue. See Helene Cooper and Jeff Zeleny, "Obama Calls for a New Era of Civility in U.S. Politics," *New York Times,* January 12, 2011; and Allie Townsend, "What's in Bill Clinton's Head?" *Time,* October 11, 2011. Clinton and Bush also serve as honorary chairmen of the National Institute for Civil Discourse at the University of Arizona; see http://nicd.arizona.edu/.

14. Bill Bishop, *The Big Sort: Why the Clustering of Like-Minded America Is Tearing Us Apart* (New York: Houghton Mifflin, 2008); Nicholas Kristof, "The Daily Me," New York Times, March 18, 2009.

15. Charles Murray, *Coming Apart: The State of White America, 1960–2010* (New York: Crown Forum, 2012).

16. "Chancellor issues statement on Arizona shootings," Public Affairs, UC Berkeley News Center, January 10, 2011, http://newscenter.berkeley.edu/2011/01/10/arizona/.

17. Eric L. Dey, Molly C. Ott, Mary Antonaros, Cassie L. Barnhardt, and Matthew A. Holsapple, *Engaging Diverse Viewpoints: What Is the Campus Climate for Perspective-Taking?* (Washington, D.C.: Association of American Colleges and Universities, 2010), available online.

18. For example, see Mary Reda, "What's the Problem With Quiet Students? Anyone? Anyone?" *Chronicle of Higher Education,* September 5, 2010; Erin E. Templeton, "Silence Is Golden," *Chronicle of Higher Education,* January 27, 2010; Martha E. Gimenez, "Silence in the Classroom: Some Thoughts About Teaching in the 1980s," *Teaching Sociology,* vol. 17 (April 1989), pp. 184–91.

19. Diana C. Mutz, *Hearing the Other Side: Deliberative versus Participatory Democracy* (Cambridge: Cambridge University Press, 2006).

20. See generally Cass R. Sunstein, *Going to Extremes: How Like Minds Unite and Divide* (New York: Oxford University Press, 2009); and *Infotopia: How Many Minds Produce Knowledge* (New York: Oxford University Press, 2006).

21. Mark Bauerlein, *The Dumbest Generation: How the Digital Age Stupefies Young Americans and Jeopardizes Our Future (Or, Don't Trust Anyone Under 30)* (New York: Penguin Group, 2008), pp. 228–29.

22. Richard Arum and Josipa Roksa, *Academically Adrift: Limited Learning on College Campuses* (Chicago: University of Chicago Press, 2011), p. 36.

23. "Wabash National Study of Liberal Arts Education, 2006–2009: Research Findings," Center of Inquiry, Wabash College, http://www.liberalarts.wabash.edu/study-research/.

24. Alan Charles Kors and Harvey A. Silverglate, *The Shadow University: The Betrayal of Liberty on America's Campuses* (New York: Free Press, 1998).

CHAPTER 1: LEARNING ALL THE WRONG LESSONS IN HIGH SCHOOL

1. David Yalof and Kenneth Dautrich, *Future of the First Amendment 2004*, John S. and James L. Knight Foundation, p. 3, http://www.knightfoundation.org/publications/future-first-amendment-2004.

2. Evan Mayor, "Parent says school broke education laws by allowing articles in paper," Student Press Law Center, May 26, 2006, http://www.splc.org/news/newsflash.asp?id=1264; Nicole Ocran, "Timberland student journalists, parents plan to speak out at board meeting," Student Press Law Center, March 10, 2010, http://www.splc.org/news/newsflash.asp?id=2047.

3. Josh Moore, "Newspaper adviser resigns following student editorial advocating marijuana legalization," Student Press Law Center, June 7, 2010, http://www.splc.org/news/newsflash.asp?id=2102.

4. Yalof and Dautrich, *Future of the First Amendment 2004*, p. 1.

5. First Amendment Center, "State of the First Amendment 2009," September 2009, p. 4.

6. Bill of Rights Institute, "42 Percent of Americans Attribute Communist Slogan to America's Founding Document," December 15, 2010.

7. U.S. Department of Education, *Advancing Civic Learning and Engagement in Democracy: A Road Map and Call to Action* (Washington, D.C., 2012), p. 7, http://www.ed.gov/sites/default/files/road-map-call-to-action.pdf.

8. *Sweezy v. New Hampshire*, 354 U.S. 234, 250 (1957), http://caselaw.lp.findlaw.com/scripts/getcase.pl?court=us&vol=354&invol=234.

9. California Education Code, sec. 94367 (Leonard Law) (1992), http://codes.lp.findlaw.com/cacode/EDC/3/d10/59/3.3/s94367.

10. We have a list of over 400 colleges and their policies in our easily searchable and routinely updated database: http://thefire.org/spotlight/.

11. Harvard College, Office of Student Life, "Free Speech Guidelines," *Student Organization Handbook*, 2010.

12. Jonathan Rauch, *Kindly Inquisitors: The New Attacks on Free Thought* (Chicago: University of Chicago Press, 1995).

13. Christopher Hitchens recounted some examples of this unenthusiastic condemnation in his writing on the topic, including Secretary of State James Baker's comment that the fatwa was merely "regrettable" and the Japanese government's statement that it was "not something to be praised." The Canadian government even went so far as to temporarily ban imports of the book, while German officials complained that it had strained German-Iranian relations. Christopher Hitchens, "Assassins of the Mind," *Vanity Fair*, February 2009.

14. Jimmy Carter wrote at the time, "While Rushdie's First Amendment freedoms are important, we have tended to promote him and his book with little acknowledgment that it is a direct insult to those millions of Moslems whose sacred beliefs have been violated and are suffering in restrained silence the added embarrassment of the Ayatollah's irresponsibility." Jimmy Carter, "Rushdie's Book Is an Insult," *New York Times*, March 5, 1989, http://www.cartercenter.org/news/documents/doc1381.html.

15. Daniel Pipes reported: "Significant voices in the West expressed sympathy for Khomeini. . . . The director of the Near East Studies Center at UCLA, Georges Sabbagh, declared Khomeini 'completely within his rights' to sentence Rushdie to death. Immanuel Jakobovits, chief rabbi of the United Kingdom, wrote that 'the book should not have been published' and called for legislation to proscribe such 'excesses in the freedom of expression.'" Daniel Pipes, "The Clash to End All Clashes?" *National Review Online*, February 7, 2006.

16. World Health Organization, "Female genital mutilation," February 2012, http://www.who.int/mediacentre/factsheets/fs241/en/.

17. For a great discussion of the importance of being wrong, see Kathryn Schulz, *Being Wrong: Adventures in the Margin of Error* (New York: HarperCollins, 2010).

18. Cass R. Sunstein, *Democracy and the Problem of Free Speech* (New York: Free Press, 1995).

19. See generally Cass R. Sunstein, *Infotopia: How Many Minds Produce Knowledge* (New York: Oxford University Press, 2006).

20. Ibid., pp. 21–26.

21. Ibid., p. 14.

22. For a more extensive discussion of group polarization, see Cass R. Sunstein, *Going to Extremes: How Like Minds Unite and Divide* (New York: Oxford University Press, 2009). As Sunstein notes, "It is an understatement to say that the literature on group polarization is vast." His appendix lists a wide variety of empirical studies on the subject.

23. Sunstein, *Infotopia*, ch. 2, "The Surprising Failures of Deliberating Groups."

24. For an easy overview of groupthink and its problems, go to http://oregonstate.edu/instruct/theory/grpthink.html.

25. See discussion of groupthink in Sunstein, *Infotopia*, p. 12ff.

26. See ibid., ch. 6, "Implications and Reforms."

27. John Stuart Mill, *On Liberty* (New York: Penguin Classics, repr., 1995).

28. Richard Arum and Josipa Roksa, *Academically Adrift: Limited Learning on College Campuses* (Chicago: University of Chicago Press, 2011), p. 147.

29. For greater detail, see Harvey A. Silverglate, David French, and Greg Lukianoff, FIRE's *Guide to Free Speech on Campus* (Philadelphia: Foundation for Individual Rights in Education, 2005), www.thefire.org/guides; Michael Kent Curtis, *Free Speech, "The People's Darling Privilege": Struggles for Freedom of Expression in American History* (Durham, N.C.: Duke University Press, 2000); David Rabban, *Free Speech in Its Forgotten Years, 1870–1920* (Cambridge: Cambridge University Press, 1999); Christopher Finan, *From the Palmer Raids to the Patriot Act: A History of the Fight for Free Speech in America* (Boston: Beacon Press, 2008).

30. *Gitlow v. People of the State of New York*, 268 U.S. 652 (1925), http://caselaw.lp.findlaw.com/scripts/getcase.pl?court=us&vol=268&invol=652.

31. Will Rahn, "Auburn student ordered to take down Ron Paul sign shares his story," *Daily Caller*, December 22, 2011.

32. Photos of Dorm Decorations at Auburn University, January 12, 2012, http://thefire.org/article/14060.html; Pictures of Window Hangings at Auburn University, Fall 2011, http://thefire.org/article/13965.html.

33. University of Oklahoma campus-wide email, September 12, 2008, http://thefire. org/article/9802.html.

34. Greg Lukianoff, "As election nears, censorship fever hits college campuses," *Huffington Post*, October 17, 2008; FIRE Letter to University of Oklahoma President David L. Boren, http://thefire.org/article/9801.html.

35. Samantha Harris, "Speech Code of the Month: Case Western Reserve University," *The Torch*, December 1, 2010, http://thefire.org/article/12552.html.

36. "Marquette University: Political Quote Banned from Office Door," http://thefire. org/case/726.html.

37. Email from OSPLD Director Joey Greenwell to College Republicans, http:// thefire.org/article/7715.html.

38. Debra Saunders, "S.F. State—Hecklers' paradise," *San Francisco Chronicle*, February 8, 2007.

39. *College Republicans at San Francisco State University* v. *Reed*, 523 F. Supp. 2d 1005 (N.D. Cal. 2007), http://www.leagle.com/xmlResult.aspx?xmldoc=20071528523 FSupp2d1005_11458.xml.

CHAPTER 2: OPENING THE COLLEGE BROCHURE

1. Yale College, "Free Expression, Peaceful Dissent, and Demonstrations," *Undergraduate Regulations, Policies and Procedures, 2011–2012*.

2. University of Texas at El Paso, "Speech, Expression, and Assembly," sec. 2.2.4, "Harassment," *Handbook of Operating Procedures*.

3. Alan Charles Kors and Harvey A. Silverglate, *The Shadow University: The Betrayal of Liberty on America's Campuses* (New York: Free Press, 1998), p. 15.

4. "Buffaloed," *Time*, November 29, 1993; Nat Hentoff, *Village Voice*, May 4, 1993; "Speech Impediment: How a Penn freshman stood up to the PC police and cracked the campus speech code," *Rolling Stone*, August 5, 1993; Alexander Chancellor, "Alexander Chancellor Column," *The Times* (London), May 1, 1993; Richard Bernstein, "Play Penn: Sheldon Hackney's dismal record," *New Republic*, August 2, 1993; NBC Nightly News, May 14, 1993; James Morgan, "As They Say in Europe: Washington Post and water buffalogate," *Financial Times*, May 8, 1993; Michael deCourcy Hinds, "A Campus Case: Speech or Harassment?" *New York Times*, May 15, 1993. Additional cites can be found in Kors and Silverglate, *The Shadow University*.

5. Gary Trudeau, *Doonesbury*, July 11, 1993.

6. Michael deCourcy Hinds, "Blacks at Penn Drop a Charge of Harassment," *New York Times*, May 25, 1993.

7. *McCauley* v. *University of the Virgin Islands*, 618 F.3d 232 (3d Cir. 2010); *DeJohn* v. *Temple University*, 537 F.3d 301 (3d Cir. 2008); *Dambrot* v. *Central Michigan University*, 55 F.3d 1177 (6th Cir. 1995); *Smith* v. *Tarrant County College District*, 694 F. Supp. 2d 610 (N.D. Tex. 2010); *College Republicans at San Francisco State University* v. *Reed*, 523 F. Supp. 2d 1005 (N.D. Cal. 2007); *Roberts* v. *Haragan*, 346 F. Supp. 2d 853 (N.D. Tex. 2004); *Bair* v. *Shippensburg University*, 280 F. Supp. 2d 357 (M.D. Pa. 2003); *Booher* v. *Northern Kentucky University Board of Regents*, No. 2:96-CV-135, 1998 U.S. Dist. LEXIS 11404 (E.D. Ky. July 21, 1998); *Corry* v. *Leland Stanford Junior University*, No. 740309 (Cal. Super. Ct. Feb. 27, 1995) (slip

op.); *UWM Post, Inc. v. Board of Regents of the University of Wisconsin*, 774 F.Supp. 1163 (E.D. Wisc. 1991); *Doe v. University of Michigan*, 721 F. Supp. 852 (E.D. Mich. 1989).

8. For more on this history, see Greg Lukianoff, "Campus Speech Codes: Absurd, Tenacious, and Everywhere," National Association of Scholars, May 23, 2008, http://thefire.org/article/10026.html.

9. Robert O'Neil, *Free Speech in the College Community* (Bloomington: Indiana University Press, 1997), pp. 20–21.

10. *Spotlight on Speech Codes 2012: The State of Free Speech on Our Nation's Campuses* (Philadelphia: Foundation for Individual Rights in Education, 2012), http://thefire.org/spotlight/speechcodes/2012.

11. Rhode Island College, "Residential Life and Housing Judicial Procedures and Policies: Code of Social Responsibility," http://thefire.org/public/pdfs/21fc11d45 80f89a042457b5b6fcc704b.pdf?direct.

12. Texas Southern University, *Student Code of Conduct*, August 2007, sec. IV, 4.6.

13. Samantha Harris, "Speech Code of the Month for January 2010: The University of Northern Colorado," *The Torch*, January 8, 2010, http://thefire.org/article/11451.html.

14. Samantha Harris, "Speech Code of the Month: Texas A&M University," *The Torch,* May 1, 2007, http://thefire.org/article/7994.html.

15. The College at Brockport (State University of New York), "Computing Policies and Regulations: Internet/E-mail Rules and Regulations," approved April 4, 2006, access via http://thefire.org/article/11344.html.

16. Samantha Harris, "Speech Code of the Month: Lone Star College," *The Torch*, December 1, 2008, http://thefire.org/article/9977.html.

17. Fordham University, "Information Technology Usage," updated August 24, 2011, http://thefire.org/public/pdfs/eb6e8bed00780c322a7f542b3e9b78cb.pdf?direct; Samantha Harris, "Speech Code of the Month: Northeastern University," *The Torch*, February 2, 2007, http://thefire.org/article/7703.html.

18. Murray State University Women's Center, "Sexual/Peer Harassment."

19. University of Idaho, "University Housing climate and safety," *Residence Hall Handbook* 2011–2012, p. 11.

20. New York University, "Anti-Harassment Policy and Complaint Procedures," *Surviving Sexual Assault: NYU Policies and Procedures Concerning Sexual Assault 2008–2009*, Appendix I, p. 13, http://www.nyu.edu/student.affairs/pdfs/Surviving_Sexual_Assault_08-09.pdf.

21. Davidson College, "Definition of Harassment," *Student Handbook*, Codes of Honor, Responsibility and Disciplinary Procedures, http://www3.davidson.edu/cms/x8905.xml.

22. San Francisco State University, "Sexual Harassment Policy and Procedures," University Executive Order #95-18, http://www.sfsu.edu/~hrwww/ueo/ueo_95_18.html.

23. University of Iowa, "Sexual Harassment Policy Update: What is Sexual Harassment?" http://www.sexualharassment.uiowa.edu/.

24. University of Tulsa, "Policy on Harassment," *Policies and Procedures Manual*, 2005, http://www.utulsa.edu/personnel/policies/index.pl?section=h.

25. Western Michigan University, "Policy on Sexual Harassment and Sexism," 2007, access via http://thefire.org/article/7795.html.

26. You can see all of these codes at http://thefire.org/spotlight/scotm/.

27. *Davis* v. *Monroe County Board of Education*, 526 U.S. 629 (1999), http://www.law.cornell.edu/supct/html/97-843.ZS.html.

28. Ibid.

29. Michael D. Shear, Jim Rutenberg, and Mike McIntire, "Cain Speaks Out to Deny Accusations; 2nd Voice Heard," *New York Times*, November 8, 2011.

30. Randy Kreider, "Chicago Woman Claims Herman Cain Wanted Her to Trade Sex for Job," ABC News, November 7, 2011.

31. Todd Tucker, *Notre Dame vs. the Klan: How the Fighting Irish Defeated the Ku Klux Klan* (Chicago: Loyola Press, 2004).

32. IUPUI AAO Letter to Sampson, November 25, 2007, http://thefire.org/article/9090.html.

33. ACLU-IN's Letter to IUPUI Counsel, January 31, 2008, http://thefire.org/article/9221.html; FIRE letter to IUPUI Chancellor Charles R. Bantz, March 28, 2008, http://thefire.org/article/9191.html.

34. Dorothy Rabinowitz, "American politics aren't 'post-racial,'" *Wall Street Journal*, July 7, 2008.

35. Melanie Asmar, "Dorm poster gets student kicked out," *Concord Monitor*, October 29, 2004, http://thefire.org/article/5014.html.

36. Flyer Posted by Timothy Garneau, http://thefire.org/public/pdfs/5005_3461.pdf?direct.

37. "UNH student back—in new dorm," *Union Leader*, November 16, 2004, http://thefire.org/article/5147.html.

38. Asmar, "Dorm Poster Gets Student Kicked Out."

39. Samantha Harris, "Speech Code of the Month: Tufts University," *The Torch*, June 2, 2008, http://thefire.org/article/9370.html.

40. "O Come All Ye Black Folk," from December 6, 2006 issue of *The Primary Source*, http://thefire.org/article/8041.html.

41. "Islam—Arabic Translation: Submission," from April 11, 2007 issue of *The Primary Source*, http://thefire.org/article/8043.html.

42. Outcome of the Tufts Committee on Student Life's Hearing on Charges against *The Primary Source*, May 10, 2007, http://thefire.org/article/8044.html; Kat Schmidt, "CSL hearing turns spotlight on controversial Source pieces," *Tufts Daily*, May 20, 2007, http://thefire.org/article/8083.html.

43. "Byline requirement on conservative student journal lifted," Associated Press, August 22, 2007, http://thefire.org/article/8337.html.

44. Samantha Harris, "Speech Code of the Month: Tufts University," *The Torch*, June 2, 2008, http://thefire.org/article/9370.html.

45. "University of Central Florida: Censorship of Internet Speech," http://thefire. org/case/706.html.

46. "Occidental College: Use of Harassment Charges to Suppress Protected Speech," http://thefire.org/case/647.html; William Creeley and Greg Lukianoff, "Occidental College's Censorship of Radio Station Marks Abuse of Power," *Daily Journal* (Los Angeles), September 22, 2004, http://thefire.org/article/4861.html.

47. Harvey A. Silverglate and Greg Lukianoff, "Speech Codes: Alive and Well at Colleges ...," *Chronicle of Higher Education*, August 1, 2003, http://thefire.org/ article/3978.html.

48. "Purdue professor's comments cause flap," United Press International, February 14, 2012, http://thefire.org/article/14183.html.

49. Kevin Simpson, "Concerns raised about academic freedom over University of Denver professor's punishment," *Denver Post*, November 30, 2011, http://thefire. org/article/13901.html.

50. Syllabus, INTS 3300 and 4141, The Domestic and International Consequences of the Drug War, Spring Quarter 2011, http://thefire.org/article/13788.html.

51. FIRE Letter to University of Denver Chancellor Robert Coombe, November 4, 2011, http://thefire.org/article/13833.html; DU AAUP Letter to DU Provost Kvistad and Chancellor Coombe, November 12, 2011, http://thefire.org/article/13850. html.

52. Letter from the United States Department of Education's Office for Civil Rights, July 28, 2003, http://thefire.org/article/5046.html.

53. *McCauley* v. *University of the Virgin Islands*, 618 F.3d 232 (3d Cir. 2010); *DeJohn* v. *Temple University*, 537 F.3d 301 (3d Cir. 2008); *Dambrot* v. *Central Michigan University*, 55 F.3d 1177 (6th Cir. 1995); *Smith* v. *Tarrant County College District*, 694 F. Supp. 2d 610 (N.D. Tex. 2010); *College Republicans at San Francisco State University* v. *Reed*, 523 F. Supp. 2d 1005 (N.D. Cal. 2007); *Roberts* v. *Haragan*, 346 F. Supp. 2d 853 (N.D. Tex. 2004); *Bair* v. *Shippensburg University*, 280 F. Supp. 2d 357 (M.D. Pa. 2003); *Pro-Life Cougars* v. *University of Houston*, 259 F. Supp. 2d 575 (S.D. Tex. 2003); *Booher* v. *Northern Kentucky University Board of Regents*, No. 2:96-CV-135, 1998 U.S. Dist. LEXIS 11404 (E.D. Ky. July 21, 1998); *Corry* v. *Leland Stanford Junior University*, No. 740309 (Cal. Super. Ct. Feb. 27, 1995) (slip op.); *UWM Post, Inc.* v. *Board of Regents of the University of Wisconsin*, 774 F.Supp. 1163 (E.D. Wisc. 1991); University of Connecticut (1990) (unpublished opinion); *Doe* v. *University of Michigan*, 721 F. Supp. 852 (E.D. Mich. 1989). Additionally, many challenges have ended in settlements, including at these schools: Citrus College, the State University of New York at Brockport, Pennsylvania State University, Georgia Institute of Technology, the University of Maryland–Baltimore, Yuba Community College, Shippensburg University, and Spokane Community College.

54. U.S. Department of Education's Office for Civil Rights "Dear Colleague" Letter, April 4, 2011, http://thefire.org/article/13143.html.

55. FIRE Coalition Open Letter to Office for Civil Rights Assistant Secretary Russlynn Ali, January 6, 2012, http://thefire.org/article/14017.html.

56. Greg Lukianoff, "Clear campus rules needed on 'harassment,'" *Washington Post*, January 5, 2012.

57. Robert C. Post, *Democracy, Expertise, and Academic Freedom: A First Amendment Jurisprudence for the Modern State* (New Haven: Yale University Press, 2012).

58. Eric L. Dey, Molly C. Ott, Mary Antonaros, Cassie L. Barnhardt, and Matthew A. Holsapple, *Engaging Diverse Viewpoints: What Is the Campus Climate for Perspective-Taking?* (Washington, D.C.: Association of American Colleges and Universities, 2010), available online.

59. Ibid., p. 7.

60. Ibid.

61. Ibid.

62. Ibid.

63. Michiko Kakutani, "Critic's Notebook; Debate? Dissent? Discussion? Oh, Don't Go There!" *New York Times*, March 23, 2002.

64. Suzanne Feigelson, "The Silent Classroom," *Amherst Magazine*, Fall 2001.

65. "University of Massachusetts at Amherst: Refusal to Permit Pro-War Speech," http://thefire.org/case/73.html.

66. "University of Massachusetts–Amherst," http://thefire.org/spotlight/codes/763.html.

67. "University May Be Infringing on Students' Rights," *Central Michigan Life*, October 24, 2011, http://thefire.org/article/5858.html.

68. Lou Marano, "School Warns Man Who Rebuked Saudis," United Press International, October 25, 2001, http://thefire.org/article/4324.html.

69. John Leo, "Don't tread on free-speakers," *U.S. News and World Report,* November 5, 2001.

70. For more on this topic, view "Portraits of Terror," a FIRE documentary posted on YouTube at http://www.youtube.com/watch?v=y_Sea_uGgHk.

71. Arlene Levinson, "College Faculty, Staff Find Chilling New Climate for Free Speech on Campus," Associated Press, October 13, 2001, http://thefire.org/article/4688.html.

72. The professor, Richard Berthold, related his story a year later in "My Five Minutes of Infamy," *History News Network*, November 25, 2002.

73. Robin Wilson, "CUNY Chancellor, Trustees Denounce Professors Who Criticized U.S. Policy After Attacks," *Chronicle of Higher Education*, October 5, 2001, http://thefire.org/article/5865.html.

74. David Folkenflik,"NPR Ends Williams' Contract After Muslim Remarks," National Public Radio, October 21, 2010.

75. Juan Williams, *Muzzled: The Assault on Honest Debate* (New York: Crown Publishers, 2011), p. 6.

76. Mark Memmott, "NPR CEO Apologizes for 'Psychiatrist' Remark," National Public Radio, October 21, 2010.

CHAPTER 3: THE COLLEGE ROAD TRIP

1. Delaney Hall, "Law student sues Texas Tech over free speech zone," *Daily Texan*, June 16, 2003, http://thefire.org/article/4456.html.

2. Texas Tech University, *Student Affairs Handbook*, 2002–2003, p. 15, http://thefire. org/article/5920.html.

3. FIRE Letter to Texas Tech University President Donald Haragan, February 6, 2003, http://thefire.org/article/5925.html.

4. *Roberts* v. *Haragan*, 346 F. Supp. 2d 853 (N.D. Tex. 2004), http://thefire.org/ article/5908.html.

5. Texas Tech University, *Student Affairs Handbook*, 2003–2004, p. 18, http://thefire. org/article/5911.html.

6. Alan Charles Kors and Harvey Silverglate, *The Shadow University: The Betrayal of Liberty on America's Campuses* (New York: Free Press, 1998), p. 149.

7. "West Virginia University Quarantines Free Speech," http://thefire.org/article/77. html.

8. Jake Stump, "Students, FIRE put heat on WVU free speech rules: Civil rights foundation joins campus protest," *Dominion Post*, March 22, 2002, http://the-fire.org/article/4584.html; Daniel Shapiro, "First Amendment only free speech policy needed," *Daily Athenaeum* (WVU), February 11, 2002, http://thefire.org/ article/5316.html.

9. Herschel Tomlinson, "The University of North Texas grants students campus wide free speech," *Examiner.com*, October 24, 2009; Mark Harper, "Students challenge UCF's 'free-assembly' policies," *Daytona Beach News-Journal*, December 6, 2006, http://thefire.org/article/7559.html; Jim Brown, "FIRE Applauds University of Nevada-Reno's Dropping of 'Speech Zones,'" *Agape Press*, July 5, 2006, http://thefire.org/article/7136.html; Jim Brown and Judy Brown, "Clemson exonerates student group, will review policy on 'free-speech zones,'" *Agape Press*, December 4, 2006, http://thefire.org/article/7558.html; Terry Webster, "Citrus College officials settle free-speech lawsuit," *San Gabriel Valley Tribune*, August 12, 2003, http://thefire.org/article/4704.html; "Florida State University," http://thefire.org/spotlight/codes/330.html; Amy Kingsley, "College groups unite for free speech at UNCG," *Yes! Weekly*, February 1, 2006, http://thefire. org/article/6767.html; "California State University–Chico," http://thefire.org/ spotlight/codes/129.html; "Students win right to protest with empty holsters," *Inside Higher Ed*, November 9, 2009, http://thefire.org/article/11264.html; Mike Adams, "Appalachian State's six-foot monument to free speech," *Townhall.com*, February 26, 2007, http://thefire.org/article/7782.html.

10. Associated Press, "Campus abolishes its free-speech zone," First Amendment Center, May 9, 2003; "Zoning free speech," *Critical Mass*, May 1, 2003, http:// www.erinoconnor.org/archives/2003/05/zoning_free_spe.html.

11. Karah-Leigh Hancock, "Policy Changed: VSU reveals new free expression rule; FIRE backs off," *The Spectator* (VSU), September 8, 2008, http://thefire.org/ article/9700.html.

12. Samantha Harris, "Speech Code of the Month: McNeese State University," *The Torch*, July 3, 2007, http://thefire.org/article/8198.html.

13. Samantha Harris, "Speech Code of the Month: Front Range Community College," *The Torch*, August 4, 2010, http://thefire.org/article/12131.html.

14. Samantha Harris, "Speech Code of the Month: University of Massachusetts Amherst," *The Torch*, September 2, 2010, http://thefire.org/article/12205.html.

15. Samantha Harris, "Speech Code of the Month: University of Missouri–St. Louis," *The Torch*, March 1, 2012, http://thefire.org/article/14254.html.

16. Samantha Harris, "Speech Code of the Month: University of Cincinnati," *The Torch*, December 5, 2007, http://thefire.org/article/8700.html; Robert Shibley, "'Right to work' students sue University of Cincinnati over 'Free Speech Area,'" *Daily Caller*, February 24, 2012.

17. Ryan Hoffman, "Temporary truce in free-speech suit," *News Record* (U. of Cincinnati), March 8, 2012.

18. Stephanee Freer, "VIDEO: NAU Administration Shuts Down 9/11 Event," CampusReform.org, September 10, 2011.

19. *Ward v. Rock Against Racism*, 491 U.S. 781 (1989), http://supreme.justia.com/cases/federal/us/491/781/.

20. Professor Steven Pinker on FIRE, Censorship, and the "Psychology of Taboo," Address given at Ford Hall Forum in Boston on March 18, 2010, http://thefire.org/index.php/article/12310.html.

21. Nat Hentoff, *Free Speech for Me—But Not for Thee: How the American Left and Right Relentlessly Censor Each Other* (New York: HarperCollins, 1992), p. 17.

22. Mary Beth Marklein, "College gender gap remains stable: 57% women," *USA Today*, January 26, 2010.

23. Enrollment data for Hunter College and Lehman College provided in *U.S. News and World Report*'s college rankings, http://colleges.usnews.rankingsandreviews.com/best-colleges.

24. Andrew Hacker and Claudia Dreifus, *Higher Education? How Colleges Are Wasting Our Money and Failing Our Kids—and What We Can Do About It* (New York: Times Books, 2010), p. 122.

25. Benjamin Ginsberg, *The Fall of the Faculty: The Rise of the All-Administrative University and Why It Matters* (New York: Oxford University Press, 2011).

26. College Board Advocacy and Policy Center, *Trends in College Pricing*, 2011, p. 13, fig. 5, http://trends.collegeboard.org/college_pricing.

27. Ibid., p. 24.

28. "Top 100: Colleges with the Highest Total Cost 2011–2012," *Campus Grotto*.

29. Ibid.

30. Carmen DeNavas, Bernadette D. Proctor, and Jessica C. Smith, U.S. Census Bureau, Current Population Reports, *Income, Poverty and Health Insurance Coverage in the United States: 2010* (Washington, D.C.: U.S. Government Printing Office, 2011), p. 5, http://www.census.gov/prod/2011pubs/p60-239.pdf.

31. Mark Kantrowitz, "Total College Debt Now Exceeds Total Credit Card Debt," *Fastweb*, August 11, 2010; "Student Loan Debt Rose 25% Since 2008," *Huffington Post*, August 16, 2011. To see the current level of student debt, visit the "Student Load Debt Clock" at the FinAid website.

32. Blake Ellis, "Average student loan debt tops $25,000," CNNMoney, November 3, 2011.

33. Alexander Eichler, "Student-Loan Delinquencies Rise, Adding to Fears of an Education Bubble," *Huffington Post*, August 17, 2011. For examples of individuals

saddled with an overwhelming amount of debt, visit http://studentloanjustice. org/victims.htm.

34. "The higher-education bubble: More on Peter Thiel," Schumpeter blog, *The Economist*, April 13, 2011.

35. Chris Staiti, "Student-Loan Debt Could Become Next Financial Bubble, S&P Says," *Bloomberg News*, February 9, 2012.

36. Hacker and Dreifus, *Higher Education?* p. 119.

37. Ibid.

38. "Halloween in the Hood" Party Invitation, posted by Justin Park on Facebook. com, October 26, 2006, http://thefire.org/article/7526.html.

39. Letter from Associate Dean of Students Dorothy Sheppard to Justin Park, November 6, 2006, http://thefire.org/index.php/article/7528.html.

40. Ibid.

41. Johns Hopkins University, "Principles for Ensuring Equity, Civility and Respect for All," http://webapps.jhu.edu/jhuniverse/administration/minutes_policies_reports/policies/equity/; William Brody, "Thinking Out Loud," *JHU Gazette*, December 11, 2006, http://www.jhu.edu/~gazette/2006/11dec06/11brody.html.

42. Josh Keller and Andrea Fuller, "Executive Compensation at Private Colleges: President Profiles: Highest Paid Private College Presidents, 2009," *Chronicle of Higher Education*, updated December 5, 2011, http://chronicle.com/article/Executive-Compensation/129979/.

43. Scott Jaschik, "The Shrinking Professoriate," *Inside Higher Ed*, March 12, 2008, http://www.insidehighered.com/news/2008/03/12/jobs.

44. L. G. Knapp, J. E. Kelly-Reid, and S. A. Ginder, *Employees in Postsecondary Institutions, Fall 2009, and Salaries of Full-Time Instructional Staff, 2009–10*, U.S. Department of Education (Washington, D.C.: National Center for Education Statistics, 2010), p. 3, http://nces.ed.gov/pubsearch/pubsinfo.asp?pubid=2011150.

45. Ginsberg, *The Fall of the Faculty*, p. 28.

46. Jay P. Greene, Brian Kisida, and Jonathan Mills, *Administrative Bloat at American Universities: The Real Reason for High Costs in Higher Education*, Goldwater Institute Policy Report no. 239 (August 17, 2011), available online, p. 1.

47. Ibid., p. 11.

48. Ibid., p. 1.

49. Staff Editorial, "Criminal charges possible for professors' role in protest," *10News San Diego*, November 5, 2009, http://thefire.org/article/11246.html.

50. "Nassau Community College: Free Speech Zone," http://thefire.org/case/871. html.

51. Kharli Mandeville, "ASU blocks petition website on campus network," *State Press* (ASU), February 2, 2012.

CHAPTER 4: HARVARD AND YALE

1. Yale College, "Freedom of Expression," http://yalecollege.yale.edu/content/freedom-expression.

2. Naomi Massave, "Hate sign removed from Durfee Hall," *Yale Daily News*, October 30, 2001, http://thefire.org/article/6056.html.

3. Ibid.

4. "Cathars," *Crusades-Encyclopedia*, http://www.crusades-encyclopedia.com/cathars.html.

5. Massave, "Hate sign removed from Durfee Hall."

6. Ibid.

7. Martha Fulford, "Administrators: protecting free speech is top goal," *Yale Daily News*, November 13, 2001, http://thefire.org/article/6059.html.

8. Jordi Gasso, "Freshman Class Council scraps offensive shirts," *Yale Daily News*, November 19, 2009.

9. Letter from Yale University President Richard C. Levin to FIRE, January 14, 2010, http://thefire.org/index.php/article/11481.html.

10. Natasha Thondavadi, "Harvard does not 'like' FCC shirts," *Yale Daily News*, November 17, 2011.

11. Jytte Klausen, *The Cartoons That Shook the World* (New Haven: Yale University Press, 2009).

12. Statement by John Donatich, Director of Yale University Press, http://yalepress.yale.edu/yupbooks/KlausenStatement.asp.

13. Letter to Yale University Opposing Removal of Mohammed Images from Book, http://thefire.org/article/11706.html.

14. Walter Reich, "Saving the Yale anti-Semitism institute," *Washington Post*, June 13, 2011.

15. Ron Rosenbaum, "Yale's New Jewish Quota," *Slate*, July 1, 2011.

16. Josh Abner and Jon Gray, "TKE privileges suspended," *Louisville Cardinal Online*, December 5, 2001, http://thefire.org/article/5996.html.

17. *Iota Xi Chapter of Sigma Chi Fraternity* v. *George Mason University*, 993 F.2d 386 (4th Cir. 1993), http://classweb.gmu.edu/jkozlows/gmu1ay.htm.

18. Jordi Gasso and Sam Greenberg, "DKE apologizes for pledge chants," *Yale Daily News*, October 15, 2010.

19. "Title IX Complaint Press Release," *Yale Herald*, March 31, 2011; Diane Orson, "Feds Launch Inquiry into Sexual Harassment at Yale," National Public Radio, April 6, 2011.

20. Lisa Foderaro, "Yale Restricts a Fraternity for Five Years," *New York Times*, May 17, 2011

21. Jordi Gasso, "DKE will continue to operate, Executive Director of DKE International says," *Yale Daily News*, June 25, 2011.

22. "News' View: Free speech and Sex Week," *Yale Daily News*, November 14, 2011.

23. Daniel R. Schwartz, "A Harvard Retrospective," *The Lantern*, January 4, 2012, http://www.thefirelantern.org/a-2011-harvard-retrospective/.

24. Ibid.

25. Ibid.

26. Ibid.

27. Ibid.

28. *Harbus* Cartoon, October 2002, http://thefire.org/article/5945.html.

29. Lauren A. E. Schuker, "Editor Resigns over Cartoon," *Harvard Crimson*, November 12, 2002.

30. Letter from Harvard Business School Dean Kim B. Clark to FIRE, January 2, 2003, http://thefire.org/article/6092.html.

31. Harvey Silverglate, "Parody Flunks Out," *Boston Phoenix*, July 30, 2008, http://thefire.org/article/9568.html.

32. Branden C. Adams, "Adams House Makes 'Barely Legal' Party Change Name," *Harvard Crimson*, April 25, 2008.

33. FIRE Letter to Harvard Adams House Resident Dean Sharon Howell, May 8, 2008, http://thefire.org/article/9378.html.

34. Letter from Harvard University Attorney Bradley E. Abruzzi, May 30, 2008, http://thefire.org/article/9379.html.

35. Subramanian Swamy, "Analysis: How to wipe out Islamic terror," *Daily News and Analysis* (India), July 16, 2011, http://thefire.org/article/13426.html.

36. Leanna B. Ehrlich, "Petition Calls Op-Ed by Harvard Summer School Instructor Offensive to Muslims," *Harvard Crimson*, July 27, 2011.

37. Letter from FIRE to Harvard University President Drew Gilpin Faust, July 27, 2011, http://thefire.org/article/13425.html.

38. Radhika Jain and Kevin J. Wu, "Faculty Cancel Controversial Summer School Instructor's Courses, Debate Reaction to 'Occupy,'" *Harvard Crimson*, December 7, 2011.

39. Ibid.

40. Stephanie B. Garlock and Hana N. Rouse, "Harvard College Introduces Pledge for Freshmen to Affirm Values," *Harvard Crimson*, September 1, 2011.

41. Harry Lewis, "The Freshman Pledge," *Bits and Pieces*, August 30, 2011, http://harry-lewis.blogspot.com/2011/08/freshman-pledge.html.

42. Ibid.

43. Greg Lukianoff, "Does Harvard Want Bold Thinkers or Good Little Boys and Girls?" *Huffington Post*, September 7, 2011.

44. Ralph Waldo Emerson, "Self-Reliance," *Essays: The First Series* (Boston: Houghton, Mifflin and Company, 1885), pp. 45–87.

45. Lawrence H. Summers, "Remarks at NBER Conference on Diversifying the Science and Engineering Workforce," Address given at National Bureau of Economic Research Conference in Cambridge, Massachusetts, on January 14, 2005, http://www.harvard.edu/president/speeches/summers_2005/nber.php.

46. Ibid.

47. Jeanna Bryner, "Men Smarter Than Women, Scientist Claims," *Live Science*, September 8, 2006; Charles Murray, "The Inequality Taboo," *Commentary*, September 2005, http://www.bible-researcher.com/murray1.html.

48. Summers, "Remarks at NBER Conference on Diversifying the Science and Engineering Workforce."

49. Marcella Bombardieri, "Harvard women's group rips Summers," *Boston Globe*, January 19, 2005; Marcella Bombardieri and David Abel, "Summers gets vote of no confidence," *Boston Globe*, March 16, 2005; Marcella Bombardieri and Maria Sacchetti, "Summers to step down, ending tumult at Harvard," *Boston Globe*, February 22, 2006.

50. "Psychoanalysis Q-and-A: Steven Pinker," *Harvard Crimson*, January 19, 2005.

51. Steven Pinker, *The Blank Slate: The Modern Denial of Human Nature* (New York: Penguin Group, 2003), pp. 108–11.

CHAPTER 5: WELCOME TO CAMPUS!

1. Alan Charles Kors, "Thought Reform 101," *Reason*, March 2000.

2. Greg Lukianoff, "Harvey Silverglate on the Importance of Fighting for Free Speech on Campus," *The Torch*, March 19, 2010, http://thefire.org/article/11670.html.

3. For more on the rise of residence life, see the arguments made by Benjamin Ginsberg in *The Fall of the Faculty: The Rise of the All-Administrative University and Why It Matters* (Oxford: Oxford University Press, 2011), pp. 20, 126ff.

4. Samantha Harris, "Speech Code of the Month: University of Nevada at Reno," *The Torch*, August 24, 2005, http://thefire.org/article/6224.html; University of Utah, "Resident Rights and Responsibilities," http://thefire.org/public/pdfs/c370e3e96871bc998dcc669dcfacb728.pdf?direct; Samantha Harris, "January 2009: University at Buffalo," *The Torch*, January 6, 2009, http://thefire.org/article/10097.html.

5. Claremont University Consortium, "The Claremont Colleges Communication Protocol for Bias Related Incidents," 2005, http://www.scrippscollege.edu/about/diversity/bias-claremont.php.

6. UGA Police Department, "Incident/Investigation Report," http://thefire.org/public/pdfs/835ccdab9aa1c63109415bf8775f3830.pdf?direct.

7. Peter Bonilla, "Police Investigate Jokes about Human Anatomy on Whiteboards in University of Georgia Residence Halls," *The Torch*, October 19, 2010, http://thefire.org/article/12383.html.

8. "University of Delaware: Students Required to Undergo Ideological Reeducation," http://thefire.org/case/752.html.

9. Adam Kissel, "Please Report to Your Resident Assistant to Discuss Your Sexual Identity—It's Mandatory! Thought Reform at the University of Delaware," *The Lantern*, October 30, 2008, http://thefire.org/article/9865.html.

10. Residence Life Escalation Procedures, October 24, 2007, http://thefire.org/article/9172.html.

11. Kissel, "Please Report to Your Resident Assistant ..."

12. In *1984*, the totalitarian villain O'Brien, while interrogating and torturing the resister Winston, says to him, "If you want a picture of the future, imagine a boot

stamping on a human face—forever." George Orwell, *1984* (New York: Plume, 1983), p. 239.

13. For more on this group, visit http://nolabels.org/.

14. University of Delaware Office of Residence Life, Diversity Training and Facilitation, August 14 and 15, 2007, presented by Dr. Shakti Butler, http://thefire.org/public/pdfs/730a8163b35b360f8edd2b889c832ce9.pdf?direct.

15. See more student reactions in the video "Think What We Think … Or Else: Thought Control on the American Campus," posted on YouTube at https://www.youtube.com/watch?v=6EbQfmVoOfM.

16. University of Delaware Office of Residence Life, "Russell Complex Curriculum 2007–2008 (first half)," p. 45, access via http://thefire.org/article/8575.html.

17. Example of Best and Worst One-on-One Sessions with University of Delaware RAs, http://thefire.org/article/8596.html.

18. Ibid.

19. Office of Residence Life Presentation on Assessment of Student Learning, p. 16, http://thefire.org/article/8545.html.

20. Jan Blits, "Are the Dorms Being Politicized?" Address given at National Association of Scholars Annual Conference in Washington, D.C., on January 11, 2009.

21. John K. Wilson, "Unsustainable? A Defense of ResLife at Delaware," *Minding the Campus*, May 12, 2008.

22. Adam Kissel, "More Delaware Students and RAs Speak Out," *The Torch*, November 1, 2007, http://thefire.org/article/8576.html; Erin O'Connor, "Delaware staff and students speak," *Critical Mass*, November 1, 2007; Adam Kissel, "Delaware: Residence Life Fighting Back?" *The Torch*, November 3, 2007, http://thefire.org/article/8605.html.

23. Adam Kissel, "Yes, Blue Hens, Your Reeducation Is Mandatory," *The Torch*, October 30, 2007, http://thefire.org/article/8557.html.

24. Eric Hoover, "U. of Delaware halts residence-life program that was criticized as 'thought reform,'" *Chronicle of Higher Education*, November 2, 2007, http://thefire.org/article/8609.html. For more media coverage, visit http://thefire.org/case/752.

25. Letter from Vice President for Student Life Michael Gilbert to FIRE, October 31, 2007, http://thefire.org/article/8598.html; Patrick Harker, "A Message to the University of Delaware Community," *UDaily*, November 1, 2007, http://www.udel.edu/PR/UDaily/2008/nov/letter110107.html.

26. Jerry Rhodes, "Kerr elected American College Personnel Association vice president," *UDaily*, March 1, 2012, http://www.udel.edu/udaily/2012/mar/kerr-acpa-030112.html.

27. Peter Wood, "Inside the ACPA Conference," National Association of Scholars, February 29, 2008, http://www.nas.org/articles/Inside_the_ACPA_Conference.

28. John L. Jackson, Jr., *Racial Paranoia: The Unintended Consequences of Political Correctness* (New York: Basic Civitas Books, 2010).

29. University of Delaware Office of Residence Life, Diversity Training and Facilitation, August 14 and 15, 2007, presented by Dr. Shakti Butler.

30. Ibid.

31. Georgetown University, "ERASE (Educating Students About Social Equality)," http://reslife.georgetown.edu/studentfamily/resources/rocc.html; Clemson University Newsroom, "Award-winning actor to speak during One World Project," April 1, 2009, http://www.clemson.edu/newsroom/articles/2009/april/OneWorld2009.php5; Washington State University, "Footsteps: A Tunnel Experience," http://reslife.wsu.edu/footsteps; University of North Carolina at Chapel Hill, "Tunnel of Oppression: Rethink Your Role," http://tunnel.unc.edu/; Florida State University, Center for Leadership and Civic Education, "Without Words Overview," http://thecenter.fsu.edu/involved/programs/wow.overview.html; Michigan State University, Events Calendar, "Tunnel of Oppression," April 13, 2011, http://events.msu.edu/main.php?view=event&eventid=1301508772185&timebegin=2011-04-13%2018:00:00; Ohio State University, "Tunnel of Oppression," http://www.units.muohio.edu/saf/reslife/tunnel/history.htm.

32. Eric Strand, "Enter the Tunnel of Oppression," *Vidette Online*, October 19, 2004.

33. Mark Schmitt, "The Legend of the Powell Memo," *American Prospect*, April 27, 2005.

34. Jonathan Allen and John Bresnahan, "Sources: Joe Biden likened tea partiers to terrorists," *Politico*, August 1, 2011; Jim Rutenberg, "Deconstructing the Bump," The Caucus blog, *New York Times*, June 11, 2008.

35. "A Relatively Closer Look – Hitler Reference," *The Daily Show*, June 16, 2005.

CHAPTER 6: NOW YOU'VE DONE IT! THE CAMPUS JUDICIARY

1. "DePaul University: Professor Suspended for Expression Without Due Process," http://thefire.org/case/678.html.

2. Ron Grossman, "'I'm not the ideal poster boy,'" *Chicago Tribune*, December 20, 2005.

3. You can see most of the materials from the seminar at http://thefire.org/case/732.html.

4. SAC Presentation, "How to Increase Student Accountability in Your Campus Community," ASJA International Conference 2002, p. 1, http://thefire.org/article/7584.html.

5. Ibid.

6. Student Accountability in Community Seminar: Faculty and Staff Guide, http://thefire.org/article/7586.html.

7. *Doe v. University of Michigan*, 721 F. Supp. 852 (E.D. Mich. 1989), http://www.bc.edu/bc_org/avp/cas/comm/free_speech/doe.html; *Dambrot v. Central Michigan University*, 55 F.3d 1177, 1184 (6th Cir. 1995), http://www.leagle.com/xmlResult.aspx?page=1&xmldoc=1995123255F3d1177_11054.xml&docbase=CSLWAR2-1986-2006&SizeDisp=7.

8. SAC "Power and Control Wheel," http://thefire.org/article/7589.html.

9. FIRE Letter to Michigan State University President Lou Anna K. Simon, November 20, 2006, http://thefire.org/article/7582.html.

10. "Victory for Freedom of Conscience: Michigan State Ends Controversial Thought Reform Program," http://thefire.org/article/8011.html.

11. Craig Brandon, *The Five-Year Party: How Colleges Have Given Up on Educating Your Child and What You Can Do About It* (Dallas: BenBella Books, 2010), pp. 116–38, 183–85.

12. Antioch's Infamous Sexual Assault Policy, http://thefire.org/article/8138.html.

13. Gettysburg College Sexual Misconduct Policy, http://thefire.org/article/7032. html.

14. Patrick Kerkstra, "Sexual-Misconduct Policy Is Faulted," *Philadelphia Inquirer*, May 12, 2006.

15. Cathy Young, "On campus, an absurd overregulation of sexual conduct," *Boston Globe*, May 22, 2006.

16. Steve Marroni, "G-burg College revises policy," *York Daily Record*, August 26, 2007, http://thefire.org/article/8348.html.

17. Stuart Taylor Jr. and KC Johnson, *Until Proven Innocent: Political Correctness and the Shameful Injustices of the Duke Lacrosse Rape Case* (New York: St. Martin's Press, 2007), pp. 31–32.

18. Chris Cuomo, Eric Avram, and Lara Setrakian, "Key Evidence Supports Alibi in Potential Rape Defense for One Indicted Duke Player," ABC News, April 19, 2006.

19. Joseph Neff, "Lacrosse files show gaps in DA's case," *News and Observer*, August 6, 2006.

20. Taylor and Johnson, *Until Proven Innocent*, p. 194.

21. Ibid., pp. 144–48.

22. "Duke Case: The 'listening' statement," *Johnsville News*, November 10, 2006.

23. The settlement may have been as high as $20 million to each student. "Were the Duke lacrosse players wrongly accused of rape paid $20 MILLION each in secret settlement?" *Daily Mail* (UK), February 28, 2011.

24. Lindsey Rupp, "Rape policy mandates reporting," *Duke Chronicle*, August 28, 2009, http://thefire.org/public/pdfs/97678c9ec697d99029ba8bc6a1238ca8. pdf?direct.

25. Ada Gregory, "Comment on rape policy not aimed at all students," *Duke Chronicle*, August 31, 2009, http://thefire.org/public/pdfs/b7554738a6d6e-255a23938e93b9bf1fd.pdf?direct.

26. Duke University's New "Sexual Misconduct" Policy, http://thefire.org/article/11723.html.

27. University of California, Berkeley, Gender Equity Resource Center, "Sexual Harassment," http://thefire.org/public/pdfs/9f7e945faae108ef612a83813f5c46d3. pdf?direct.

28. Alabama State University, "Discrimination and Harassment Policy," http://thefire.org/spotlight/codes/3.html.

29. Iowa State University, Policy Library, "Discrimination and Harassment," updated August 9, 2011, http://policy.iastate.edu/policy/discrimination/.

30. U.S. Department of Education's Office for Civil Rights "Dear Colleague" Letter, April 4, 2011, http://thefire.org/article/13143.html.

31. "Standard of Evidence Survey: Colleges and Universities Respond to OCR's New Mandate," http://thefire.org/article/13796.html.

32. "University of North Dakota: Accuser Is Criminally Charged with Lying to Police, but School Refuses to Reopen Misconduct Case," http://thefire.org/case/868.html.

33. Harvey Silverglate, "Yes Means Yes—Except on Campus," *Wall Street Journal*, July 15, 2011.

34. Wendy Kaminer, "The SaVE Act: Trading Liberty for Security on Campus," *The Atlantic*, April 25, 2011.

35. "Editorial: Fairness first," *Akron Beacon Journal*, March 24, 2006, http://thefire.org/article/14306.html.

36. Judge Learned Hand, "The Spirit of Liberty," Speech given in Central Park, New York, on May 21, 1944, http://www.providenceforum.org/spiritoflibertyspeech.

37. Ibid.

CHAPTER 7: DON'T QUESTION AUTHORITY

1. Video of these incidents is posted on YouTube: "University of Florida student Tasered at Kerry forum," http://www.youtube.com/watch?v=6bVa6jn4rpE; and "UC Davis Protestors Pepper Sprayed," http://www.youtube.com/watch?v=6AdDLhPwpp4.

2. Emails between Professor James Miller and Chief of Police Lisa Walter, September 16, 2011, http://thefire.org/article/13592.html.

3. Email to James Miller from Chief of Police Lisa Walter, September 20, 2011, http://thefire.org/article/13593.html.

4. FIRE Letter to UW–Stout Chancellor Charles W. Sorensen, September 21, 2011, http://thefire.org/article/13590.html.

5. Adam Baldwin and Liberty Chick, "University Professor Censored Over ... Firefly Poster?" *Big Hollywood*, October 4, 2011; Lauri Apple, "Theater Professor's Firefly Poster Declared a Threat," *Gawker*, September 27, 2011; Sean O'Neal, "College campus police save students from threat of Firefly poster," *A.V. Club*, September 27, 2011; Jacob Sullum, "The Clear and Present Danger Posed by Space Captains," *Reason*, September 26, 2011, http://thefire.org/article/13599.html.

6. Email from University of Wisconsin–Stout Chancellor Charles W. Sorensen to all faculty and staff, September 27, 2011, http://thefire.org/article/13621.html.

7. University of Wisconsin–Stout Statement from Chancellor Sorensen, Provost Julie Furst-Bowe, and Vice Chancellor Ed Nieskes to Students, Faculty, and Staff, http://thefire.org/article/13658.html.

8. Rob Capriccioso, "Facebook Face Off," *Inside Higher Ed*, February 14, 2006, http://www.insidehighered.com/news/2006/02/14/facebook.

9. Brent Schrotenboer, "College Athletes Caught in Tangled Web," *San Diego Union Tribune*, May 24, 2006, http://thefire.org/article/7068.html.

10. Roman Caple's Facebook Message, http://thefire.org/article/13247.html.

11. Letter to Roman Caple from Vice President for Student Development and Services Eric W. Jackson, April 27, 2011, http://thefire.org/article/13251.html.

12. Ibid.

13. Response from Saint Augustine's College, April 29, 2011, http://thefire.org/article/13243.html.

14. Saint Augustine's College Attorney Letter to FIRE, May 24, 2011, http://thefire. org/article/13244.html.

15. Saint Augustine's College Student Handbook and Academic Calendar, 2009–2011, pp. 58–50, 100, http://thefire.org/article/13245.html.

16. Complaint Filed by Roman Caple in Wake County (N.C.) Superior Court, against Saint Augustine's College and President Dianne Boardley Suber, July 8, 2011, http://thefire.org/article/13360.html.

17. William Creeley, "St. Augustine's College Extends Punishment, Bans Graduate from Homecoming for Facebook Post," *The Torch*, October 19, 2011, http://thefire. org/article/13764.html.

18. Ann Carrns, "Some Students Grumble About Higher One's Debit Card Fees," Bucks blog, *New York Times*, November 14, 2011.

19. Ibid.

20. Ibid.

21. Marc Bechtol's Comments on Catawba Valley Community College's Facebook page, September 28, 2011, http://thefire.org/article/13708.html.

22. Notice of Suspension from CVCC to Marc Bechtol, http://thefire.org/article/13703.html; FIRE Letter to Catawba Valley Community College President Garrett D. Hinshaw, October 10, 2011, http://thefire.org/article/13706.html.

23. Carrns, "Some Students Grumble About Higher One's Debit Card Fees"; "Students Against HigherOne," Facebook, http://www.facebook.com/pages/Students-Against-HigherOne/176918409063183.

24. "Michigan State University: Student Government Official Threatened with Suspension for E-mailing Faculty about University Scheduling Concerns," http://thefire.org/case/773.html.

25. Email from Kara Spencer to Selected Faculty, http://thefire.org/article/9992.html.

26. Disciplinary Allegations Letter against Kara Spencer, http://thefire.org/article/9991.html.

27. Email to Kara Spencer from the Judicial Affairs Office, http://thefire.org/article/10019.html.

28. Open Letter to Michigan State University President Lou Anna K. Simon, http://thefire.org/article/10045.html.

29. "Appropriate Use of MSU Email Services by Internal Users on MSUnet," http://thefire.org/article/11044.html.

30. "Petition to Save Peace College," http://www.zoomerang.com/Survey/WEB-22CJ3GDWJJ5.

31. Letter from Catharine Biggs Arrowood, Parker Poe, November 1, 2011, http://thefire.org/article/14259.html.

32. Ibid.

33. William Peace University, "Speech, Expression and Assembly," *Campus Information and Policies*, p. 63.

34. Letter from Catharine Biggs Arrowood, Parker Poe, November 1, 2011, http://thefire.org/article/14259.html.

35. *New York Times Co.* v. *Sullivan*, 376 U.S. 254 (1964), http://www.law.cornell.edu/supct/html/historics/USSC_CR_0376_0254_ZO.html.

36. Ken, "All We Are Asking Is That You Give Peace a Chance. Also, Shut Up Or Else," *Popehat*, March 6, 2012.

37. Samantha Harris, "Speech Code of the Month: Coast Community College District," *The Torch*, June 1, 2006, http://thefire.org/article/7078.html; Samantha Harris, "Speech Code of the Month: University of Mississippi," *The Torch*, October 3, 2006, http://thefire.org/article/7330.html; Samantha Harris, "Speech Code of the Month: Lone Star College," *The Torch*, December 1, 2008, http://thefire.org/article/9977.html; Samantha Harris, "Speech Code of the Month: Moorpark College," *The Torch*, November 4, 2010, http://thefire.org/article/12436.html; Samantha Harris, "Speech Code of the Month: Sam Houston State University," *The Torch*, October 3, 2011, http://thefire.org/article/13645.html.

38. Samantha Harris, "Speech Code of the Month: James Madison University," *The Torch*, October 1, 2009, http://thefire.org/article/11147.html.

39. Samantha Harris, "Speech Code of the Month: Barnard College," *The Torch*, April 4, 2006, http://thefire.org/article/6945.html.

40. Author interview in Tom Wolfe, *I Am Charlotte Simmons* (Audio Renaissance Audiobook, 2004).

41. Tom Wolfe, *I Am Charlotte Simmons: A Novel* (New York: Farrar, Straus & Giroux, 2004), pp. 35–36.

42. Charges against Isaac Rosenbloom, http://thefire.org/article/11885.html.

43. You can listen to the hearing yourself at http://thefire.org/article/11881.html.

44. *Papish* v. *Board of Curators of the University of Missouri et al.* 410 U.S. 667 (1973), http://caselaw.lp.findlaw.com/scripts/getcase.pl?court=us&vol=410&invol=667.

45. *Cohen* v. *California*, 403 U.S. 15 (1971), http://caselaw.lp.findlaw.com/scripts/getcase.pl?court=us&vol=403&invol=15.

46. Charges against Isaac Rosenbloom, http://thefire.org/article/11885.html.

47. "Victory for Free Speech on Campus: Mississippi College Reverses Punishment of Student for Swearing Outside of Class," http://thefire.org/article/12101.html.

48. Emails between Jacob Lovell and UGA Parking Services, August 17 and 18, 2010, http://thefire.org/article/12270.html.

49. University of Georgia Letter to Jacob Lovell, September 3, 2010, http://thefire.org/article/12274.html.

50. Valerie Strauss, "Student gets in trouble for email on scooter parking," *Washington Post*, September 26, 2010.

51. Check from Jacob Ramirez to Western Washington University, October 6, 2011, http://thefire.org/article/13794.html.

52. "The RS 500 Greatest Songs of All Time," *Rolling Stone*, December 9, 2004.

53. Notice of Investigation from Michael L. Schardein to Jacob Ramirez, October 19, 2011, http://thefire.org/article/13791.html.

54. Response from Associate Dean of Students Sherry L. Mallory to FIRE, October 28, 2011, http://staging.thefire.org/article/13809.html.

55. See California Education Code, sec. 94367 (Leonard Law) (1992), http://codes.lp.findlaw.com/cacode/EDC/3/d10/59/3.3/s94367.

56. Illinois College Campus Press Act (2007), 110 ILCS 13, http://www.splc.org/pdf/ilcollegepresslaw.pdf.

57. Oregon Student Free Expression Law (Public Colleges and Universities) (2007), Ore. Rev. Stat. sec. 351.649, http://www.splc.org/knowyourrights/law_library.asp?id=43.

58. Arizona Senate Bill 1467, 50th Legislature, Second Regular Session (2012), http://e-lobbyist.com/gaits/text/557056.

59. Angus Johnston, "Arizona Law Would Make It Illegal to Teach Law, History or Literature," *The Nation*, February 10, 2012.

60. Greg Lukianoff, "Arizona State Senate to Colleges: Get Rid of Those Non-G-Rated Professors!" *Huffington Post*, February 8, 2012.

61. Erika Woodward, "It's Not About Porn Say Maryland Students," *Southern Maryland Online*, April 3, 2009, http://somd.com/news/headlines/2009/9780.shtml.

62. Laura Fitzpatrick, "Pirates XXX: One University's Battle over Porn," *Time*, April 8, 2009.

63. Todd Thomsen, "Oklahoma legislator proposes resolution to condemn Richard Dawkins," The Richard Dawkins Foundation for Reason and Science, March 5, 2009, http://richarddawkins.net/articles/3641.

64. Greg Lukianoff, "Oklahoma Legislature: Do You Plan to Keep Investigating Richard Dawkins' Speech?" *Huffington Post*, March 23, 2009.

65. FIRE's Open Letter to President Barack Obama, http://thefire.org/index.php/article/10141.html.

66. Mark Viera, "Former Coach at Penn State Is Charged with Abuse," *New York Times*, November 5, 2011.

67. Kevin Dolak and Colleen Curry, "Penn State Scandal: Sandusky Allegedly Confessed to Boy's Mother," ABC News, November 9, 2011.

68. Ibid.

69. Ibid.

70. Viera, "Former Coach at Penn State Is Charged with Abuse."

71. Ivan Maisel, "Joe Paterno: I Met My Responsibilities," ESPN, November 7, 2011.

CHAPTER 8: STUDENT ACTIVITIES FAIR

1. Harvey Silverglate, "Parody Flunks Out," *Boston Phoenix*, July 30, 2008.

2. You can see an extended speech by Chris Lee about his case on a YouTube video posted by the Campus Freedom Network, "How Washington State Censored a Student Musical," https://www.youtube.com/watch?v=bmA3sORy5rM. A shorter explanation of his ordeal was posted under the title "New Threats to Freedom," May 17, 2010, https://www.youtube.com/watch?v=_g94EziXwlo.

3. Note that even in an attempt to deny they had organized a disruption of the play, administrators admitted to advising students to go and yell "I'm offended" during the play. Obviously, such an en masse protest not only could but actually did get out of hand. See: Email from Rich Kelley to Charlene Jaeger, July 19,

2005, http://thefire.org/article/6239.html. Given the hostility the administration felt towards Chris and the play, I believe that even the claim that they intended a more limited disruption of the play is disingenuous. See: Email from Raul Sanchez to Various Washington State Administrators, April 29, 2005, http://thefire.org/article/6331.html. On the FIRE website you can also see: Washington State University Interdepartmental Invoice for 40 Tickets to "Passion of the Musical," http://thefire.org/article/6104/html.

4. Shawn Vestal, "WSU chief stands by protesters at biting play," *Spokesman-Review*, July 14, 2005, http://thefire.org/article/6108.html.

5. Washington State University "Mangina Monologues" Notice, http://thefire.org/article/6580.html.

6. Gary A. Tobin and Aryeh K. Weinberg, *Profiles of the American University*, vol. 2, *Religious Beliefs and Behavior of College Faculty* (San Francisco: Institute for Jewish and Community Research, 2007).

7. Letter from Indian River Community College's Attorney to FIRE, December 22, 2004, http://thefire.org/article/5110.html.

8. Jim Brown and Judy Brown, "College Bans Gibson's Passion—but Allows Blasphemous, Sexualized Skit," American Family Association, January 17, 2005, http://thefire.org/article/5121.html.

9. Statement of Indian River Community College, February 1, 2005, http://thefire.org/article/5212.html. (Now called Indian River State College.)

10. Letter from Associate Director of Housing and Residence Life Deborah Newman to Bible Study-Leading RAs, July 26, 2005, http://thefire.org/article/6376.html.

11. Email from Associate Director of Housing and Residence Life Deborah Newman to Lance Steiger, September 22, 2005, http://thefire.org/article/6377.html.

12. James Brunmeier, "Conquering the world with a smile," *The Spectator* (UWEC), April 29, 2004, http://thefire.org/public/pdfs/a47775ee0e3f958234b2ec82c88f6545.pdf?direct.

13. Letter from University of Wisconsin System President Kevin Reilly to Wisconsin Attorney General Peggy A. Lautenschlager, November 14, 2005, http://thefire.org/article/6465.html.

14. University of Wisconsin–Eau Claire RA Letter and Job Description, http://thefire.org/article/6414.html.

15. Letter from University of Wisconsin System General Counsel Patricia Brady to FIRE, November 8, 2005, http://thefire.org/article/6421.html.

16. UWEC's Bid for the GLACURH Commitment to Diversity Award, 2005, http://thefire.org/article/6442.html; UWEC's Proposal to Host the GLACURH Conference in 2006, http://thefire.org/article/6443.html.

17. UWEC's Bid for the GLACURH Commitment to Diversity Award, 2005, p. 6.

18. Nathan Burchfiel, "Update: University Committee Approves Bible Study Ban," *Cybercast News Service*, January 19, 2006, http://thefire.org/article/6707.html.

19. "University of Wisconsin System Board of Regents, March Meeting, Day Two News Summary," *UW System News*, March 10, 2006, http://www.wisconsin.edu/news/2006/r060310.htm.

20. *Roberts* v. *U.S. Jaycees*, 468 U.S. 609 (1984), http://www.law.cornell.edu/supct/html/historics/USSC_CR_0468_0609_ZO.html.

21. Ibid.

22. "Louisiana State University: Threat to Muslim Group's Freedom of Association," http://thefire.org/case/671.html.

23. Alliance Defense Fund, "Arizona State University: *Christian Legal Society at Arizona State University College of Law* v. *Crow*," http://www.speakupmovement. org/Map/CaseDetails?Case=180; "Brown University: Wrongful Suspension of Religious Student Group," http://thefire.org/case/728.html; "California State University at San Bernardino: Refusal to Recognize Christian Group," http:// thefire.org/case/696.html; William Creeley, "Following President's Statement, Cornell's Religious Student Groups Should Brace for Disparate Treatment," *The Torch*, April 15, 2010, http://thefire.org/article/11768.html; "The State of Religious Liberty at America's Colleges and Universities," http://thefire.org/public/pdfs/e1dd72051b3e54ee12895963ee94a25c.pdf?direct; "Ohio State University: Refusal to Allow Religious Clubs to Decide Membership Based on Religious Belief," http://thefire.org/case/643.html; "Pennsylvania State University: Charges of 'Discrimination' Due to Religious Language in Club Constitution," http:// thefire.org/case/65.html; "Princeton University: Refusal to Recognize Religious Group," http://thefire.org/case/677.html; "Purdue University: Refusal to Allow Christian Women's Group to Require Christian Membership," http://thefire. org/case/641.html; "Rutgers University: Refusal to Allow Christian Clubs to Require Christian Leadership," http://thefire.org/case/24.html; "Tufts University: Refusal to Allow Evangelical Christian Club to Reject Homosexual Leadership," http://thefire.org/case/54.html; Alliance Defense Fund, "Texas A&M University: Freshmen Leaders in Christ," http://www.speakupmovement.org/Map/CaseDetails?Case=230; "University of Arizona: Pro-Life Group Denied Recognition over Belief Requirement," http://thefire.org/case/825.html; Alliance Defense Fund, "University of Florida: *Beta Upsilon Chi* v. *Machen*," http://www. speakupmovement.org/Map/CaseDetails?Case=189; Alliance Defense Fund, "University of George: *Beta Upsilon Chi* v. *Adams*," http://www.speakupmovement.org/Map/CaseDetails?Case=191; Alliance Defense Fund, "University of Mary Washington: Robert Simpson," http://www.speakupmovement.org/Map/CaseDetails?Case=233; Alliance Defense Fund, "University of New Mexico: Christian Legal Society Chapter at the University of New Mexico School of Law," http://www.speakupmovement.org/Map/CaseDetails?Case=210; "Washington University: Mandatory University Viewpoint," http://thefire.org/case/33.html.

24. Young Americans for Freedom, "The Sharon Statement," http://www.yaf.org/sharon_statement.aspx.

25. For more on a student's personal experience in this case, see "Penn State's Problem with 'God-Given Free Will'" on YouTube, http://www.youtube.com/watch?v=Au-mUOjnVOw.

26. Letter from Penn State President Graham B. Spanier to FIRE, March 12, 2001, http://thefire.org/article/4960.html.

27. Screenshots of Facebook Group Entitled "People who believe the Young Americans for Freedom is a Hate Group," http://thefire.org/article/7878.html.

28. Email from YAF President Dennis Lennox II to Director of Student Life Thomas Idema, Jr., February 20, 2007, http://thefire.org/article/7885.html.

29. Email Response from Director of Student Life Thomas Idema, Jr., to YAF President Dennis Lennox II, http://thefire.org/article/7886.html.

30. Letter from Central Michigan University President Michael Rao to FIRE, March 27, 2007, http://thefire.org/article/7880.html.

31. Petition for Writ of Certiorari, *Christian Legal Society* v. *Martinez*, No. 08-1371 (U.S. May 5, 2009), http://www.scotusblog.com/wp-content/uploads/2009/10/08-1371_petition.pdf.

32. *Christian Legal Society* v. *Martinez*, 130 S.Ct. 2971 (2010), http://www.supremecourt.gov/opinions/09pdf/08-1371.pdf.

33. Ibid.

34. *Healy* v. *James*, 408 U.S. 169 (1972), http://supreme.justia.com/cases/federal/us/408/169/case.html.

35. *Rosenberger* v. *Rector and Visitors of University of Virginia*, 515 U.S. 819 (1995), http://supreme.justia.com/cases/federal/us/515/819/case.html; *Board of Regents of the University of Wisconsin System* v. *Southworth*, 529 U.S. 217 (2000), http://www.law.cornell.edu/supct/html/98-1189.ZS.html.

36. *Christian Legal Society* v. *Martinez*, 130 S.Ct. 2971 (2010).

37. *Healy* v. *James*, 408 U.S. 169 (1972).

38. Ibid.

39. "Hampton University: Gay and Lesbian Student Group Denied Recognition Without Explanation," http://thefire.org/case/736.html.

40. Michael Paul Williams, "Hampton's philosophy: 'Don't speak,'" *Richmond Times-Dispatch*, February 26, 2007, http://thefire.org/article/7776.html.

41. Elia Powers, "No Room for a Gay Group," *Inside Higher Ed*, February 26, 2007, http://www.insidehighered.com/news/2007/02/26/hampton.

42. *Bowers* v. *Hardwick*, 478 U.S. 186, 106 S. Ct. 2841 (1986), http://www.law.cornell.edu/supct/html/historics/USSC_CR_0478_0186_ZS.html.

43. *Lawrence* v. *Texas*, 539 U.S. 558 (2003), http://www.law.cornell.edu/supct/html/02-102.ZS.html.

44. This changed when the Supreme Court, in a rare moment of solidarity for a normally hotly divided Court, *unanimously* held in 2006 that colleges could not deny military recruiters access to campus. *Rumsfeld* v. *Forum for Academic & Institutional Rights, Inc.*, 547 U.S. 47, 68 (2006), http://www.law.cornell.edu/supct/html/04-1152.ZS.html.

45. *Alpha Delta Chi-Delta Chapter* v. *Reed*, 648 F.3d 790 (9th Cir. 2011), http://www.ca9.uscourts.gov/datastore/opinions/2011/08/02/09-55299.pdf.

46. Ibid.

47. Ibid.

48. Jeff Schapiro, "Vanderbilt's Nondiscrimination Policy May Discriminate Against Religious Groups," *Christian Post*, September 28, 2011.

49. Video posted on YouTube, "Vanderbilt University 1/31 Town Hall Meeting," February 1, 2012, http://www.youtube.com/watch?v=pUdGSHoXLuo.

50. Transcript of Vanderbilt University Town Hall Regarding Non-discrimination Policy, January 31, 2012, http://thefire.org/article/14375.html.

51. Annalisa Musarra, "Vanderbilt faith groups follow Catholics off campus," *Washington Post*, April 10, 2012.

52. Email Exchange between Seminole Community College Administrator Gail Agor and Eliana Campos, http://thefire.org/article/5730.html.

53. "Community College of Allegheny County: Student Denied Right to Start Advocacy Organization," http://thefire.org/case/787.html.

54. "Tarrant County College Bans Symbolic 'Empty Holster' Protest," http://thefire.org/case/763.html.

55. *Smith v. Tarrant County College District*, No. 4:09-CV-658-Y (N.D. Tex. Mar. 15, 2010), http://thefire.org/article/11657.html.

56. Glenn Garvin, "Why can't students say 'guns' in school?" *Miami Herald*, April 21, 2009, http://thefire.org/article/10496.html.

57. "Lone Star College: Student Group Threatened with Probation and Derecognition for Posting Flyer," http://thefire.org/case/767.html.

58. "Colorado College: Students Found Guilty for Satirical Flyer," http://thefire.org/case/759.html.

59. Scott Jaschik, "Worried About Guns? Ban a Campus Musical," *Inside Higher Ed*, February 22, 2008, http://www.insidehighered.com/news/2008/02/22/arktech.

60. Joe Murray, "Minnesota College suspends student for advocating gun rights," *The Bulletin* (Philadelphia), October 15, 2007, http://thefire.org/article/8503.html; "Professor Fired over Discussion of VT Shootings," *USA Today*, April 24, 2007; Elia Powers, "Stage Fright," *Inside Higher Ed*, April 23, 2007, http://www.insidehighered.com/news/2007/04/23/weapons.

CHAPTER 9: FINALLY, THE CLASSROOM!

1. Lynn Weber's Guidelines for Classroom Discussion, http://thefire.org/index.php/article/6041.html.

2. Ibid.

3. Lynn Weber Cannon, "Fostering Positive Race, Class and Gender Dynamics in the Classroom," *Women's Studies Quarterly*, vols. 1 and 2 (1990), pp. 129–33.

4. Lynn Weber, "Classroom Discussion Guidelines: Promoting Understanding Across Race, Class, Gender, and Sexuality," in *Teaching Sociological Concepts and the Sociology of Gender*, ed. Marybeth C. Stalp and Julie Childers, 2nd ed. (Washington, D.C.: American Sociological Association Teaching Resources Center, 2005).

5. Steven Pinker, *The Blank Slate: The Modern Denial of Human Nature* (New York: Penguin Group, 2003), pp. 287–92.

6. FIRE Letter to University of Colorado at Boulder Interim Chancellor Philip P. DiStefano, February 9, 2005, http://thefire.org/article/5252.html; "FIRE Issues Analysis of Churchill Report," http://thefire.org/article/5469.html.

7. Greg Lukianoff, "Protecting Free Speech Means Rising Above Professor's Words," *Daily Journal* (Los Angeles), February 15, 2005, http://thefire.org/article/5305.html.

8. Terry Webster, "Assignments get teacher in trouble," *San Gabriel Valley Tribune*, March 11, 2003, http://thefire.org/article/4051.html; C. M. Gaston, "Controversy prompts national attention," *The Clarion* (Citrus College), March 19, 2003, http://thefire.org/article/4656.html.

9. Letter from Citrus College President Louis E. Zellers to FIRE, March 7, 2003, http://thefire.org/article/5860.html.

10. Lou Marano, "College to apologize to Bush for professor," United Press International, March 7, 2003, http://thefire.org/article/4029.html.

11. Email from Rhode Island College Professor James Ryczek to Bill Felkner, October 15, 2004, http://thefire.org/article/5343.html.

12. Letter from Rhode Island College Master's of Social Work Program Chair Lenore Olsen to Bill Felkner, May 11, 2005, http://thefire.org/article/5680.html.

13. To hear firsthand about Emily's experiences, see FIRE's documentary "Threats, Coercion, and Bullying at Missouri State," on YouTube, https://www.youtube.com/watch?v=avEeswjaqaQ.

14. "Missouri school sued by student who refused to support gay adoptions," *USA Today*, November 2, 2006.

15. Missouri State University School of Social Work Site Visit Report, http://thefire.org/article/12121.html.

16. Ibid.

17. "JUSTICESPEAKS" Poster, http://thefire.org/article/9921.html.

18. Written Plan for Andre Massena, http://thefire.org/article/9922.html.

19. New Allegations from Laura Bronstein, http://thefire.org/article/9930.html.

20. Email from Laura Bronstein to Andre Massena, http://thefire.org/article/9943.html.

21. KC Johnson, "Disposition for Bias," *Inside Higher Ed*, May 23, 2005, http://thefire.org/article/6250.html.

22. Letter from Brooklyn College School of Education to Professor K. C. Johnson, June 20, 2005, http://thefire.org/article/6251.html.

23. Letter from Brooklyn College President Christoph M. Kimmich to FIRE, September 7, 2005, http://thefire.org/index.php/article/6264.html.

24. Paula Wasley, "Accreditor of Education Schools Drops Controversial 'Social Justice' Language," *Chronicle of Higher Education*, June 16, 2006, http://thefire.org/article/7168.html.

25. Teachers College "Conceptual Framework," http://thefire.org/article/7386.html.

26. Greg Lukianoff, "Social justice and political orthodoxy," *Chronicle of Higher Education*, March 30, 2007, http://thefire.org/article/7857.html.

27. FIRE Letter to Columbia President Lee Bollinger, September 15, 2006, http://thefire.org/article/7361.html; New York Civil Rights Coalition Statement on "Thought Reform" at Columbia's Teachers College, http://thefire.org/article/7366.html.

28. Columbia University Teachers College, "Critiquing TC's Conceptual Framework," October 20, 2006, http://www.tc.columbia.edu/news.htm?articleId=5906.

29. FIRE Letter to Columbia University President Lee Bollinger and Teachers College President Susan Fuhrman, October 18, 2006, http://thefire.org/article/7405.html.

30. Ibid.

31. Letter from Teachers College President Susan Fuhrman to FIRE, May 11, 2007, http://thefire.org/article/8066.html.

32. *West Virginia State Board of Education* v. *Barnette*, 319 U.S. 624, 642 (1943), http://www.law.cornell.edu/supct/html/historics/USSC_CR_0319_0624_ZO.html.

33. Letter from Jeffery A. Mangram to Matthew Werenczak, September 7, 2011, http://thefire.org/article/14070.html.

34. Facebook comments, July 20, 2011, http://thefire.org/article/14069.html.

35. Letter from Jeffery A. Mangram to Matthew Werenczak, September 7, 2011, http://thefire.org/article/14070.html.

36. Denis Carter, "Syracuse Reverses Course After Expelling Student for Facebook Post," *eCampus News*, January 23, 2012, http://thefire.org/article/14089.html.

37. Richard Arum and Josipa Roksa, *Academically Adrift: Limited Learning on College Campuses* (Chicago: University of Chicago Press, 2011).

38. "Keeping a Writer's Daybook," Pamela Mitzelfeld, English 380, September 1, 2011, http://thefire.org/article/14149.html.

39. Oakland Community College, "2009–10 Student Essay Competition," http://www.oaklandcc.edu/essay/2009-10.aspx.

40. Joseph Corlett's Daybook, November 1, 2011, http://thefire.org/article/14153.html.

41. Email from Pamela Mitzelfeld to Sherry Wynn Perdue, November 29, 2011, http://thefire.org/article/14150.html.

42. Letter to Joseph Corlett from Assistant Vice President for Student Affairs and Dean of Students Glenn McIntosh, January 20, 2012, http://thefire.org/article/14152.html.

43. "Oakland University Student Suspended after Writing Essay Titled 'Hot for Teacher,'" *Van Halen News Desk*, February 14, 2012.

44. Denial of Appeal from Mary Beth Snyder to Joseph Corlett, March 5, 2012, http://thefire.org/article/14284.html.

45. Karen Gutiérrez, "Abortion display destroyed," *Northern Kentucky Enquirer*, April 14, 2006.

46. Ibid.

47. "President issues statement," *Cincinnati Enquirer*, April 18, 2006.

48. Bill Bishop, *The Big Sort: Why the Clustering of Like-Minded America Is Tearing Us Apart* (New York: Houghton Mifflin, 2008), p. 21.

49. Ibid., p. 3.

CHAPTER 10: IF EVEN YOUR PROFESSOR CAN BE PUNISHED …

1. Eric L. Dey, Molly C. Ott, Mary Antonaros, Cassie L. Barnhardt, and Matthew A. Holsapple, *Engaging Diverse Viewpoints: What Is the Campus Climate for*

Perspective-Taking? (Washington, D.C.: Association of American Colleges and Universities, 2010), available online, p. 7.

2. Letter from Provost Marty Krauss to Professor Donald Hindley, October 30, 2007, http://thefire.org/article/8853.html.

3. Brandeis University Faculty Senate Resolution, November 8, 2007, http://thefire.org/article/8851.html; Report from Committee on Faculty Rights and Responsibilities, December 10, 2007, http://thefire.org/article/8847.html; Report from Committee on Faculty Rights and Responsibilities, December 19, 2007, http://thefire.org/article/8849.html.

4. "Editorial: There is such a thing as bad publicity," *Brandeis Hoot*, February 1, 2008, http://thefire.org/article/8918.html.

5. "Brandeis University: Professor Found Guilty of Harassment for Protected Speech," http://thefire.org/index.php/case/755.html.

6. Wendy Kaminer, "Can Educators Ever Teach the N-Word?" *The Atlantic*, February 21, 2012.

7. "Editorial: Prof. Hindley deserves better," *The Justice* (Brandeis), November 6, 2007.

8. Petition from Shaw University Professor Gale J. Isaacs to Shaw University President Talbert O. Shaw, October 24, 2002, http://thefire.org/article/5853.html.

9. Letter from Shaw University President Talbert O. Shaw to Dr. Gale J. Isaacs, November 16, 2002, http://thefire.org/article/5845.html.

10. Ibid.

11. Cindy George, "Shaw professor fired over letter," *News and Observer,* December 12, 2002, http://thefire.org/article/4850.html.

12. Stephen Kershnar, "Are Conservatives Being Shut Out of the Academy?" *Dunkirk-Fredonia Observer*, February 15, 2006, http://thefire.org/article/7155.html; Stephen Kershnar, "Against Affirmative Action at Fredonia," *Dunkirk-Fredonia Observer*, February 1, 2006, http://thefire.org/article/7154.html.

13. Letter from SUNY Fredonia President Dennis L. Hefner to Stephen Kershnar, April 27, 2006, http://thefire.org/article/7159.html.

14. Contract Drafted by SUNY Fredonia President Dennis L. Hefner, http://thefire.org/article/7160.html.

15. Greg Lukianoff and Robert Shibley, "No free speech for SUNY profs?" *New York Post*, August 1, 2006, http://thefire.org/article/7188.html.

16. Promotion Letter from SUNY Fredonia President Dennis L. Hefner to Stephen Kershnar, August 11, 2006, http://thefire.org/article/7208.html.

17. "Glendale Community College: Professor Sanctioned for Sending E-Mail," http://thefire.org/index.php/case/743.html.

18. "Quick Takes: Glendale settles e-mail dispute," *Inside Higher Ed*, June 26, 2007, http://thefire.org/article/8172.html.

19. *Rodriguez* v. *Maricopa County Community College District,* 605 F.3d 703 (9th Cir. 2010), http://www.ca9.uscourts.gov/datastore/opinions/2010/05/20/08-16073.pdf.

20. "The Source of the Controversy," http://thefire.org/article/4949.html.

21. Ibid.

22. FIRE's Letter to Chancellor Leutze, http://thefire.org/article/4950.html.

23. *Garcetti v. Ceballos*, 547 U.S. 410 (2006), http://www.supremecourt.gov/opinions/05pdf/04-473.pdf.

24. *Adams v. Trustees of the University of North Carolina–Wilmington, et al.*, 640 F.3d 550 (4th Cir. 2011), http://thefire.org/article/13051.html.

25. Stanley Bermudez's Rebel Flag Statement, http://thefire.org/article/12929.html.

26. Southern Heritage Alerts Blog Entry, January 25, 2011, http://thefire.org/article/12930.html.

27. Letter to Gainesville State College President Martha T. Nesbitt, March 7, 2011, http://thefire.org/article/12927.html.

28. Gainesville State College President's Statements, February 4, 2011, http://thefire.org/article/12928.html.

29. Peter Bonilla, "Gainesville State College Remains Unaccountable for Censorship of Faculty Artwork," *The Torch*, April 15, 2011, http://thefire.org/article/13089.html.

30. Peter Bonilla, "Gainesville State College President Censors Faculty Art Critical of Confederate Heritage," *The Torch*, March 8, 2011, http://thefire.org/article/12932.html.

31. FIRE Letter to Brooklyn College President Karen L. Gould, January 28, 2011, http://thefire.org/article/12800.html.

32. Ibid.; and Justin Elliot, "Backlash over firing of pro-Palestinian professor," *Salon*, January 28, 2011, http://thefire.org/article/12795.html.

33. Adam Kissel, "Brooklyn College Reinstates Professor after Controversy," *The Torch*, February 1, 2011, http://thefire.org/article/12809.html.

34. "UN human rights official: Gaza evokes memories of Warsaw Ghetto," *Haaretz*, Janaury 23, 2009.

35. Scott Jaschik, "Crossing a Line," *Inside Higher Ed*, April 23, 2009, http://www.insidehighered.com/news/2009/04/23/ucsb.

36. FIRE Letter to University of California–Santa Barbara Chancellor Henry T. Yang, http://thefire.org/article/10733.html.

37. Letter to Professor William Robinson from UCSB Executive Vice Chancellor Gene Lucas, http://thefire.org/article/10786.html.

38. Linda McCarriston's "Indian Girls," http://thefire.org/article/4944.html.

39. Victoria Kondor, "Professor's poem draws fiery conflict," *Northern Light*, January 16, 2001.

40. President Hamilton's Memo, http://thefire.org/article/4943.html.

41. FIRE Letter to Rhode Island College President John Nazarian, August 2, 2004, http://thefire.org/article/6067.html.

42. An Open Letter to President John Nazarian and Rhode Island College, http://thefire.org/article/4869.html; Letter from Rhode Island ACLU to Rhode Island College President John Nazarian, September 10, 2004, http://thefire.org/article/6065.

html; "Rhode Island College Union Files Free Speech Grievance," http://thefire. org/article/4888.html.

43. Ed Achorn, "Attacking speech at RIC," *Providence Journal*, August 31, 2004, http://thefire.org/article/5282.html; "Professor faces deadline for hearing on discrimination complaint," Associated Press, September 1, 2004, http://thefire. org/article/5160.html; "Free Speech Victory at Rhode Island College," http:// thefire.org/article/4864.html.

44. Professor Thomas Thibeault's Notes from EGC's Sexual Harassment Training, http://thefire.org/article/11076.html.

45. Professor Thomas Thibeault's Written Account of the Meeting with President Black, http://thefire.org/article/11074.html.

46. Letter from East Georgia College President John Black to Professor Thomas Thibeault, October 20, 2009, http://thefire.org/article/11229.html.

47. Thomas Thibeault Settlement with East Georgia College, http://thefire.org/ article/13520.html.

48. Philip Roth, *The Human Stain: A Novel* (New York: Houghton Mifflin, 2000), p. 6.

49. Dean Shabner and Matt Negrin, "Rush Limbaugh Apologizes for Calling Sandra Fluke a 'Slut,'" ABC News, March 3, 2012.

50. Kirsten Powers, "Rush Limbaugh Isn't the Only Media Misogynist," *Daily Beast,* March 4, 2012.

51. Jennifer Epstein, "De Niro suggests it's 'too soon' for another white FLOTUS," *Politico*, March 19, 2012; Elicia Dover, "Gingrich Says De Niro's 'White First Lady' Crack Is 'Inexcusable,'" ABC News, March 20, 2012.

52. Bill Maher, "Please Stop Apologizing," *New York Times*, March 21, 2012.

CHAPTER 11: STUDENT DRAFTEES FOR THE CULTURE WAR

1. Michael Edwards, "Estimated 10,000 issues of *Daily Wildcat* stolen at University of Arizona," Student Press Law Center, October 9, 2008, http://www. splc.org/news/newsflash.asp?id=1975; Kate Maternowski, "Catholic University newspapers stolen, area police refuse to investigate," Student Press Law Center, April 2, 2009, http://www.splc.org/news/newsflash.asp?id=1894; Marnette Federis,"Committee, editor clash over police report for stolen papers," Student Press Law Center, October 20, 2006, http://www.splc.org/news/newsflash. asp?id=1355; Marnette Federis, "Two Indiana papers have homecoming week issues stolen," Student Press Law Center, October 20, 2006, http://www.splc. org/news/newsflash.asp?id=1356; Ricky Ribeiro,"Nearly 5,000 copies of Rhode Island student newspaper stolen," Student Press Law Center, April 28, 2006, http://www.splc.org/news/newsflash.asp?id=1255; Kim Peterson, "More than 8,500 student newspapers stolen at University of Utah," Student Press Law Center, November 15, 2005, http://www.splc.org/news/newsflash.asp?id=1128; Diane Krauthamer, "Students admit to theft of 4,000 copies of Calif. university student newspaper," Student Press Law Center, March 29, 2005, http://www.splc. org/news/newsflash.asp?id=994.

2. Casey Wooten, "Issue with article on student's rape charge stolen from news-stands," Student Press Law Center, November 12, 2007, http://www.splc.org/news/newsflash.asp?id=1644; Anne Elliott, "Police investigate newspaper theft at Vincennes University," Student Press Law Center, October 21, 2009, http://www.splc.org/news/newsflash.asp?id=1983.

3. Catherine MacDonald, "Investigation into theft of more than 1,200 student newspapers halts at UC Riverside," Student Press Law Center, June 4, 2009, http://www.splc.org/news/newsflash.asp?id=1912.

4. Brian Hudson, "Papers stolen from UNC-Charlotte after staff neglects to feature presidential candidate," Student Press Law Center, April 18, 2007, http://www.splc.org/news/newsflash.asp?id=1508.

5. Erica Walters, "Newspaper estimates loss of $2,750 after 3,500 copies of paper stolen," Student Press Law Center, October 14, 2008, http://www.splc.org/news/newsflash.asp?id=1823; "One student disciplined for theft, others go unpunished," Student Press Law Center, Spring 2004, http://www.splc.org/news/report_detail.asp?id=1107&edition=29.

6. Brian Hudson, "Rowan University newspapers stolen after article named alleged drug distributors," Student Press Law Center, March, 9, 2007, http://www.splc.org/news/newsflash.asp?id=1461.

7. Marnette Federis, "UNC fraternity claims responsibility for theft of 10,000 newspapers," Student Press Law Center, December 1, 2006, http://www.splc.org/news/newsflash.asp?id=1380.

8. Marnette Federis, "Sorority suspected in Stetson newspaper theft," Student Press Law Center, October 25, 2006, http://www.splc.org/news/newsflash.asp?id=1357.

9. Judith Patton, "Bucknell students reprint trashed newspaper edition," *Penn Live*, March 11, 2008.

10. Katie Maloney, "Eagle's racks emptied after publication of controversial column addressing rape," Student Press Law Center, March 29; 2010, http://www.splc.org/news/newsflash.asp?id=2058.

11. Peter Bonilla, "At American University, Newspaper Theft Goes Unpunished, and Leaves Questions About Commitment to Free Speech," *The Torch*, August 6, 2010, http://thefire.org/article/12143.html.

12. Associated Press, "Campus newspapers featuring nude picture stolen from racks," First Amendment Center, October 17, 2006.

13. Phil Taylor, "Judge acquits former student of torching newspapers," First Amendment Center, June 17, 1998.

14. Erin O'Connor, "Of spines and student papers," *Critical Mass*, September 20, 2005; Chris Beam, "Cartoon Scandals So Hot Right Now," *Ivy Gate*, November 8, 2006; "Student leader uses papers for bonfire," Student Press Law Center, Spring 2007, http://www.splc.org/news/report_detail.asp?id=1335&edition=42.

15. Beam, "Cartoon Scandals So Hot Right Now."

16. For just two recent examples, see Amir Taha, *Nietzsche, Prophet of Nazism: The Cult of the Superman—Unveiling the Nazi Secret Doctrine* (Bloomington, Ind.: AuthorHouse, 2005); and Stephen R. C. Hicks, *Nietzsche and the Nazis* (Loves Park, Ill.: Ockham's Razor Publishing, 2010).

17. Beam, "Cartoon Scandals So Hot Right Now."

18. *Texas* v. *Johnson*, 491 U.S. 397 (1989), http://caselaw.lp.findlaw.com/scripts/getcase.pl?court=us&vol=491&invol=397.

19. Brian Hudson, "Student leader admits to taking newspapers and using them as kindling at frat party," Student Press Law Center, April 5, 2007, http://www.splc.org/news/newsflash.asp?id=1489.

20. "Berkeley mayor admits to *Daily Cal* theft after police investigate," Student Press Law Center, December 6, 2002, http://www.splc.org/news/newsflash.asp?id=518.

21. Erica Walters, "University of Tampa orders newspaper thief to pay $150, spend 20 hours working for paper," Student Press Law Center, September 9, 2008, http://www.splc.org/news/newsflash.asp?id=1805.

22. Jenna Johnson, "Christopher Newport admission staffers hid newspapers headlined: 'Suspected meth lab on East Campus,'" *Washington Post*, April 11, 2012.

23. Katie Maloney, "No charges filed in Texas newspaper theft," Student Press Law Center, March 4, 2010, http://www.splc.org/news/newsflash.asp?id=2042.

24. Adam Goldstein, "Coach Proud of Team's Newspaper Theft Should Resign," *Huffington Post*, March 3, 2010.

25. University of Wisconsin-Milwaukee Student Association, "SA Sedition Act," *UWM Post*, http://www.uwmpost.com/archives/images/article-photos/861_full.jpg.

26. *UWM Post, Inc.* v. *Board of Regents of the University of Wisconsin System*, 774 F. Supp. 1163 (E.D. Wis. 1991), http://www.mit.edu/activities/safe/legal/uwm-post-v-u-of-wisconsin.

27. Kevin Lessmiller, "Sedition Act Shot Down at Meeting," *UWM Post*, February 18, 2008, http://www.uwmpost.com/2008/02/18/sedition-act-shot-down-at-sa-meeting/.

28. Matthew Daneman, "College settles case, will revise its speech code," *Rochester Democrat and Chronicle*, May 11, 2005, http://thefire.org/article/5657.html.

29. Christopher Wells, "BSG's lawyer alleges libel," *The Stylus* (Brockport), February 17, 2011.

30. Harvey Silverglate, "What Characterizes the Modern Totalitarian, Corporatized University?" *Minding the Campus,* March 17, 2011.

31. "University of Massachusetts at Amherst: Student Newspapers Stolen while Police Officer Watches," http://thefire.org/case/780.html.

32. S. P. Sullivan, "Administration rejects SGA suspension of *The Minuteman*," *Massachusetts Daily Collegian*, April 21, 2009, http://thefire.org/article/10508.html.

33. Brian Schraum, "R.I. college paper staff locked out of their newsroom," Student Press Law Center, August 27, 2010, http://www.splc.org/news/newsflash.asp?id=2126.

34. Liz White, "West Georgia SGA passes bill to freeze money to student newspaper after publishing anti-Greek column," Student Press Law Center, May 8, 2009, http://www.splc.org/news/newsflash.asp?id=1905.

35. "East Carolina University: Viewpoint Discrimination Against Student Organization," http://thefire.org/case/860.

36. Jacob Sullum, "What's a Group Gotta Do to Post a Flyer Around Here?" *Reason*, December 8, 2010.

37. Greg Lukianoff, "The 'No Viewpoint' Viewpoint," *Inside Higher Ed*, June 6, 2005, http://www.insidehighered.com/views/2005/06/06/lukianoff.

38. Nicole Santa Cruz, "11 Muslim Student Union members charged with disrupting Israeli ambassador's speech at UC Irvine," *Los Angeles Times*, February 5, 2011.

39. You can watch the video, "Uncivilized Tactics at UC Irvine (Rough Cut)," on YouTube, http://www.youtube.com/watch?v=7w96UR79TBw.

40. You can watch the video, "Minutemen Protest Storming at Columbia University," on YouTube, http://www.youtube.com/watch?v=PuNXmyoe5fc.

41. You can watch the video, "Tancredo at UNC," on YouTube, http://www.youtube.com/watch?v=aaTkGgE-hXA.

42. You can watch the video, "Don Feder Protested at UMass Amherst," on YouTube, http://www.youtube.com/watch?v=cJPmv1vTbjc.

43. Stephen Erfelt, "Missouri State University Students Vandalize Campus Pro-Life Cross Display," *LifeNews.com*, October 10, 2008, http://www.lifenews.com/2008/10/10/state-3545/.

44. You can watch the video, "UM Bears for Life: Interview with student that vandalized the 'Graveyard of the Innocents,'" on YouTube, http://www.youtube.com/watch?v=vexOiSRpdTM.

45. You can watch the video, "Cemetery of Innocents conflict," on YouTube, http://www.youtube.com/watch?v=t5NeLyMZUYM.

46. Scott Jaschik, "Dissent vs. Vandalism," *Inside Higher Ed*, April 19, 2006.

47. "Suspected vandals say destroying anti-abortion display is free speech," *KYPost.com*, April 11, 2012.

48. J. D. Wallace, "Conservative Author Is Attacked with Pies," *Tucson News Now*, October 22, 2004; Patrick X. Coyle, "How About Some 'Civility' toward College Conservatives?" *Human Events*, January 30, 2011.

49. Scott Jaschik, "Speech Interrupted," *Inside Higher Ed*, April 8, 2005, http://www.insidehighered.com/news/2006/04/19/nku.

50. "Two Horowitz Protestors Arrested," *Ball State Daily News*, November 10, 2006.

51. Salvador Rizzo, "Outside Group Stifles Horowitz Speech," *Emory Wheel*, October 25, 2007, http://www.emorywheel.com/detail.php?n=24510.

52. Scott Jaschik, "Still Banned at Saint Louis U.," *Inside Higher Ed*, February 8, 2010, http://www.insidehighered.com/news/2010/02/08/slu.

53. Ibid.

54. Ibid.

55. Ibid.

56. Peter Wood, "Mobbing for Preferences," *Chronicle of Higher Education*, September 22, 2011.

57. Adelaide Blanchard, "Report Stirs UW Students to Action," *Badger Herald*, September 13, 2011, http://badgerherald.com/news/2011/09/13/report_spurs_uw_stud.php.

58. Deborah Ziff and Devin Rose, "UW-Madison faculty, students fight admissions discrimination charge," *Wisconsin State Journal*, September 14, 2011; Linda Chavez, "How Campus Thugs Defend Racism," *New York Post*, September 17, 2011.

59. Wood, "Mobbing for Preferences."

60. Randy Hall, "University Restricts Students Over 'Hate' Speech," CNS News, October 6, 2003, http://thefire.org/article/4114.html.

61. "Gonzaga University: Censorship of 'Hate Speech,'" http://thefire.org/case/22.html.

62. "South Park creators warned over Muhammad depiction," BBC News, April 22, 2010; "Protest Cancels Coulter Speech in Ottawa," Fox News, March 24, 2010; Cathy Young, "Before you know it, your speech could be offensive," *RealClearPolitics*, April 22, 2009, http://thefire.org/article/10505.html; Jayson Rodriguez, "Kanye West Crashes VMA Stage During Taylor Swift's Award Speech," MTV News, September 13, 2009.

63. Jinjoo Lee, "Students Deface Posters They Call Racist Against Asians," *Cornell Daily Sun*, March 26, 2012.

64. Ibid.

65. Margaret Cho, "Chop Suey Font," *Margaret Cho* website, March 21, 2012, http://www.margaretcho.com/2012/03/21/chop-suey-font/.

66. You can watch the video here: Stephen Gutowski, "Students Who 'Support' Free Speech Want to Ban Conservatives From Radio and TV," MRC TV, May 20, 2011.

67. Email from Professor Gregory Germain to Len Audaer, October 15, 2010, http://thefire.org/article/12613.html.

68. Greg Lukianoff, "The 12 Worst Colleges for Free Speech," *Huffington Post*, January 27, 2011.

69. "Constitutional Law – First Amendment – Third Circuit Holds University Sexual Harassment Policy Unconstitutional," *Harvard Law Review*, vol. 122 (2009): 1772–1779.

70. Kelly Sarabyn, "*Harvard Law Review* Gets Lazy: Prestigious Journal Publishes Article Ignoring Case Law, Defending Speech Codes," *The Torch*, August 3, 2009, http://thefire.org/article/10932.html.

71. Samuel D. Warren and Louis Brandeis, "The Right to Privacy," *Harvard Law Review*, vol. 4, no. 5 (1890); Zecharia Chafee, *Freedom of Speech* (New York: Harcourt, Brace and Company, 1920).

72. Michael Kent Curtis, *Free Speech, "The People's Darling Privilege": Struggles for Freedom of Expression in American History* (Durham, N.C.: Duke University Press, 2000).

73. Harvey Silverglate, "Tyler Clementi: What's hate got to do with it?" *Boston Phoenix*, September 30, 2010.

74. Caroline Black, "Tyler Clementi Suicide Prompts Anti-Bullying Legislation from N.J. Senator," CBS News, November 19, 2010; Debra J. Saunders, "Life gets better—politics get worse," *San Francisco Chronicle*, October 19, 2010.

75. *Davis* v. *Monroe County Board of Education*, 526 U.S. 629 (1999), http://www.law.cornell.edu/supct/html/97-843.ZS.html.

76. Winnie Hu, "Bullying Law Puts New Jersey Schools on Spot," *New York Times*, August 30, 2011.

77. Derek Bambauer, "Cyberbullying and the Cheese-Eating Surrender Monkeys," *Concurring Opinions*, February 21, 2012.

78. Arizona House Bill 2549, 50th Legislature, Second Regular session (2012).

79. Jared Newman, "Arizona Looks to Outlaw Internet Trolling," Techland, *Time*, April 3, 2012.

80. Liz Goodwin, "Arizona lawmakers to review cyberbullying bill over free speech concerns," Yahoo News, April 9, 2012; Heather Campobella, "Arizona's Cyber-Bullying Law May Be Revised," WebProNews, April 6, 2012.

81. Eugene Volokh, "A Crime to Use 'Any Electronic or Digital Device' 'And Use Any Obscene, Lewd or Profane Language' 'With Intent to … Offend'?" *The Volokh Conspiracy*, March 31, 2012; Harvey Silverglate, "The Arizona Legislature Tries to Bully the Constitution," *Forbes*, April 5, 2012.

82. Frank LoMonte, "From the 'Right Not to Be Annoyed' Department … where do you go to report annoying legislation?" Student Press Law Center, March 28, 2012, http://www.splc.org/wordpress/?p=3428.

83. Eugene Volokh, "Crime to Post Images That Cause 'Emotional Distress' 'Without Legitimate Purpose,'" *The Volokh Conspiracy*, June 6, 2011.

84. Joseph Cohn, "Alabama Bill Would Make It a Crime to Annoy Someone Online," *The Torch*, March 6, 2012, http://thefire.org/article/14265.html.

Index